# Colonial Rosary

# COLONIAL

**Swallow Press**

Ohio University Press

*Athens*

# ROSARY

The Spanish and Indian

Missions of California

*Alison Lake*

Swallow Press / Ohio University Press, Athens, Ohio 45701
www.ohio.edu / oupress

Swallow Press / Ohio University Press books are printed on acid-free paper ⊗ ™

12 11 10 09 08 07 06 05 04   5 4 3 2 1

*Library of Congress Cataloging-in-Publication Data*

Lake, Alison.
  Colonial rosary : the Spanish and Indian missions of California / Alison Lake.
    p. cm.
  Includes bibliographical references and index.
  ISBN-13: 978-0-8040-1084-9 (cloth : alk. paper)
  ISBN-10: 0-8040-1084-6 (cloth : alk. paper)
  ISBN-13: 978-0-8040-1085-6 (pbk. : alk. paper)
  ISBN-10: 0-8040-1085-4 (pbk. : alk. paper)
  1. Missions, Spanish—California—History. 2. Indians of North America—Missions—California—History. 3. Spaniards—California—History. 4. Franciscans—California—History. 5. California—History—To 1846. 6. California—Social life and customs. 7. California—Race relations. 8. California—Church history. I. Title.

F864.L1655 2006
979.4—dc22

2006006072

*In remembrance of a year of*

*birth, love, and progress.*

# Contents

# Illustrations

*Figures*

*Tables*

# Foreword

All Californians grew up with a special fondness for California's twenty-one Franciscan missions. Perhaps we loved these reconstructed tile-roofed mud-brick compounds because they were near the Pacific coast in beautiful places like San Diego, San Luis Obispo, Carmel, or Monterey rather than in arid and land-locked Modesto, Fresno, or Tulare. On visits the weather and the missions' lush gardens were as enticing as the accompanying stories of Father Serra civilizing the natives and introducing irrigated agriculture and Spanish architecture to a once-harsh landscape.

In the last thirty years that romance has pretty much disappeared. The story of civilization building has been replaced by the more sinister story of Spanish religious zealots whipping native Californians, destroying indigenous cultures, and using Indian labor to build an oppressive new world of colonial Spanish California.

Of course, neither extreme view is the entire story. Father Junípero Serra was a visionary of the eighteenth century, with all the good and bad that such an image entails. In his relentless trek up and down the California coastal mountains, Serra accomplished feats of physical and mental courage that we moderns can only shudder at.

Natives were routinely beaten, killed, and herded into missionary settlements, but not always with simple economic coercion in mind. Just as often, priests and clerics felt that they were saving souls, ending abortion and infanticide, introducing literacy, offering instruction in agriculture and settled life, and ensuring that Christianization and assimilation might offer real material improvement to the impoverished.

As *Colonial Rosary* demonstrates, history is not melodrama, but tragedy. Sometimes good intentions have good, bad, and ambiguous results that take centuries to sort out. Although we may wish the Spanish had been far more humane and tolerant in their efforts to bring what they saw as Western civilization to California, we were not around in the eighteenth century to philosophize in a climate without electricity, modern medicine, plentiful food, or much law. We English-speakers like to think that after statehood in 1850, religious diversity, democracy, Anglo-Saxon jurisprudence, and the emergence of a middle class made California a different—and far better—place to live than it was in its Spanish past.

Perhaps; but such sweeping chauvinism ignores more subtle questions of demography, technology, and geopolitics. And we should have the intellectual integrity to acknowledge that the California we take for granted today, with its bountiful agriculture, easy transportation, and materially rich cities, is more or less the vision of the early missions, which are emblems, again both salutary and ambiguous, of what we have become.

While history is never static, it is always ironic: given the radically changing demographics and multiculture of present-day California, Father Serra's dream of a largely Catholic, Spanish-speaking, and assimilated Native American population inheriting the culture of Western civilization may not seem so fantastic in another two hundred years.

Yet the history of the California missions is more than a morality tale. It is a fascinating story of architecture, viticulture and arboriculture, cattle ranching, religion, and road building—the skeleton of sorts of what we successors to the Spanish have fleshed out in the two centuries since the missions.

It is to Alison Lake's credit in her richly documented and well-written history that for all the sins and transgressions we read about, we come away more rather than less intrigued with the California missions. Indeed, in a time of rampant suburbanization, radically changing demography, and exhausted state treasuries, Lake reminds us that California's missions require new investment to ensure maintenance, necessary ongoing reconstruction, and simple attention apart from the rapidly growing housing tracts in their midst.

The final irony is that Father Serra and his missionaries knew California perhaps better than we; centuries later, we all seem to want to live precisely where he and his clergy did. These early observers were astute regarding the weather, resources, topography, and natural landscape of this enormous and richly endowed state.

*Victor Davis Hanson*
*Senior Fellow, The Hoover Institution, Stanford University*

# Acknowledgments

Although the bulk of this book was written over countless hours alone in the library and at the computer, it could not have been accomplished without the help of academic professionals and their years of expertise on the subject of California Indians, Spanish missions, and colonial history. The bibliography reflects extensive material available on these subjects. The California Mission Studies Association and San Diego Historical Society also played critical roles in my research.

Individuals with intimate knowledge of American Indian culture and mission history lent a personal perspective. Russell Imrie of Los Gatos, California, cheerfully provided input throughout the research and writing process. His viewpoint as a Canadian mission Indian and his experience working with the California Ohlone and Indian Canyon communities provided invaluable food for thought.

I was fortunate to have input from Ruben Mendoza, Director of the Institute for Archaeological Science at California State University, Monterey Bay. Ruben read parts of the manuscript and shared his contacts and experiences with mission archaeological digs. Thanks also go to the following experts who took time out of their busy days to read and comment on parts of the manuscript: Carmen Boone, an independent historian in Mexico City and member of the California Mission Studies Association board of directors; Brother Guire Cleary, Curator of Mission San Francisco de Asís; William Warwick, Retired Curator of Mission Santa Inés; Dennis Sharp, archivist/oral historian of the San Diego Historical Society Research Library; Rebecca Lawrence, San Diego; and Dr. Knox Mellon, State Historic Preservation Officer, Department of Parks and Recreation.

I will never forget how Vernon Lidtke, PhD, taught me at Johns Hopkins University that the study of human history can be a source of excitement and wonder. I appreciate his encouragement in the early stages of the research process. I am also thankful for the assistance of family and friends in helping with final line edits of the manuscript. I want to thank Sandy Van Densen for her ongoing help and encouragement and endless efforts for the book's success. Finally, thanks go to Gillian Berchowitz, David Sanders, and John Morris of Ohio University Press and Swallow Press for their enthusiasm and support of this project.

# Tables

## Table 1.1 Native American languages of California

| Stock | Family | Group or language | Language or dialect |
|---|---|---|---|
| Hokan | | Salinan (isolate) | |
| | | Esselen (isolate) | |
| | Chumashan | | |
| | Yuman | Diegueño | Ipai, Tipai |
| | Pomoan | | |
| Penutian | Utian | Miwokan, Costanoan | Mutsun, Rumsen, Cholan (Soledad) |
| | Yokutsan | | |
| | Wintun | Patwin | |
| Aztec-Tanoan | Uto-Aztecan | Numic | Western Shoshone |
| | | Takic | Gabrielino-Fernandeño Luiseño-Juaneño |

Source: Christopher Moseley and R. E. Asher, eds., *Atlas of the World's Languages* (London: Routledge, 1994).

## Table 1.2 Tribes or tribal groups incorporated by missions

| Tribe or group | Mission |
|---|---|
| Cholon (Soledad) | Soledad |
| Chumash | Buenaventura, Purísima, San Luis Obispo, Santa Barbara, Santa Inés |
| Costanoan/Ohlone | San Antonio, San Francisco, San Juan Bautista, Santa Cruz, Soledad |
| Diegueño (Yuman) | San Diego |
| Esselen | San Antonio, San Carlos (Carmel), possibly Soledad |
| Gabrielino | San Fernando, San Gabriel |
| Juaneño | San Juan Capistrano |
| Luiseño | San Luis Rey |
| Miwok | San Francisco, San José, San Rafael, Santa Clara, Sonoma |
| Patwin | San Francisco, San José, Sonoma |
| Pomo | San Francisco, San Rafael, Sonoma |
| Salinan | San Antonio, San Miguel, Soledad |
| Yokuts | San José, San Juan Bautista, Soledad, Santa Clara, Santa Cruz (all from different Yokuts regions) |

Map of California mission system.

# Introduction

## *The Missions*

California would be a wholly different place today without the imprint of Spanish culture and legacy of Indian civilization. The colonial Spanish missions that dot the coasts and foothills between Sonoma and San Diego are relics of a past that transformed California's physical and cultural landscape, and above all its native peoples.

Today cactus and Castilian roses continue to grow in mission courtyards. Wine is still sold from crops of mission grapes. Olive presses, wine cellars, and leather-tanning rooms all stand as reminders of California's first commercial industries. Weatherworn adobe bricks shaped by human hands remain from the first colonial buildings. These frontier churches and outbuildings still standing today connect modern California with a rich and traumatic history forged by European colonists and diverse native populations.

Well before the American Revolution, the kingdom of Spain's mission system was entrenched in Mexico and South America. Two centuries of imperial rule set a precedent for Spain's colonization of California. Beginning in Florida with the settlement of St. Augustine in 1565 and continuing into Mexico, Texas, New Mexico, and Arizona, mission territories were the primary instruments of Spanish rule across North and South America. California missions appeared after Spanish missions were already established in the Baja Peninsula of present-day Mexico and were the logical next step of colonization.

For two and a half centuries, Spain sent soldiers and Catholic priests of several orders to the Americas to facilitate the spread of Spanish rule and Christian faith. Starting in 1769, Franciscan priests and Spanish soldiers founded twenty missions in California. The twenty-first appeared after Mexico's independence from Spain in 1823.

Indian tribes were the focus of conversion and a source of labor. Designed to sustain missionaries, soldiers, and converted native populations, each mission maintained its own network to produce food, provide shelter, and ensure military protection. Mission buildings surrounded a central church and became the early settlements of California's first towns. Today California's Spanish missions remain as both remote outposts in the coastal hills and landmarks in bustling city centers. These centers of California's colonial past not only provide retreats for Catholics and history enthusiasts, but also provoke thought and controversy on colonial treatment of native peoples and California's Hispanic heritage.

Mission buildings standing today in California are mere suggestions of the active complexes they once were. With an understanding of the society that composed these centers of Spanish colonial culture, one's imagination and historical readings can accommodate gaps of time and decay. Some missions remain in operation today as parishes. Nearly all suffer from limited funds and crumbling walls. Those open to the public require constant upkeep and funding to continue as museums. Only with sustained interest and public support can California's missions be saved and preserved for future generations.

Reminders of the Spanish mission period flourish across the lower half of today's California, from streets and districts named for the missions to city and residential buildings crafted in the Spanish colonial style. Hispanic ambiance saturates California place-names and architecture and is manifest in the adobe arcades of historic districts such as San Diego's Old Town. The vineyards of Sonoma, ranchlands of Santa Barbara, and widespread red tile roofs are all signs of the missions' economic and architectural imprint on California's coastal and inland regions.

Spanish settlers also introduced significant agricultural innovations to the state, such as cattle and horse ranches, farming tools and methods, olive cultiva-

Mission courtyard. © iStockphoto.com/Aaron Whitney.

tion, and viticulture (the cultivation of grapes for wine). California's thriving
cattle trade, wine industry, and agriculture all began with the missions.

Small townships grew up around the Spanish missions all along the California coast, from San Diego to Sonoma. *El Camino Reál* (the royal road), named in
honor of the king of Spain, was first scratched out as a foot trail winding up the
Pacific coast of Alta California. As religious settlements increased in number
and substance, the route became the main land artery for settlers traveling between Mexico and California. Today, the Camino Reál correlates approximately
with California's Highway 101.

California's Indian civilization varied widely in language, practices, and use
of resources. Spain's drive to colonize California began and drove a decline of
Indian culture, independence, and population similar to that which occurred
elsewhere in the Americas. The shock wave of civilization shook these civilizations and complex cultures to their roots. Mission life undermined cultural dis-
tinctions among tribes while inadvertently importing diseases that wiped out
significant groups.

Thrown together into the structured and unfamiliar mission environment,
groups from different tribes were expected to work, sleep, and eat together in

close quarters while following orders from the missionaries and soldiers. Throughout the mission period, Indian groups coped with this upheaval in many ways—
by assimilation, resistance, obedience, or adaptation.

Tragically, with the imposition of Spanish Catholic ways, rich cultural differences began to blend together or disappear. The combination of Spanish and
later Mexican and American colonial culture, along with sweeping epidemics of
European-imported diseases, spelled the end of many Indian languages and cultures, not to mention lives. Most of the languages spoken before the arrival of
the Europeans were lost before the end of the nineteenth century. Some, however, are still nurtured today by various tribal groups as part of the effort by
many California tribes to continue the practice of their ancestral customs.[1] The
mission Indian tribes that exist today confront their unique ancestries in different ways. Some still identify with mission culture, while others actively condemn its imposition.

## About This Book

This look at California's mission story begins with the array of subcultures that
occupied the coasts, plains, deserts, and mountains of California long before any
European set foot on its shores. Initial interactions between Indian and Spaniard
were harbingers of the approaching upheaval of the area's social and economic
environment. Each mission developed a culture particular to the region, its resources, its unique Indian tribes, and the men in charge, and this culture quickly
replaced centuries-old social institutions among the native peoples.

Colonial history is reflected in the period of mission occupation: Spain's decline as a world power, Mexico's growing presence in the region, and eventually
America's inclusion of California as a state.

The geographic scope of this book is the coastal and inland regions of California between San Diego and Sonoma, home to the twenty-one missions of
California. In this book, "California" means the area now occupied by the state
of California, unless otherwise noted, while "New Spain" means the area now
occupied by Mexico. Pre-mission Indians, however, used no single name for the
area we know as California. During the Spanish colonial period, before establishment of the first mission in San Diego, "California" meant the great peninsula now called Baja California (lower California). During the colonial mission
period, the name came to include the area from Cape San Lucas at the southern
tip of the Baja Peninsula up to Puget Sound. It was then divided into *Alta* and

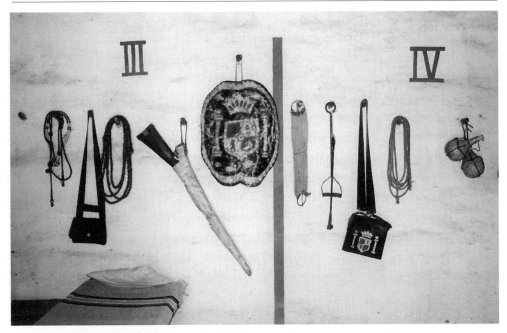

Armor, gun, and riding gear, La Purísima.

*Baja* (upper and lower) California. Spanish settlers called Alta California *Nueva* (new) California and the peninsula *Antigua* (old) California, but by 1800, when the colonial government in Mexico City reorganized the provinces into administrative sections, the names reverted officially to Alta and Baja.[2] After the Treaty of Guadalupe Hidalgo in 1848, Baja California remained part of Mexico.

California's mission story is a poignant and provocative tale of American history. Students of history and culture, along with travelers and the general reader, will discover lesser-known but meaningful scenes from America's past in these pages.

## Understanding the Indians of the Missions

Most of the numerous books and documents from the last two hundred years that deal with the California missions tell the story from the perspective of the European colonists, rather than of the Indians. For an understanding of the Indian perspective, primary research materials—letters, documents, and literature written and passed down by Indians who lived in the missions—are essential. Regretfully, such materials are limited in scope and are frequently based on a few written accounts of the period, secondhand reports, and oral histories.

One reason for this disparity in documentation is the low literacy rate among mission Indian populations. The purpose of missionary teachings was religious education, not the creation of a literate society. Consequently, Indians did not commonly learn to read and write Spanish.

Despite these research obstacles, a wealth of information, including that gained from recent archaeological finds, is available to illuminate the life and culture of California's Indians before the Spanish moved in. With these data, along with detailed mission records of incorporated tribal groups and their occupations, one can gain a basic understanding of the California mission Indians before, during, and after Spanish settlement. This understanding is based in part on educated conclusions, recent ethnographic and ethnohistoric research, and reasoned speculation. In the future more primary research, with the help of further archaeological and anthropological studies, may add details about these native populations, who outnumbered early colonists and soldiers by the thousands.[3]

## Terms and Definitions

To this day controversy rages over the status and definitions of Indian cultures in the United States. How to define oneself and one's connection to one's ancestors is a sensitive and intimate topic. In part, this situation results from the relative lack of historical resources that offer the tribal peoples' own perspective during the mission colonization period.

The term "Indian" originated as a colonial construct based on Columbus's thinking he had landed in the Indies and accordingly giving that name to the islands he discovered. During Spanish colonization of California, Indians were then further historically defined as "neophytes" or "converts" in the missions, as workers in the ranchos, and as residents of the reservations.[4]

Many Native Americans still refer to themselves today as "Indians." "Native American," "Indian," or "American Indian" is commonly used when referring generally to Indians of North America or a particular region. More often, individual tribal names are used.

In California, since before European settlers and explorers arrived, native groups have been identified with specific names for their own cultural subset, village, or language groups. In some instances, this practice has led to the adoption of ethnic terms derived from original village names in mission California, such as Ohlone village.[5]

While "neophytes" and "converts" may seem preferable to earlier terms such as "natives" and "Diggers," which we would consider derogatory, they are misleading in their assumption of a particular state of mind on the part of the Indians. The drastic change from native systems of beliefs to Christianity was extremely complex and is difficult to measure. Debates continue over how Indians were brought into the mission system. To what degree were they coerced? How often did they willingly choose mission life? Although mission Indians during the years of early contact allowed themselves to be baptized and incorporated and no longer publicly practiced many of their previous rituals, we cannot know to what extent a *spiritual* change was made. Calling the mission Indians "converts" is therefore presumptuous.

"Neophyte" presents a similar problem. Traditionally, a neophyte is a person new to the church who is undergoing the process of becoming a Catholic. Not yet baptized and confirmed, but studying Catholic doctrine, a neophyte plans to fully join the faith. Histories that refer to mission residents as "neophytes" neglect to specify whether a person is a full member of the church or is on the path to becoming so.

The terms "heathen" and "gentile," which have been used to refer to Indians outside the mission system, are inappropriate to a balanced study of the Indian peoples.

For consistency and accuracy, the individual cultural names are used within this book when possible; the term "Indians" is used more generally. The above considerations should be kept in mind when reading this and other materials pertaining to the missions of California.

# 1

## Native California before the Missions

EIGHTEENTH-CENTURY HISTORICAL DOCUMENTS and one's imagination can only hint at what transpired during the early meetings between Spaniard and Indian in the native settlements of California, when two worlds collided in a land that had been untouched by outside groups for centuries, even millennia. The Spanish found an established Indian culture that their settlement would forever change.

Spain's colonial mission settlements progressed naturally from occupation of Baja California, south of present-day San Diego, into the coastal regions of central and southern California, including the Pacific shore and the Coast Ranges. The region south of Los Angeles, including San Diego, was the first to be grasped. As a rule, the coastal area was the most accessible and would remain the focus of settlement. The areas occupied by the Colorado River tribes, such as the Mojave and Yuma, living in southwestern California, were more remote, although efforts were made to set up mission sites there.

While Indian knowledge of Europeans was minimal at best, the Spaniards arrived in California with some understanding of native peoples after their colonization of Mexico and Central and South America in the previous centuries.

Still, the Indian cultures north of the Baja Peninsula differed greatly from their southern counterparts and would provide many surprises for the new arrivals.

California and Mexico are rich in archeological findings dating back to approximately 18,000 BCE. California's Indian population in the late eighteenth century has been estimated as the densest in North America at that time, with estimates ranging from 700,000 up to one million people.[1] California's pre-mission Indian cultures were delineated by tribal, territorial, and geographical boundaries created by inland basins, the coast, deserts, waterways, and mountains. Self-contained and cooperative communities evolved within each physically distinct geographic region. Valleys were heavily populated due to their concentrations of vegetation, animals, and water.

Some Indian historians see central California as most typically Californian in its Indian tribal attributes and the northwest coast and the southwest as heavily influenced by British Columbia and the southwest Pueblo culture, respectively. Central California, the bulk of which is the great Central Valley, includes the coasts and stretches from Tehachapi, where the Sierra Nevada joins the Coast Ranges, up through the San Joaquin and Sacramento valleys. While the tribes of central California absorbed and diffused some traits from outlying areas, they also maintained unique and distinct cultures, exemplified by the complex tribal organization of the Yokuts Indians.

The tribes discussed in this book are the major groups of Indians influenced by the Spanish missions of California: the Chumash, Costanoan, Diegueño (Ipai-Tipai), Gabrielino, Juaneño, and Luiseño. (The last four were named after the mission settlements with which they were associated.) These groups encompassed more numerous tribal and cultural subgroups.

While the California Indians shared many culture and lifestyle traits, the large geographic area they lived in also ensured great diversity among them. There were approximately one hundred tribes or similar units in California, along with hundreds of subcultures and villages. The variety of California Indian languages was staggering: California's five primary language groups consisted of twenty-one language families, along with eighty mutually unintelligible languages further sorted into hundreds of dialects.[2]

Customs, spiritual beliefs, modes of survival, and dress also varied across the tribal sections. Group traits accorded with available natural resources and other geographic characteristics of each locale. Major Indian cultural centers of the time were found in widely differing topographies, from the great Central Valley to California's mainland shore and islands. Some village communities differed more by dialect than by political organization. Except between communities that traded with one another, communication across tribal boundaries was limited, resulting in widely differing dialects and languages. Despite these significant variations, some generalizations can be offered about the California Indians' way of life.

### Natural Opportunism

The California Indians' use of land and resources was reflected in broad choices of shelter, tools, and food. Fishing, hunting, and foraging were the primary means of survival among these tribes, known as the most omnivorous group of tribes in North America.[3]

Most pre-mission Indians and their ancestors lived in densely settled valleys along the central and southern coasts. Organized agriculture as we know it today was absent in native California except near the Colorado River, where the Yuma cultivated squash and corn. Elsewhere, food in its natural and ready-to-eat form was so abundant that formal cultivation was unnecessary. Indians did use techniques to facilitate their foraging, such as regularly burning brush to hinder wildfires and increase the growth of new plants.

Occasional droughts, floods, earthquakes, and fires upset the balance of human consumption, but on the whole California's pre-mission Indians enjoyed a bountiful and regular food supply in comparison to those in other regions of North America. Their food typically consisted of seeds and acorns, as well as fish and small game, shellfish and sea mammals on the coast, and larger game animals in the interior. As a result, settlements around lakes and river regions were plentiful. Foothill communities consumed acorns, vegetables, fish, and some game animals. Across California, plants, seeds, and insects were eaten more frequently than mammals, reptiles, and birds.

Acorns were the most common staple of Indian domestic economy throughout California. Acorns had multiple uses in food, but procuring and preparing them was not a simple task. Before they could be consumed safely, their tannic acid had to be removed using a lengthy process. After knocking the acorns to the ground using long poles, the Indians either buried the unshelled acorns in mud for several months to neutralize the acid or used hot water to leach the acid from ground and shelled acorns.[4]

Rivers and streams of the San Joaquin Valley, the lower half of the great Central Valley, provided a bounty of fish and waterfowl. Rain runoff from the Sierra Nevada irrigated the valley and nourished inland Indian cultures with fish and plants. California's southwest coast offered plenty of shellfish and sea mammals.

Tools were crafted to meet the unique needs of particular communities. Indians used the bow in all areas where game was available, and clubs and harpoons on the coasts. Skilled boatmen, the Chumash Indians gained access to the entire coast with their canoes made from wooden planks and tar. The southern Coast Ranges tribes, which had to contend with tall bluffs that obstructed the sea and its fishing grounds, instead harvested wild seeds for sustenance.

Basketry was widespread across California for the collection and storage of materials. It was the most developed art form in California's Indian civilization. Women made rugs and clothing from animal skins, rushes, and anything else available in nature. Mines and quarries provided materials for tools and trade, as well as decorative and ceremonial objects. Tools were also crafted from stone, wood, bones, and shells. Sandstone was a common material on the coast, as was soapstone for vessels in the Channel Islands region.

Along the coast, families occupied basket-like huts of tule, a kind of bulrush. Chumash houses, made of tree branches and reeds, were dome-shaped. Inland, huts were constructed from brush or branches.[5]

By contrast, the nomadic Indians of Baja California struggled to survive in extremely arid and grassless conditions. Mountains and dry land spanned almost the entire length of the peninsula. Life in the Mojave Desert was equally spartan; the Indian tribes who lived there were not targeted by the missionaries, who instead concentrated on Alta California, with its abundant raw foodstuffs and building materials.

## Cultural and Political Division

The word "tribe" should be used carefully when describing Indians in California, who varied somewhat in their organization. Typically, Indians lived in small village units of fifty to five hundred people. The village community was usually a land tract of individually owned property; some five hundred such groupings existed during the precolonial era. Some settlements were communities composed of a collection of villages under a chief's leadership. Ritual and kinship were important ties that strengthened and legitimized each local settlement.

Physical land features marked tribal boundaries, creating insular societies deeply attached to place of birth. Villages were named for their locations and physical attributes. Many groups clearly defined their land-use rights and divisions with regard to neighboring communities.

The Yokuts tribe inhabited the San Joaquin Valley plains and the western Sierra foothills. Along with the Yuma and Mojave, the Yokuts were the closest approximation to a tribal organization, with forty political entities supporting up to a thousand people. Each tribe or subtribe was distinguished by its own language and customs. The Yokuts were truly tribal, with a name, dialect, and designated territory for each subtribe. By the time Spanish settlements appeared on the coast, between fifteen and twenty thousand Yokuts Indians lived in the San Joaquin Valley.

For survival, California's Indian civilization developed its own political systems to oversee these communities sustained by local resources. Across pre-mission California, tribal regions often had a central village that served as a political and economic center. Adjacent groups and villages traded with one another and conducted intertribal trade across ecologically distinct regions. Beyond the hills or boundaries of a territory, ruling chiefs exchanged baskets and shells with neighboring tribes or communities. Shells and shell beads were also traded widely, as were goods such as food, ornaments, household wares, clothing, tools, baskets, and raw materials.

Chiefs typically held the highest position of leadership in California's Indian villages and tribes. The chief directed the daily cycle of village life, overseeing the political and economic activities of each local settlement. The production and distribution of trade items and food also fell under the chief's management of the village economy. For example, the Costanoan, who were hunters and gatherers, left their base villages at certain times of the year under the direction of their chiefs and traveled in search of supplies and resources.

Answering to each chief was a village or tribal council, which was responsible for the administration and execution of the chief's policies. Chiefs at times doubled as religious leaders or shamans. Village and tribe members displayed great respect and deference for their leaders. The chief's position was typically hereditary and associated with wealth accumulated during his term of power. In Salinan culture, men and women inherited chiefdoms patrilineally.

The Chumash lived in villages under regional federations ruled by chiefs. Chumash society was tiered, from poor laborers to skilled craftsmen to the chiefs, shamans, and healers. Both women and men were chiefs and shamans. Chiefs were the most powerful and wealthy of the Chumash and oversaw several villages. Salinan hereditary chiefs also ruled multiple villages and solidified political ties with neighboring groups and territories through marriage.

The traditional California Indian family was more a web of associations than a conjugal unit. These ties were often economic, political, and kinship based. Although marriage customs varied from region to region, marriage usually occurred within social and economic ranks, and tribal leaders promoted economically productive family relationships within tribes. Marriage followed strict rules and was often arranged by village elders or parents. Sometimes a price was involved. The groom's family would give the bride's parents a gift, a bride price, to recognize the status of her family and compensate them for the loss of her labor—a kind of reverse dowry. Marriages that solidified ties between neighboring villages or families in prominent positions of leadership were encouraged. Such ties helped maintain economic prosperity and limited the possibility of warfare between groups.

Although Indian society, like Catholic Spanish society, prohibited incest, sexual behavior and attitudes tended to be more tolerant in Indian society and less punitive of premarital, extramarital, and polygamous associations, as well as divorce. In the *berdache* tradition, men assumed female traits and were accorded social status as transvestites, a recognized third gender.[6]

The social structure and interrelationships came under the supervision of the chief. In general, California chiefs settled disputes among village families and saw that the laws of the tribe were followed, sometimes meting out punishment for crimes. Disagreements between leaders over the balance of trade, land and resources, and encounters with occasional trespassers from outside tribes were the most common reasons for conflict in pre-mission California. The crossing of another tribe's boundary to hunt or fish was forbidden. These and other territorial altercations were usually settled early by tribal chiefs. Widespread war and conquest by invasion were uncommon events. Local conflicts were no doubt a regular fact of life, as described by mission Indian Pablo Tac of Mission San Luis Rey: "[A]lways there was a war, always strife day and night with those who spoke in another language." Writing in the mid-nineteenth century, Tac referred to Indian conflict prior to mission settlements. Life "was very miserable, because there was always strife." Tac's observation also illuminates the sometimes stark differences among Indian cultures. He concluded: "Thus we lived among the woods until merciful God freed us of these miseries through Father Antonio Péyri, a Catalan, who arrived in our country in the afternoon with seven Spanish soldiers."[7] This individual perspective from an educated Indian suggests that the Spanish missionaries saved his people from their warring tendencies.

### Earth, Spirit, and Kin

A belief system that intimately connected each person with the earth guided the behavior and spirituality of California's Indians. Plants, animals, land, and cosmology were crucial to their understanding of the world. The Indian concept of time, as in many human societies, followed the seasons and the phases of the moon and sun. All pre-mission Indians were hunters, gatherers, and fishermen whose ceremonies centered on the seasons and the fall harvest. They attributed the gifts of a mild climate and rich land to their creator, or to a family of gods and spirits who watched over them.

Transcending the differences between Indian groups, social customs and spiritual beliefs sustained the symbiosis between nature and humanity across California. While each tribe and community maintained its local traditions, some general social and spiritual behaviors spanned the tribes. For example, women followed their own rituals associated with childbirth and other stages of life. Tribes valued the sweathouse as a communal institution where men and adolescent boys met daily to promote kinship and friendship and for physical and spiritual purification, more for ritual than for medicinal purposes.[8] Frederick Beechey, commander of the British ship *Blossom*, which anchored at California in 1826 en route to a northern polar expedition, observed:

> At some of the missions they pursue a custom said to be of great antiquity among the aborigines and which appears to afford them much enjoyment. A mud house or rather a large oven, called *temescál* by the Spaniards, is built in a circular form, with a small entrance and an aperture in the top for the smoke to escape through. Several persons enter this place quite naked and make a fire near the door, which they continue to feed with wood as long as they can bear the heat. In a short time they are thrown into a most profuse perspiration; they wring their hair and scrape their skin with a sharp piece of wood or an iron hoop, in the same manner as coach horses are sometimes treated when they come in heated; and then plunge into a river or pond of cold water, which they always take care shall be near the *temescál*.[9]

Rather than one organized religion, California's Indians followed a complex web of beliefs about their earthly and spiritual worlds as manifested in daily life. Shamans were the religious leaders throughout California. Each region's intricate spiritual heritage was characterized by the shaman's exercise of power. Healer, medicine man or woman, and priest, the shaman ranked second to the chief in authority and prestige in each village. Widely accepted as a healer of disease, the shaman spent a lifetime caring for the sick, settling disputes, and comforting with wisdom passed through the ages. A bridge between humans and the spiritual world, the shaman was believed to possess supernatural powers and a connection with guardian spirits. Above all, the shaman nourished the spiritual life of the villagers, joining them with the gods and spirits who surrounded them.

In central and southern California, the shaman's power carried different characteristics, ranging from benevolent to evil. The nature and source of shaman power differed among tribal regions, as did the associated customs. Rain and rattlesnake doctors were other breeds of shaman in the pre-mission areas. The bear doctor's ability to transform into a grizzly bear allowed him or her to destroy enemies and evil spirits.

Inanimate objects were also assumed to embody spirits. On the coast, during the winter solstice, Chumash shamans led festivals in honor of the sun, known as the fiery giver and taker of life. Indians paid attention to the stars, and village shamans were trusted as astrologers who helped guide the way and make predictions.

The Indian spiritual belief system included creation mythology: one or more gods were seen as responsible for the creation of the earth and its inhabitants. Indian religion also explained natural occurrences. A giant, possibly the creator himself, caused earthquakes by rolling over during his underground sleep. A Costanoan creation myth described a primeval flood that inundated the universe. Subsequently, earth and man were formed from mud with the help of a turtle.[10] Indians of the inland valleys believed the eagle to be the earth's creator. The Gabrielino, Juaneño, and Luiseño Indians believed porpoises watched the world, circling it to be sure it was safe.[11] Such myths explained reality for California Indians. Gods or natural and supernatural forces were the cause of all events, good and bad. Shamans were expected to listen to these gods and communicate appropriate action to the community.

Clans and totems were especially common in the Central Valley region on the outskirts of the mission yoke. Totemic religion was present in southern and south-central California among such tribes as the Miwok, Central Yokuts, Salinan, and Luiseño. Totemic philosophy was based on a symbiosis between humans and animals that enforced both taboos and privileges, depending on the tribe's customs and animal beliefs. The moiety defined rituals and helped maintain man's balance with nature.

Often animals such as the bear and eagle were personified and had spectacular powers attributed to them. Many California Indians did not eat bear meat because they believed bears resembled humans. On the coast, as mentioned above, the porpoise was considered guardian of the world.[12] Costanoan groups, for spiritual or superstitious reasons, avoided eating animals such as eagles, owls, ravens, buzzards, frogs, and toads.

Totems and the structure of Indian cults varied widely from place to place. Some cult practices were common across California, such as war and victory dances; female adolescent ceremonies that incorporated singing, dancing, fasting from meat, and other rituals; and other adolescent rites of initiation.

Southern California and the Sierra region practiced a "mourning anniversary" ceremony to honor dead tribe members. The death of a loved one was initially recognized by his property being destroyed and his name no longer being mentioned. His thatched house, like that of his ancestors before him, would be burnt to the ground and scattered in the river with his ashes.

During the mission period, the Franciscans often recorded their observations of seemingly religious aspects of Indian culture. For instance, one prominent missionary in San Luis Rey recorded that the Indians had "an idea of a rational soul, which they call *chamson,* and believe that when they die this goes below to *tolmar,* where all come together and live forever in much happiness. With this they have, however, no idea of reward or punishment."[13]

With these timeless rituals, the Indians dealt with grief and other emotions through their greater connection with ancestral spirits and the earth. Like their ancestors before them, members of a tribal group may have expected this and other traditions to repeat themselves in generations to come and made efforts to perpetuate them. The Kuksu cult, common to the western Coast Ranges, San Francisco Bay, eastern Sacramento Valley, and northern San Joaquin Valley, is a well-known example. Especially among the Yokuts, this cult, a complex and formal organization with secret administrative societies, focused its spiritual attention on ghosts and spirits. Shamans and other participants impersonated gods and spirits in intricate dances, and the dance for the dead was a salient tradition.

Indian medicine used shamanistic and ceremonial practices as well as pharmaceutical remedies. In the south, the Chumash, Yokuts, Gabrielino, Juaneño, and Luiseño practiced various cults based on the narcotic plant *toloache* (datura, or jimsonweed). Among the Chumash, for example, the drug was used in puberty rites and the interpretation of dream visions, and a network of priests moved from village to village to participate in rituals.[14]

All tribes followed their own taboos, omens, origin myths, lore, and guides for behavior. Mythology presented a narrative example for behavior and differed according to the region of origin. Central California myths perpetuated by the Costanoan, Esselen, Miwok, and Yokuts focused on contests between animals. Instead of one creator, a hierarchy of animals governed the world. Southwest

Courtyard, Mission San Miguel.

legends made more abstract references to the human spirit and soul, to life and death, and to an "earth-female" and "sky-male" duality.[15] Tribal and interfamily history were passed through the generations through stories and legends.

Most Indians were animists who viewed animate creatures and inanimate objects as carriers of spirit, both good and evil. Dancers played a strong supernatural role as communicators with the spirits. Prayers and offerings were prominent in the Costanoan religion, along with dream interpretations. Shamans were believed to control the weather and cure disease. Such religious and ceremonial practices were broadly labeled as idolatry by the Spanish and considered antithetical to Christian belief. However, as in other cultures influenced and converted by Catholicism elsewhere in the world, some local Indian customs were incorporated into mission life or allowed to remain to a certain degree.

With the arrival of Spanish missionaries, the California Indians' spiritual and temporal existence was drastically uprooted. Seen by the missionaries as incompatible with Catholicism, Indian religions were replaced, at least superficially, with the dogma and practice of the Catholic Church. Personification of animals and nature was discounted as superstition, idolatry, or even devil worship. Other rituals such as animal and human sacrifice and infanticide were eliminated and replaced by the missionaries with a new set of rules, some enforced with capital

Entrance to La Purísima.

punishment. No priest could change or enter the minds of the Indians completely, however. As in other cultures converted to Catholicism elsewhere in the world, some local Indian customs were allowed to remain to a certain degree. The result was a metamorphosis of two cultures and the first immigrant transformation of California's population.

*Yokuts Indian Prayer*

My words are tied in one
With the great mountains,
With the great rocks,
With the great trees,
In one with my body
And my heart.[16]

# 2

## All the World's a Stage for Spain

*Divine Rule and Foreign Policy*

Spain, a country twice the size of today's Oregon, once ruled almost half the world. As the leading European power and with an unparalleled colonial presence, Spain in the fifteenth and sixteenth centuries controlled a land area twenty times the size of the ancient Roman Empire. Hernando Cortés, the original Spanish conquistador, captured the Aztec capital Tenochtitlán (Mexico City) in 1521 and oversaw more missions in Mexico and the East Indies.[1] Mexico then blossomed into the center of Spanish colonial power in the Americas.

By 1540 the Spanish empire base had spread from the Iberian Peninsula across Europe, South America, Asia, and the Caribbean. While instituting military settlements, Spain also attempted to implant its religion and culture in the New World. California in the eighteenth century was the last extension of the Spanish empire.

Spain asserted its colonial goals through military strength and religious doctrine. Popular in Europe since medieval times was the belief that kings and queens, as God's representatives on Earth, possessed a divine right to rule in

Moorish gate in Spain. © iStockphoto.com/Charles Humphries.

God's name. Each Spanish king thus had a divine duty to protect the interests of his empire.

Imposition and promotion of Christianity were official policy in Spain long before the Franciscans trudged through the coastal mountains of California. Spain set out to convert, civilize, and exploit the new subjects in its American possessions,[2] imposing Catholic values and practices in its territories while trying to protect Christendom and Spanish lands from foreign enemies. To that end, religious conformity was brutally enforced in Spain for centuries under the Inquisition; when King Ferdinand II of Aragon (1479–1516) and Queen Isabella I of Castile (1474–1504), joint rulers of Spain from 1479, expelled Jews and Moors from Spain in 1492; and later in the rigid atmosphere of the Counter-Reformation under King Philip II (1556–98).

Ferdinand and Isabella were granted the unusual right of patronage, usually reserved for the pope, which allowed them to appoint bishops and clergy to serve in the Americas. Spanish monarchs championed the conversion of native North and South Americans to Roman Catholicism, strengthening their claim to the colonies with instant populations of Spanish subjects. They sent home-grown missionaries and soldiers to complete the task of settling Mexico and South America. In South America, conquistadores—the Spanish conquerors of Indian societies—and Catholic missionaries worked to help increase Spain's wealth, territory, and cultural domination.

Religious conversion was one way to acquire a cooperative labor force. Spain used its Catholic subjects to exploit resources and produce exportable goods. Taxation and conscripted labor in the colonies yielded profits for the kingdom. In California, Indians were intended to become the lower class, supporting Spanish colonial society with inexpensive labor.

Over a period of two centuries, missions became the tool on the local level for managing Indians and turning them into Spanish subjects. Spain further secured its power in the Americas through the creation of a colonial society living in towns, forts, and other settlements. In time, Indians became dependent on agriculture, livestock, and nearby water sources for their survival and remained in these settlements.[3] "Incorporation" was a commonly used term in seventeenth-century government documents when discussing the process of Indian conversion.[4] The Spanish viewed Indians predominantly as inferior peoples subject to control.

By the time Spain settled California at the end of the eighteenth century, its presence in Mexico and Central and South America was firmly established. The history and development of the New World missions is therefore most appropriately framed in the context of Spain's role as colonizer of parts of North America, South America, and the West Indies.

Colonization was manifest in Mexico and South America in the *encomienda*, a colonial land system. First applied to the Moors in Spain, the encomienda supported the colonial network by extracting tribute and labor from the Indians as it "civilized" and converted them. The system gradually slowed after its prohibition in the New Laws of the Indies in 1542, but its underpinnings of forced labor survived to the end of Spanish rule in California in 1821.

In 1520, just before King Charles I (1516–56) left Spain to assume his inherited position as Holy Roman Emperor, he and his deputies were counseled during a meeting with advisers: "Spain's glory, long asleep, has now returned. Those who have sung its praises tell us that when other nations sent tributes to Rome, Spain sent emperors. . . . Now the empire has come to Spain in search of an emperor and our King of Spain has, by God's grace, become King of the Romans and emperor of the world."[5] Such a bold declaration of power illustrates Spain's imperial and religious ambitions in the New World. Spain's colonial objectives for the Indians of New Spain were driven by a mix of international politics, economic motives, and evangelism.

### God's Foot Soldiers

The mission soon became the best tool for settlement in the Americas. Spain's economy contracted in the late sixteenth century, the beginning of a century-long depression that called for increased territorial expansion to fill in the holes.[6] Though colonial policy was intended to bolster Spain's wealth with mining and exports, output and wealth did not increase in the long term. Spain's depleted treasury soon gobbled up profits, and New Spain was left with rising costs, labor and supply shortages, and fixed prices for mining products.

For these reasons, Spain began to use missionaries, who were cheaper than soldiers, to extend its frontiers in the Americas. The Royal Order for New Discoveries of 1573 established missionaries as the agents for colonial occupation in New Spain.[7] In 1591, the Spanish crown ordered missionaries to convert Indians in New Spain. Spain's own settlers overseas were limited in number, and missionaries were able to help Spain obtain and keep land in newly explored parts of the world. Before the missionaries of Alta California set their first wooden crosses in the ground, missions played a primary role in dominating large native populations from South America to Baja California. The Jesuit missions in Paraguay, for example, and missionaries and their soldiers in central and northern Mexico ruled vast territories and many thousands of Indians.

Throughout their occupation, the Franciscan, Dominican, and Jesuit orders worked to convert and educate Indians. Spain established the Apostolic College of San Fernando in Mexico City to facilitate the acquisition of new territories. This college was the seat of government for Spain's colonies in the New World, and would be the headquarters of the Franciscans.

## The Jesuits

The Society of Jesus was founded by the Spanish priest St. Ignatius of Loyola in 1540. Jesuits came from noble and educated families and studied philosophy and theology at Spain's universities. With the order's focus on education, it became popular with young intellectuals from around the world. Also known as "soldiers of God," the Jesuits organized their communities along military lines and carried on the Catholic fight against Protestantism in Europe, Asia, and elsewhere. The military nature of the Jesuit organization was well suited to Spain's colonial effort, and the kingdom sent Jesuit missionaries to the New World.

Although Spanish settlements were confined to small areas in New Spain and South America, the mission system controlled most of the territory.[8] In Baja California, the Jesuits maintained order with a small peninsular army. With soldiers on constant watch at the missions, Jesuit superiors retained any soldiers they could afford to pay and had the power to hire and dismiss officers.

Jesuits immediately settled and converted parts of Mexico. In 1697 the Spanish government officially authorized the Society of Jesus to establish colonial missions in California. Mexico City became the administrative center, and the Jesuits, to help create a society based on law, order, religion, and education, set up colleges for both Spaniards and Indians.

The Jesuit order began its colonization of most of Baja California that same year, eventually establishing eighteen missions and several smaller settlements. Geographic isolation and financial strength allowed the missionaries to operate with great autonomy. The Jesuits also assumed absolute authority in administrative and spiritual affairs on the Baja Peninsula and elsewhere. The Pious Fund for the Californias allowed the Jesuits to fund their own governmental organization of the province, keeping it from being a burden on the Spanish treasury. Supported by gifts from private parties and powerful allies in the royal and noble elite and directly administered by representatives from the missions, the fund supported Jesuit civil and political administration.

The fund courted benefactors in the late seventeenth century, when the Jesuit mission cause was highly regarded in both Spain and New Spain. Donated monies were also used to buy haciendas—rural properties that raised sheep or cattle for profit. Monies earned went right back into the fund and helped sustain it.

While on the whole the Jesuits worked independently, they still relied on infusions of royal gold. The royal treasury paid expenses approved by the king, in whose name the Jesuits controlled territory for Spain. The kingdom provided fixed stipends to Jesuits who independently conducted expeditions and enlisted soldiers as guards. Jesuit landholdings, agriculture, and industry paid less in taxes and tithes than other colonists.[9]

The Jesuits' military and political autonomy and their success and influence with Spain's upper classes eventually backfired and caused suspicion amid royal and elite circles. The crown accused the Jesuits of concealing wealth in their missions and interfering in politics and suspected them of plotting to establish independent Jesuit states in South America.

At the same time that King Charles III (1759–88) was increasing Spain's presence in Alta California, he abruptly expelled the Jesuits from New Spain in 1767. All leaders of territories under Spain were ordered to arrest Jesuits, send them home, and confiscate their land and property. This was part of a general campaign to reform Spain, create a more secular society,[10] and modernize the Spanish empire. The church and the more conservative aristocrats were stripped of power, and expelling the Jesuits was an indirect way to attack both groups. Portugal had already expelled Jesuits from the homeland and the colonies in 1759, as had France in 1764, and the Society of Jesus was dissolved altogether by papal order in 1773.

As the king's agent for reform, José Gálvez arrived in Mexico City in 1765 to serve as *visitador general* (inspector general), Charles's highest representative in New Spain. Gálvez remained until 1771 and instituted new conscription and taxation laws as well as a stronger imperial defense. The Jesuits became Gálvez's scapegoat for the financial problems of the Baja Peninsula missions.[11] He objected to the large farms that exploited and enslaved Indians, and it was by his order that the Jesuits in New Spain were deported from the region. Spain confiscated all Jesuit holdings and transferred them to royal ownership, and military officials took over missions in New Mexico, Arizona, and Texas before they were converted to secular parishes.[12]

### A Precedent to Follow, and One to Avoid

The first Alta California missions soon followed the Jesuit ousting. Members of the Franciscan and Dominican orders were sent to replace Jesuit leaders in several missions in central Mexico and Baja California. At this time the missions in Baja California were in severe decline, and the rural estates that supplied the Pious Fund also suffered. Stored food, tools, and clothing were scarce. In 1768 the Franciscans assumed control of fourteen Jesuit missions in Baja California.

Thirteen of these were transferred to the Dominicans in 1774, allowing the Franciscans to concentrate their numbers in Alta California. The Dominicans founded seven more missions between 1774 and 1797.

Rather than use Baja California missions as prototypes for Alta California, New Spain looked to central Mexico as the model for new mission settlements. Evidently missions were most successful in areas with plentiful natural resources. Spanish colonists had settled in Sonora to establish mines, and during the late seventeenth century the Jesuits built missions in northern Sonora, near present-day southern Arizona. These missions were familiar features in Sonora, where many generations of converts lived and produced goods long before the first California mission in San Diego. Located in fertile valleys, the Sonoran missions provided the first livestock and supplies to new missions across the Gulf of California.

After Cortés conquered Mexico in 1521 and became governor and captain general of New Spain, he sent an expedition in 1535 across the Gulf of California to the newly discovered "island" of California (that is, Baja California) to set up a base for further expansion and search for pearl beds. A romantic saga popular in Spain soon after the time of Columbus was set in the New World on an island called California, located "on the right hand of the Indies."[13] This fictional island beckoned adventurers with its stores of gold and pearls, and it was natural to christen the new land after it. Despite being discovered in 1539 (by Francisco de Ulloa) to be a peninsula, California was depicted on maps as an island as late as the mid-1750s, even after Ferdinand VI (1746–59) officially proclaimed, "California is not an island."[14]

Cortés's new colony suffered from a lack of resources and supplies, including pearls, and was abandoned in 1536. The first permanent Spanish settlement in the Baja Peninsula was the Jesuit mission in Loreto, on the eastern coast of the peninsula, in 1697. Though Loreto developed into a major mission and pueblo, subsequent settlements on the peninsula were not as fortunate. Spain fell short of its goal of colonizing the Indians in the Baja Peninsula, setting a poor example for the Alta California missions.

The peninsula's remote location and barren resources made survival arduous, and attracting converts became a problem. On the other hand, the unforgiving environment was an opportunity for missionaries to draw Indians in with food, both imported and locally grown, and to hold them for indoctrination, at least initially. One Jesuit in Baja California described their method: "We left many gates in [the fort] through which the Indians could go and come at their pleasure before we took up our residence within. We did this in order that the heathen

Baja California desert. © iStockphoto.com/Mike Marketello.

might not understand how we were going to use this fort. . . . The following morning, the California Indians were surprised when they saw that the gates had been closed and that, within this short time, we had settled ourselves inside a new stronghold."[15]

By the time New Spain founded its first Alta California mission in San Diego in 1769, the missions of the Baja Peninsula were crumbling. Indians there reportedly lived peacefully under the mission system, adopting basic farming techniques and learning Christian doctrine and tradition. Some learned to speak Spanish. However, missions drained Spain's colonial coffers. The revenue from royal duties on pearls and silver was not enough to maintain the province's army.[16]

Finding adequate resources to support the missions was a difficult task. Agricultural success in the Baja Peninsula was undermined by a declining population, drought, and famine. While the coast of Alta California had fertile land and abundant food sources, the Baja Peninsula was barren and not conducive to permanent settlement. Clouds of locusts had destroyed crops in all but the northernmost missions in Baja California, and the herds had been reduced by half.[17] The population was constantly on the lookout for food. Roots, stems, seeds, insects, small animals, and occasional larger game were indispensable to survival, and water was a constant concern.

Soldiers on garrison duty were poorly paid and equipped. Miners quickly picked over the ore districts, and commercial manufacture and agriculture hovered at a paltry level of output. Some Baja Indians had been driven from their native lands and transferred to remote regions of the peninsula, and the displaced population succumbed to diseases such as smallpox, syphilis, tuberculosis, measles, typhus, and malaria. The native mission population of the Baja Peninsula was reduced to a tenth of its original number, with "the survivors living quietly in the missions as neophytes, toiling in the mines or on the *haciendas* practically as slaves."[18] Less labor was available for the construction and maintenance of religious and civil buildings, mining, agriculture, and hunting. Tributes and administrative fees imposed on the Indians also disappeared as sources of income.

The Franciscans removed supply stores from the Baja Peninsula missions and took them north to the more fertile mission sites of California. By 1772, the devastated Baja Peninsula missions were taken over by the Dominicans. Spanish settlers began to move into the mission sites, where they raised cattle and worked small plots of land.

Frontier plans and goals for Baja California fell flat. A program to distribute Jesuit mission lands and communal land and water rights to Spanish settlers and converts was never carried out. Militia companies were planned, as well as schools to help mission children learn trades, but these were never realized either.[19] The necessary supplies and money were simply unavailable.

The Baja chain of missions was one of the least fruitful colonial efforts of the Spanish frontier. The changeover from Jesuit to Franciscan, then to Dominican administration began a new era of mission building for Spain, its future difficulties foreshadowed by the ailing Baja Peninsula missions.

## Exploration of an Unknown Coast

Because of war in Europe and a constrained treasury, the budget for additional exploration was limited. As a result, incursions into California from Mexico were sporadic, and it was almost two centuries before any permanent settlements were planted. Instead, Spain devoted its resources to the exploration and settlement of other New World colonies.

In 1542 Spain enlisted Portuguese admiral Juan Rodriguez Cabrillo to explore the coast of Alta California for further harbors and potential colonies. It was also Cabrillo's job to find the Northwest Passage, or the Straits of Anian, which supposedly connected the Atlantic and Pacific oceans, providing a route to the Spice Islands. Cabrillo discovered San Diego Bay and sailed north to explore and map California's coast. His crew ended up just north of San Francisco Bay. San Diego Bay was highly desirable for its strategic location against possible incursions from other countries and as a safe harbor for Spanish ships. As traveler Henry Miller observed two centuries later during his tour of the missions, "The

Bay of San Diego is, next to the Bay of San Francisco, the best on this coast. The entrance is very narrow, but deep enough for any vessel."

Cabrillo suffered an infection from a broken bone and died on an island in the Santa Barbara Channel. His crew dutifully pressed on to Cape Mendocino and up near southern Oregon, returning to Mexico the following year. While gathering information about the upper half of the California coast, Cabrillo's crew had failed to locate the Northwest Passage.

Although Spain based its imperial claim to Alta California on the findings of Cabrillo's voyage, it was afraid and jealous of the English, Portuguese, and Dutch explorers and guarded the details of this and other explorations. Cabrillo and his crew's official charts of their voyage were kept secret. All that survives of Cabrillo's ship's log is a poor copy that contains the first place-names and descriptions of California Indians, with particular emphasis on the Chumash.

In the mid- to late sixteenth century, during the reign of Queen Elizabeth I (1558–1603), England was actively exploring the Pacific coast of North America and New Spain. English sailors such as Sir Francis Drake posed a constant threat to Spanish colonial towns and ships on the western coasts of the Americas. After plundering coastal towns in South America, Drake traveled to California in 1579. Fog kept Drake away from the narrow entrance to San Francisco Bay, and he docked to the north in Miwok territory and explored the interior for several weeks. Not finding the Northwest Passage as he had hoped, Drake backtracked down the coast.

Drake claimed northern California for England, calling it "New Albion," after the ancient name for England. It is believed that the California coast reminded Drake of the white cliffs of Dover.[20] Drake's return, even without the discovery of the Northwest Passage, was a triumph, with newly claimed land and abundant treasure stolen from Spanish caravans and South American coastal towns and a galleon from the Philippines.

The Philippines became part of the Spanish empire in 1522. Galleons, large three-masted merchant ships, picked up luxury goods traded in Manila in exchange for Mexican silver and brought them back for the new Mexican landed aristocracy. Starting in 1565, Spanish merchant galleons traveled once a year from Acapulco to the Philippines. They returned by sailing north to Japan, east to North America, and southeast along the western coast back to Acapulco.[21] California was the first stop after long months at sea, with the ships low on food supplies and fresh water and the crews often suffering from the dramatic climate changes. Nineteenth-century California historian Hubert Bancroft wrote: "Year after year the Manila galleon, coming from the west by the northern route sadly in need of a refitting and relief station, had borne her strained timbers and oriental treasure and scurvy-stricken crew down past the California ports."[22] In this condition, the galleons were easy prey for English and Dutch pirates near Cape San Lucas.[23]

Merchants and trade were vital to Spain's economy; each trip usually brought at least $25,000 in profit.[24] In 1595, King Philip II of Spain sent Sebastián Cermeño on a Manila galleon to explore the upper California coast for a safe harbor. Cermeño shipwrecked in the same place Drake had landed, and he and his crew limped back to Mexico in a small boat. However, during the return trip he completed a detailed survey of the California coast. In the long term this was extremely valuable, though in the short term it was overshadowed by his loss of a valuable galleon.

In 1602, King Philip II sent Basque soldier and merchant Sebastián Vizcaíno on the same mission that Cermeño had undertaken. Vizcaíno was instructed to explore the coast carefully from Cape San Lucas to Cape Mendocino in northern California, and as far north as Cape Blanco in Oregon. Though he too was forced to return fraught with scurvy after an arduous voyage up the California coast, his expedition produced a detailed charting of the coast. Vizcaíno christened land features with Spanish names that still remain, including San Diego and Monterey, which featured suitable harbors for galleons, and the Santa Barbara Channel and its islands. He managed to bypass the great San Francisco Bay, which would not be discovered by the Spanish until 1769. Despite his efforts, more than a century and a half passed before Spain again attempted to colonize Alta California.

By the middle of the seventeenth century, Spain's superior military and political power in Europe had begun to diminish. Spain lost Portugal in 1640, and by 1700 was losing its grip on the Spanish Netherlands. Preoccupied with war and local bureaucratic concerns, the Spanish government became reluctant with its funds. Exploration stagnated.

Throughout the eighteenth century, Spain was reluctant to commit resources to colonizing a remote land with natives who might be hostile. Alta California was too far from supply centers in Mexico and was overwhelming to navigate without established land routes: the dry, mountainous overland route through California was as grueling as traveling by sea.

## The Bourbon Transformation, and Competition

By the reign of King Charles III (1759–88), Bourbon reformism had reached the New World, along with a desire to expand use of America's raw materials. Colonial spoils had financed wars and paid debts for imperial defense overseas in the seventeenth century, and further wealth beckoned. Gold and silver were still essential resources to be gleaned from the New World, and a continued search for riches and pearl beds, the desire to incorporate more lands and people into the empire, and the search for ship havens reignited Spain's probe north of Mexico.

Spanish foreign policy during the Bourbon period focused on improved commerce and trade, in part to maintain imperial control. Spain acknowledged the possibility of war with England, along with colonial and commercial competition in the West Indies, on the Gulf of Mexico coast, in the Caribbean, and on the Atlantic coast. Though Spain lost Florida in 1763, the possession of New Spain (Mexico) was more assured. Colonial production of materials in Mexico grew while Spain's administrative control over New Spain tightened.

In Alta California, the British and Russians presented a potential threat from the north. In the hands of a foreign power, Alta California could have served as a base for conquest of northern Mexico's mines, a Spanish interest for more than two centuries.[25] Russian exploration of the Alaskan coast in the 1740s through 1760s had put Spain's absentee claim to Alta California at risk. Russian fur traders and explorers had erected small outposts along the coasts of Alaska and California, and by 1783 Russia had extended its fur trade to the Alaskan mainland (the profitable Russian fur trade monopoly in the region lasted well into the nineteenth century). Russian settlements spanned from Alaska to Point Reyes, north of San Francisco Bay.

This threat, the idea of establishing a protective zone between warring Indian tribes and northern New Spain,[26] and the need for expansion eventually overrode the state of Spain's finances and the poor results in settling the Baja Peninsula, and Spanish attention turned to California in earnest in 1765. Spain quickly formed a mission plan. Replacements were needed for the positions that had been held by Jesuits. Cheap labor was now even more essential to colonial plans. Viceroy Carlos Francisco de Croix, second in charge to the visitador general, was the man to carry out the king's order.[27] As soon as the Jesuit expulsion was official news in Mexico City, de Croix granted the Franciscan order permission to establish missions in California. In 1768 de Croix received orders from King Charles that San Diego and Monterey should be occupied and fortified in response to the Russian presence on the northwest coast.[28] The Franciscan headquarters in New Spain were in Mexico City, at the Apostolic Missionary College of San Fernando.

De Croix and Gálvez were the individuals behind the "Sacred Expedition" of 1769, the first stage of Spain's consolidation of power in Alta California. Franciscans, soldiers, and settlers were sent to California. The official expedition order for land and sea stated: "The High Government of Spain being informed of the repeated attempts of a foreign nation upon the northern coasts of California with aims by no means favorable to the Monarchy and its interests, the King gave orders to the Marques de Croix, his Viceroy and Captain General in New Spain, that he should take effective measures to guard that part of his dominions from all invasion and insult."[29] Gálvez was told to secure the whole northwest coast of California as far as it had been discovered and explored by Cabrillo in 1542 and by Vizcaíno in 1602 and 1603. San Diego was intended as an intermediate base between Monterey and Loreto. An expeditionary force of soldiers and settlers would hold the country, along with missionaries to convert the Indians. Gálvez was given the task of organizing the conquest of Alta California, and he ordered the creation of missions in the Colorado River region in 1777.

Two other Spanish leaders were at the forefront of this new colonization effort. In 1768, under orders from Charles III, Don Gaspar de Portolá arrived in Baja California with fourteen Franciscan friars to become the military administrator of both Alta and Baja California. And the most famous Spaniard associated with the California missions, their founder, Franciscan Father Junípero Serra, frequently consulted with Visitador General Gálvez to plan the first Alta California expedition. Serra's life story would become central to the establishment and maintenance of a mission chain in Alta California.

# 3

## Exploration and Settlement

*By Land or by Sea*

The proposed expedition and future trips to Alta California faced a host of problems. Where Baja California had been remote from Mexico City and mission supply centers, Alta California was even farther away. Travelers faced unexplored land, mountain chains, deserts, and a lack of supplies.

Periodic pirate raids from Europe made travel by sea risky and unpredictable. Because local ship design and construction were poorer than in Europe and the Caribbean, the ships and the iron used for fastenings and fittings were of poor quality and repairs were always needed.[1]

Ocean winds and unknown rocks and islets threatened voyages to San Diego and Monterey. No fresh food or water made illnesses such as scurvy a constant threat. Father Junípero Serra's account of sailing to San Diego from Baja California in the winter of 1774 explains: "Before we had been at sea a fortnight, cold fits and recurrent fevers took hold of the Father, my companion, and, although he tried to shake them off, they still hold him in their grip."[2]

The journey through Baja California was barren and without adequate water supply. A new land route was desperately needed to transport settlers, missionaries, soldiers, animals, arms, and food supplies, as well as to facilitate communication with the government in New Spain. Administrators in New Spain evaluated possible routes from New Mexico, Arizona, and Sonora. The old Camino Reál, which the Jesuits had used throughout the seventeenth century, ran through settled areas between Mexico City and Guadalajara, continued northwest along an ancient trade route through the Sierra Madre[3] and the plains to Sonora, then proceeded northeast to the pueblos of New Mexico. A new route was intended to extend from Sonora to Monterey.

Spanish captain Juan Bautista de Anza explored a possible overland route in 1774–75, traveling through Yuma territory in present-day Arizona. Anza started at Tubac, Sonora, in January of 1774, crossed through the Colorado Desert, and ended at Mission San Gabriel in March of 1775, having traveled some one thousand miles. When he returned, he quickly organized an expedition of soldiers and settlers from Sonora to the coast of Alta California. This expedition opened the overland route to the new mission sites in Alta California. In 138 days, Anza guided 240 colonists, the largest party of Mexican settlers to California at one time, along with one thousand head of livestock. Thirty-four families, with all the supplies needed for the expedition and settlement, trudged the rough overland route with mules, cattle, and horses. The goal of the expedition was to populate and settle two new missions and a presidio at San Francisco Bay. The promise of pay and luxuries such as tobacco, brandy, and wine attracted settlers to join.

The expedition passed through deserts and forded the Colorado River, pressed northwest, was welcomed at Mission San Gabriel, and arrived in Monterey in March of 1776. Anza, Franciscan Father Pedro Font, and a company of soldiers left the colonists in Monterey and hiked toward San Francisco Bay to choose the mission site. Anza and the colonists followed in June after permission to build the mission was granted, and at the end of the month the group pitched seventeen tents at the bay.

To protect the new overland route from Mexico to Alta California, the Spanish founded a small mission settlement at Yuma in 1780. The plan for the Colorado River missions was to set up Spanish towns with small bands of soldiers for protection. Franciscan priests would minister to the Spaniards and Indians. The settlers used Yuma Indian fields for planting and grazing livestock.[4] However, in 1781 the Yuma revolted against the incursion, destroyed two settlements, and massacred the settlers. This turn of events cut overland connections between Sonora and California, sealing off the lower Colorado River region to settlers until the conquest of northwest Mexico by the United States. The government of New Spain tried to retaliate against the Yuma with limited Spanish forces, but soon abandoned its plans for missions and presidios along the Colorado River.

### Establishing the First Missions in Alta California

In 1769 an expedition of three ships and two overland parties was sent out to construct missions and presidios at San Diego and Monterey. The ships would carry supplies and church furniture. Commander Don Gaspar de Portolá, the first governor of Baja California and leader of the colonial effort in Alta California, was assigned to supervise the expedition of soldiers, settlers, Indians, and missionaries to San Diego. Father Junípero Serra, a learned Franciscan from the island of Majorca, Spain, led the group of missionaries. Serra had worked as a missionary in Mexico for nineteen years, and before that had been a professor of philosophy in Majorca's capital, Palma. He was accompanied by Father Juan Crespí, a former student who served as Serra's assistant and official diarist of the expedition.

In March 1769 Serra and his entourage of sixteen Franciscan brothers from the San Fernando headquarters in Mexico City departed with soldiers and supplies for San Diego. On the way, they founded Mission San Fernando Velicatá in Ensenada, which would be the only Franciscan mission in Baja California. The Franciscans were instructed by their superior father "to work in that mystic vineyard of California which our Catholic monarch has confided to us." To help accomplish this task, Indian conscripts armed with bows and arrows traveled from the missions of Baja California to serve as protectors and intermediaries with Indian tribes in the north. The party's forty scouts, soldiers, and assistants were to collect cattle along the way.[5]

In June 1769 Serra, astride a mule, led his small procession along the marshy shore of San Diego Bay. Meanwhile, two ships from Cape San Lucas and La Paz, the *San Antonio* and *San Carlos,* were sent to San Diego, and the second overland expedition was sent to meet them. When he arrived at San Diego, Serra found, instead of the bustling community of colonists he had expected, the stranded remainder of a crew that had faced great illness and death during its journey. In the days following the ships' landing, more than sixty men, mostly from the sea expedition, died on the beach in a makeshift tent hospital built of sail canvas.[6] A third ship never arrived, while the crews of the other two suffered from scurvy and dysentery.

Lack of food and living supplies was an ongoing problem for the mission. The annual visit of supply ships from San Blas, unpredictable at best, was not enough to support the new settlement. The supply problem grew so dire that the mission plan faced probable extinction. Serra and his group waited months in San Diego for needed supplies and animals: "[I]f (the captain) does not bring along with him the . . . loads and stock, there is nothing else to do than leave it all; and have the religious come away from there, and wash our hands completely of California."[7]

Despite such setbacks, Portolá's land party pressed north to Monterey Bay, leaving Father Serra behind. On July 16, 1769, Serra raised a cross on the site of the first mission in Alta California. After saying mass, he dedicated the mission to St. Didacus (San Diego) of Alcalá, a Franciscan friar, after whom Vizcaíno had named the site in 1602. On the day of its founding, the mission was a brush chapel, but within a short time the group had constructed a small adobe church. The mission sat on today's Presidio Hill, commanding a view of Mission Valley, its native population, and San Diego Bay. Serra also blessed a new presidio, Spain's first spiritual and political stronghold in Alta California.

The mission's early days were spent primarily in caring for the sick and dying crewmen of the *San Carlos*. Indians attacked the newcomers, killing some of the Baja California Indians and wounding other members of the nascent community, including a priest. Afterward, Spanish soldiers erected a rudimentary stockade around the mission building, and Indians from outside the mission were forbidden entry.[8] Such problems illustrate the need to combine mission settlements with military installations.

Meanwhile, Portolá's party struggled north for thirty-eight days. At Monterey they found no sign of the port that Vizcaíno had described as "sheltered" and "very secure against all winds." Before turning back in disappointment, Portolá erected a cross on the shore of the open, windy bay with an inscription that read: "The overland party from San Diego returned from this place . . . starving."[9] The party averted starvation on its return trip by eating twelve of its mules.[10]

The San Diego settlement suffered a major food shortage in February and March of 1770. Portolá vowed to cancel the whole operation and return to Mexico unless the overdue supply ships arrived by March 19, the birthday of the expedition's patron saint, San José. Father Serra began a novena, a nine-day period of prayer with the rosary, which would end on the 19th. By coincidence or divine intervention, late on the last afternoon of the novena, the *San Antonio* crept forward on the horizon. Most of its crew had died of scurvy, but the ship's cargo of maize, flour, and rice remained intact. The settlement was saved and the stage was set for future missions.

Now convinced that the northward port where they had lodged the cross in the rocky shore was indeed Monterey Bay, Serra and Portolá made plans to return there and establish a mission. Voyaging by land and sea in June 1770, the party found the cross on the bay surrounded by offerings of meat, fish, and feathers from the Indians. A soldier and sailor were sent on horseback to deliver the news to San Diego and Baja California.

Historian Frances Rand Smith eloquently created an image of the day Monterey's discovery was announced in Mexico City:

> Let us recall a scene of long ago, when upon the presentation of a message within the City of Mexico there was sung a solemn High Mass within the great cathedral. Gathered together were the court and tribunal as well as the people in celebration of that happy achievement, the discovery of the bay of Monterey. It was on the tenth of August, 1770, that the populace heard the ringing of the chimes and the answering bells in all the churches, for this was an occasion for spreading a generous spirit of joy among the inhabitants. Rapidly the people repeated the story told by the Viceroy, Marquis de Croix, and the Inspector-General, Don José de Gálvez, which informed them that the expeditions both by land and sea had extended their dominions more than three hundred leagues along the coast "toward the north in this America." Fully grasping the importance of the occasion, the throngs gathered and passed on to the palace that all might share in a demonstration of good fortune.[11]

With the construction of Mission San Carlos Borromeo and a presidio, two frontier settlements, both mission and military sites, had been established in Alta California. In the next few years more exploratory expeditions traveled from Mexico, each time venturing a little farther into the San Francisco Bay and its surrounding shore.

In 1776 plans were under way for two more settlements to fully secure the port: Mission San Francisco de Asís and Mission Santa Clara de Asís. Serra supervised the building of three more missions along the coast between San Diego and Monterey: San Antonio de Padua, San Gabriel Arcángel, and San Luis Obispo de Tolosa. After a dispute with the president of the Monterey presidio, he moved Mission San Carlos Borromeo to the banks of the Carmel River to shelter his neophytes from the rowdy behavior of the soldiers at the presidio.

The overriding goal now was to follow the long-term mission agenda in Alta California set forth by Visitador General Gálvez: install a Catholic conversion society, set up a local civil government ruled from Mexico City, colonize the Indians, and create a thriving economy. In addition, San Diego and Monterey would be used as bases for New Spain's power and deterrents to foreign exploration.[12]

In reality, mission establishment and settlement was a complex undertaking that varied with local Indian society, landscape, demographic factors, and the degree of Indian resistance. The choice of land for each mission was based on the number of natives, agricultural potential, and available water resources. In central Mexico Indians already lived in settlements and often practiced sedentary agriculture, whereas the Alta California Indians tended toward temporary seasonal settlements and dispersed communities with looser political structures (with the exception of more complex chiefdoms such as among the Santa Barbara Channel Chumash).[13] These rich cultures, along with their lifestyles, which contrasted with those of the Baja Indians, presented the Spaniards with unique challenges at every turn.

## First Meetings

The Franciscan missionaries, often born of bourgeois educated families in Spain and schooled in Spain and Mexico City, were assigned to carry out the bulk of colonial tasks on the ground. Missionaries searched inhospitable, strange land for future converts and a place to put up stakes. Four or five armed soldiers accompanied each expedition and oversaw the trip's logistics.[14] More than excursions of conquest, at least from the perspective of their executors, the expeditions were meant to test local reaction and kindle the Indians' interest.

*Reducción* missions were established by gathering natives from small scattered villages at one central site.[15] Throughout Spanish America, missions were often placed near existing indigenous villages. The *entrada* was a crucial stage of mission development—an expedition seeking to find friendly Indians and map territories for mission settlement. Before a mission was built, one logistical goal for the Spanish colonists was to attract and hold the attention of regional Indians. But before that could happen, the missionaries had to make contact with Indian groups and communicate their intentions. Converted Indians accompanied missionaries to translate unfamiliar languages and help bridge the gap between local populations and the newcomers. Indian reaction to the Spanish arrivals was unpredictable, with a natural mixture of fear, anger, curiosity, and friendliness.

Serra recorded the reactions of the Indians along the proposed mission route through the Camino Reál: "[Their] gentleness and peaceful dispositions . . . are an incentive to travel by that route, and although in some parts they show signs of being troublesome, it is a matter of small importance; we all have to put up with some annoyance for God."[16]

The meetings between Europeans and American Indians caused bewilderment and surprise on both sides, as recorded by the missionaries. Father Serra asked a convert, a young boy in Monterey, to describe what he and his people first thought of the cross planted there by the first expedition. The native people had decorated the cross with fish, meat, feathers, and broken arrows. The boy told Serra that "they had done so to keep [the cross] from doing them harm, because they were in deadly fear of it."[17] When Indians of the San Gabriel mission (the Gabrielinos) first met the Spaniards, they accepted every gift, but secretly buried all their own food. They believed every nation possessed its own food, which could cause the Gabrielinos illness if mixed with that of other groups.[18]

Confusion and surprise were present on both sides. During his journey to set up the San Diego mission, when Serra and his pack train visited local Indians after celebrating mass, he was shocked at the group's nakedness: "I . . . found myself in front of twelve of them, all men and grown up, except two who were boys. . . . I saw something I could not believe when I had read of it, or had been told about it. It was this: they were entirely naked, as Adam in the garden, before sin . . . not for one moment, while they saw us clothed, could you notice the least sign of shame in them for their own lack of dress. One after the other, I put my hands upon the head of each one of them, in sign of affection."[19]

The chaplain of the *San Carlos,* Father Vicente Santa María, kept a journal in 1775 of his encounters with Indians living along San Francisco Bay.

> As we came near the shore, we wondered much to see Indians, lords of these coasts, quite weaponless and obedient to our least sign to them to sit down, doing just as they were bid. There remained standing only one of the eldest, who mutely made clear to us with what entire confidence we should come ashore to receive a new offering, which they had prepared for us at the shore's edge.
>
> Keeping watch all 'round to see if among the hills any treachery [was] afoot we came in slowly, and when we thought ourselves safe we went ashore. . . . There came forward . . . the oldest Indian, offering him at the end of a stick a string of beads like a rosary, made up of white shells interspersed with black knots in the thread on which they were strung.[20]

The rest of the crew disembarked from the longboat, and the Indians offered them a collection of baskets containing pine nuts and other foods. In exchange, the crew gave the Indians earrings and glass beads. Father Santa María commented on the demeanor and behavior of these natives in the presence of foreigners.

It would have seemed natural that these Indians, in their astonishment at our clothes, should have expressed a particular surprise and no less curiosity—but they gave no sign of it. Only one of the older Indians showed himself a little unmannerly toward me; seeing that I was a thick-bearded man, he began touching the whiskers as if in surprise that I had not shaved long since. We noticed an unusual thing about the young men: none of them ventured to speak and only their elders replied to us. They were so obedient that, notwithstanding we pressed them to do so, they dared not stir a step unless one of the old men told them to; so meek that, even though curiosity prompted them, they did not raise their eyes from the ground; so docile that when my companions did me reverence by touching their lips to my sleeve and then by signs told them to do the same thing, they at once and with good grace did as they were bid.

The time we were with them seemed to us short, but it was enjoyable, all the more when, upon my pronouncing the most sweet names of Jesus and Mary Most Holy, they repeated them clearly, a great satisfaction and pleasure to me and to my companions. We observed a singular thing about the gift of glass trinkets that we had presented to them: not knowing what to do with them, or what not to do, they had put them aside until we should demonstrate how they should be used; so they brought in their hands the earrings and glass beads we had given them and, reaching them out to us, made gestures with them as if asking us what they were for and how to use them. Then all of us began putting the earrings in their ears, at which they were much pleased, as they showed with faces full of joy. We urged them to come onboard the ship, but with long speeches they avoided doing so, and by signs they invited us to come with them, pointing out the way to their *rancherías*. We took leave of them, however, setting out in the longboat for the ship, and they went home.[21]

Father Santa María and a group of six men, "sustained only by our Catholic faith and . . . impelled by godly zeal lest our gains be lost," walked inland "about a league from the shore" to explore an Indian ranchería. The group proceeded with some fear and apprehension. "As soon as the Indians saw that we were near their huts, all the men stood forward as if in defense of their women and children, whom undoubtedly they regard as their treasure and their heart's core. They may have thought, though not expressing this openly to us, that we might do their dear ones harm; if so, their action was most praiseworthy."[22]

## Tangible Incentives for Conversion

To build trust and encourage interaction, Franciscan missionaries handed out food, useful trade goods, colorful glass beads, and gifts such as blankets and steel knives. The missionaries had to be creative in their approach because the Alta California Indians, unlike those in Baja California, had adequate food and shelter except during drought and floods. Material offerings and objects never seen before such as food brought from New Spain, trinkets, clothing, and simple manufactured items helped arouse curiosity.

Approaching an Indian village near San Francisco, Father Francisco Palóu and his group

> came to a large grove of trees, cottonwoods, alders, willows, and blackberries . . . [and] many Indians armed with bows and arrows came out. When we called to them they came at once, and many of them gave me arrows, which among them is the greatest demonstration of friendship. . . . I made the sign of the cross on everyone that came up, and not one resisted, being very attentive to the ceremony, as though they understood it. They gave us some baskets of *atole* [porridge], *piñole* [pine nuts], and seeds, and . . . the skin of a wildcat. The women and children did not come near, being more timid.[23]

Father Serra noted that Indian women of the Los Angeles basin area were attracted to the missionaries' painting of the Virgin Mary and brought grain, seeds, and food as offerings.[24] He described how Indians approached another mission, attracted by the church and its cornfields, along with "throngs of children and all the rest of the people, how they are all clothed, and sing and eat in plenty, even though they have to work."[25]

The friars and soldiers staged demonstrations for their future converts. During entradas, the soldiers led neophytes in Catholic chants, responses, and choruses. Others demonstrated agricultural techniques by planting small plots or garden patches. One mission Indian in the nineteenth century wrote how the priest made camp with the Indians and lived with them until the buildings were erected. During this time the priest baptized them.[26] On-the-spot baptisms were common, and dozens of Indians could be baptized in a single day.

Once the essential mission buildings stood at the new site, other techniques were used to encourage more members. A convert at Mission Santa Cruz explained how Indians were drawn to the mission: "The padres would erect a hut and light candles to say Mass, and the Indians, attracted by the lights—thinking they were stars—would approach, and soon be taken."[27]

Using an interpreter, Serra spoke with the Indians he met on his way to San Diego to found the first mission. He assured them that "a Father would stay with them" and that they should come to visit without fear and bring their friends. "The Father would be their best friend" and the soldiers "would do them much good and no harm." In return, he asked them not to steal the cattle and always to call on the Father for their needs. Serra and his group came upon "an old Indian man, just as naked as all the rest. . . . [T]he interpreters asked him if he wanted to become a Christian. He said he did . . . [and] since the Father was there he could baptize him that afternoon. They told him that first he must be taught the law of God. He answered that they should teach it to him. And in fact the interpreter began to explain to him the first lessons of the catechism. . . . The old man did his best to learn."[28]

Pablo Tac, in about 1835, described the arrival of the Spaniards, an event that transformed his people's lives forever:

> When the missionary arrived in our country with a small troop, our captain and also the others were astonished, seeing them from afar, but they did not run away or seize arms to kill them, but having sat down, they watched. But when they drew near, then the captain got up . . . and met them. They halted, and the missionary then began to speak, the captain saying perhaps in his language *hichsom iva haloun, pulluch ajama cham quinai* "What is it that you seek here? Get out of our country!" But they did not understand him, and they answered him in Spanish, and the captain began with signs, and the Fernandino, understanding him, gave him gifts and in this manner made him his friend.
>
> The captain, turning to his people[,] . . . found the whites all right, and so they let them sleep here. . . . This was that happy day in which we saw white people, by us called *Sosabitom*. O merciful God, why didst Thou leave us for many centuries, years, months and days in utter darkness after Thou camest to the world? Blessed be Thou from this day through future centuries. . . . It was a great mercy that the Indians did not kill the Spanish when they arrived, and very admirable, because they have never wanted another people to live with them.[29]

Tac's is one of the few surviving written accounts told from an Indian's perspective. Tac worked closely with the missionaries and traveled to Italy to attend seminary, so his perspective and perceptions are not typical of missionized Indians. Indian reaction was also noted in accounts from Spanish colonists and other Europeans visiting the California coast. Sign language, flight, friendliness, and hostility were recorded. Father Francisco Palóu described their encounter during their arrival and founding of Mission Dolores in San Francisco:

We arrived in the vicinity of this port [San Francisco Bay], and a camp was made composed of fifteen bell-shaped tents on the shore of a large lagoon that empties into the arm of the bay, which extends fifteen leagues to the southeast. The purpose was to await here the arrival of the ship so that the site for the presidio might be selected with reference to the best anchorage. As soon as the expedition halted, many peaceful Indians approached. They expressed pleasure at our arrival, and especially after that had experienced the friendliness with which we treated them and the little presents of glass beads and food that we gave to attract them. They visited us frequently, bringing us little presents as their poverty afforded—nothing more than mussels and wild grass-seeds.

The day after the arrival, a shelter of branches (*enramada*) was built and an altar set up on it, and there I said the first Mass on the day of the Holy Apostles SS. Peter and Paul. My fellow priest immediately said another, and we continued saying Mass every day of the whole month that we remained at that place. During that time, as the ship did not appear, we occupied ourselves in exploring the country and visiting the villages (*rancherías*) of the Indians, who all received us peacefully and expressed themselves glad of our arrival.[30]

Some Indians came to the Spanish missions and accepted Christianity for different reasons, whether motivated by fear that the new settlers possessed supernatural powers or driven in search of food. Others were gathered and brought there, sometimes by force. Food, supplies, and technology, in relieving Indians of the need to forage for sustenance, may have provided a tradeoff. Subject to ongoing debate is the balance of free will and coercion in the conversion of mission Indians, and when force was involved, its degree and nature.

# 4

# Establishment of the Missions

## Building and Stocking the Missions

Franciscan missions across Spanish America followed a generally prescribed format. Missionaries worked in pairs at each location, with one appointed as the superior. The priests in charge blessed the chosen site, and building began as soon as possible.

At the first mission site in San Diego, once the supply ship finally arrived, Fathers Palóu and Serra could start the building of the mission inside the presidio walls. Wrote Palóu: "With the aid of the sailors whom the master of the ship divided between the presidio and the mission, two structures were built at the presidio, one for a chapel and another for a storeroom for provisions, and at the mission one likewise for a chapel and another divided into living quarters for the fathers. The soldiers made their own houses at the presidio and at the missions as well, all of wood with roofs of tule thatch."[1]

Mission location was chosen based on the area's farming potential and water supply. Water was necessary to a mission settlement's survival. For example, Mission San Miguel was built on a low mesa, ideal because it offered sufficient

Irrigation ditch, La Purísima.

space for the numerous buildings and corral. Drinking and irrigation water were close by, along with poplar, alder, and willow trees, limestone in the hills, clay for tile, and abundant pasture land. Father Palóu suggested the site for Mission Santa Cruz, the twelfth mission, saying, "It lacks nothing that is necessary, and in abundance and close to the beach of Monterey."[2] Friendly Indians and four natural springs influenced the site choice of Mission San Fernando in 1797.

In California, missions tended either to need water desperately or to have too much, depending on the area and time of year. In the early years of the missions,

Bell tower (*campanario*). © iStockphoto.com/Luis Lotax.

heavy rains and poor drainage forced some settlements, like the pueblo of San José, out of their original settings and onto higher ground. A half dozen missions were relocated because of misjudgments about water. Mission San Diego suffered from alternate periods of floods and drought, a problem to which San Diego's native population was already accustomed. They would migrate to the coast during periods of ample rain and retreat to the mountains when the weather was dry for an extended time.

Heavy rain and floods destroyed the first San Diego mission buildings and crops. The missionaries transferred their buildings and crops to a higher elevation about six miles upstream in 1774. As Serra said, "[The new site is] more suitable both for the purpose of building a settlement and securing good water and proximity to lands suited for cultivation. The Indians call it Nipaguay."[3]

Mission San Carlos was first built in Monterey and then moved to a new location in the Carmel River valley, said by Palóu to have water year-round. After the water issue was addressed, land was cleared and roads and buildings were planned. Military escorts helped erect temporary shelters.

Once the mission site was deemed safe for permanent building, missionaries ordered the Indians to gather stone for the building foundations, make bricks and roof tiles from stone and mud, and cut beams and reeds.[4] Master artisans helped the Indians in these tasks and with the building of the new church. Pablo Tac remembered the building of the church at San Luis Rey: "They made a church with three altars for all the neophytes, two chapels, two sacristies, two choirs, a flower garden for the church, a high tower with five bells, two small and three large, the cemetery with a crucifix in the middle for all those who die there."[5]

Furniture and everyday supplies were also needed for each mission. Church furnishings and supplies came from other missions. The San Diego mission was stocked with contributions such as vestments, clothing, cooking utensils, and Guadalajara pottery from Mexico. Supplies for cooking, living, and church services were always limited and, when possible, were sent by ship or mule train from missions like Loreto in the Baja Peninsula. Father Palóu described how the Franciscans took inventory of previous Jesuit missions: "The fathers having reached their missions, each took charge of the church and sacristy, with all the vestments, sacred vessels, and utensils, making a formal inventory signed by the father missionary who received it and the soldier commissioner who delivered it."[6]

From Monterey in July 1775, Serra made a "list of requirements for a mission unnamed," in preparation for building the next mission:[7]

- First, a devotional Crucifix . . . the principal object of our preaching . . .
- [A] painting of the Patron or Titular Saint of the mission. Let it be by a good painter.
- Six small copper pots, soldered of diverse sizes for the kitchen for other uses, as for instance for washing, etc.
- Six frying pans of the same material and soldered
- Six flat-iron pans with their handles
- A large pail, or a large *pozole* (porridge) pot for meals for the Indians
- Two large dippers . . .
- A box of beads and some trinkets, such as combs, scissors, etc.
- Shoe papers of shoemaker's needles to be used by the Indian women
- A gross of small crosses, of metal
- Twelve gross of rosaries; let the wiring be good and durable
- Six carpenter axes and twelve axes suitable for chopping wood to make charcoal
- Two dozen hoes
- Five Castilian plowshares (shod)
- Six corn grinders with their pestles
- Four small metal candlesticks with extinguishers

- Two sets of inkwells with sand boxes of bronze or lead
- Six untrimmed Mexican skins
- Two dozen raw cowhides for yoke thongs
- Two dozen leather bags
- Twelve sets of leather harness
- Two outfits for the equipment of a pack train
- Six skeins of thread for sewing leather
- Two cowboy's saddles with their accessories
- Two riding saddles for the trips and journeyings of the Fathers
- Six blank record books bound in sheepskin, for baptism records, burials, marriages, inventories, etc.
- One *arroba* [heap] of Castilian wax for Mass
- Wine for Mass
- A bottle case to keep it under key
- Two large bolts with their fastenings, one for the Church and the other for the granary
- Six door locks and two dozen hinges
- A dozen plates, and another of cups of china, metal or some such material
- Two pitchers for drinking water, of metal or soldered copper
- Two wire strainers to strain corn flour
- A case of shaving knives with strop and whetstone [for honing tools]
- A small tin cup for shaving
- Some balance scales with its [*sic*] weight of eighteen pounds
- A Roman scale with its ball or weight
- A jointing plane, jack plane, and carpenter's hammer
- To be able to make a start in clothing the naked: Six bolts of coarse cotton cloth
- A hundred sheepherders' blankets for all

Other cooking supplies sent from existing missions included large copper kettles, *atole* kettles and sieves, pozole ladles, frying pans, and copper jars.[8]

Once a minimum of supplies, men, and pack animals had arrived, only the first step of founding the missions had been accomplished. The missionaries and colonial military would continually be faced with the challenges of physical survival on the frontier. To create productive missions, more and more groups of Indians would need to be recruited and brought to the settlements. Missionaries would then have to share their authority with a civil provincial government. Nothing was guaranteed in these flagship settlements of colonial California.

Sacristy chest, ca. 1799, La Purísima.

## Gathering More Recruits

Up-and-running missions did not guarantee instant populations of loyal con-verts. Father Palóu observed Indians living near Mission San Luis Obispo on the central coast of California:

> [I]t will not be so easy to induce them to live at the mission, for they have the custom of building their towns in places where the seeds are, and as soon as they are all gone or gathered they move to another place, moving at the same time their little house, which they make of tule mats. Hence it would only be through their interest in clothing, which they like and desire very much, that they can be reached. They are in the habit of frequenting the mission and stop-ping there several days at a time, lodging in houses near the stockade in which live the relatives of the Christians, who have finally become permanent resi-dents. It is expected that through their example others will do the same, and as they go on being baptized they will go on building houses to form a town.[9]

As the mission chain expanded, bands of soldiers and missionaries hiked out one or two days' journey from each mission in search for new recruits. After

Fencing to keep out predators, La Purísima.

1800, when disease and the loss of mission Indians who fled their Spanish captors had led to a decline in the mission population, soldiers would venture into the interior to capture new groups of Indians.[10]

There was general colonial interest in expanding the mission chain and increasing the overall number of converts. The Spanish missionaries eyed the southern part of the San Joaquin Valley in California's inland region as a place to extend their influence. In 1804 a friar from Mission San Miguel, Juan Martín, led an expedition into the San Joaquin and valleys farther south and visited a village on Tulare Lake. After later expeditions explored the area, the village of Talame was chosen as a mission site.[11] These explorations were often the first occasions of contact between the local Yokuts and the Spaniards.

In the first decade of the nineteenth century, the search for new converts extended into the Colorado Desert, the Sacramento Valley, and northern California.[12] Although expeditions conducted site surveys and mapped the inland, resource limitations prevented expansion of the mission chain into the Central Valley. One padre selected a mission site near the King's River, close to the future town of Visalia, but funds from Mexico failed to appear and no mission was built.[13]

Father-President Mariano Payeras continued to press the home government for an additional group of missions. When he wrote to Mexico City in early 1820, his request was denied based on the lack of available friars and funds, as well as the political turmoil in Mexico.

## Founding and Organizing the Missions

Once the rudimentary mission buildings were established, each mission was dedicated with a festival. Roman Catholic saints dating from the start of the Christian era provided names for the missions, as well as cause for activities and celebration. Saints' biographies inspired the missionaries and provided stories and legends to pass along to converts. Mission San Diego, like many churches in Spain, was named after the Franciscan friar San Diego de Alcalá (St. Didacus of Alcalá), who was canonized in 1588. Palóu mentioned the fanfare associated with the completion of San Diego's presidio: "Formal possession of the presidio was taken on the 17th of September, the day of the Impression of the Wounds of our Holy Father St. Francis, patron of the presidio and of the port. I sang the first Mass that day, after blessing, venerating, and raising the Holy Cross. When the service ended with Te Deum, the *señores* went through the ceremony of taking possession in the name of our Sovereign, amid much firing of cannon from ship and shore, and shooting of muskets by the troops."

Mission San Diego, established in 1769 and constructed at its present site in 1774, was both the first mission and the first permanent European settlement in California. It was the flagship mission for other missions to follow. San Diego's appeal as a harbor, its proximity to Mexico, and the large population of local Indians made the area an obvious choice for the first settlement. However, after the mission party arrived and erected temporary buildings, strong resistance from Indians and difficulty finding water caused the Indian population to be limited in the mission's early years. Conversions were few, and for eight years the presidio was little more than an armed camp.

The early mission days might have been short-lived had it not been for the leadership of Franciscan friar Junípero Serra. His motto for the founding of the missions was "Always to go forward, and never to turn back." Though the first mission was slow in taking off, Father Serra and his mission leaders persisted in gathering converts, and gradually San Diego began to prosper.

Once a mission home base was established, Indians living farther away were set up with *asistencias*. These satellite or assistant missions were usually adjacent to Indian settlements or *rancherías*—organized bands of tribes in a defined territory. When some missionized Indians were granted short terms of leave to return to their original homes, these trips were defined as visits to the rancherías. Asistencias were more common in the San Diego area, where rules requiring Indians to live inside mission walls were looser. Asistencias were not given military protection, and missionaries, rather than living on-site, typically traveled regularly to administer sacraments.

Unlike the missions, these satellites did not maintain an extensive system of trades and crafts. Santa Ysabel chapel was founded in 1818 to serve a small group of Indians who lived in the mountains near the Colorado Desert, seventy-one miles east of San Diego. Unable to receive government money to establish services for Indians living outside the San Diego area, the padres set up a temporary chapel, followed later by an adobe chapel, granary, and houses. Another type of Indian settlement were the pueblos, hybrid communities formed adjacent to the missions. These were populated by both converted Indian families and Hispanic settlers, as well as farmers and families of soldiers. Pueblos eventually grew into towns like Los Angeles and San Diego.

## Bureaucratic Obstacles

The Franciscans were not independent agents in mission development. The Spanish missions were also political and civilizing agents of the state as well as the church. They relied on stipends, military protection, and initial grants for materials such as vestments, bells, and tools. Mission administration was complex, with overlapping jurisdictions in civil, military, and religious affairs.[14] Spain was the overseeing power, New Spain ruled from afar, and the local provincial government ruled alongside the Franciscan missionaries.

The Franciscan father-president of the missions in Alta California was allowed authority in all spiritual and religious aspects of the system. The provincial governor ruled what remained, namely the military and civil institutions. Civilian authorities oversaw local administration of Spain's colonial institutions, including the pueblos, presidios, and missions. This system remained until the Mexican Revolution and the separation of the Americas from Spain.

Colonial protocol had a long history. In 1524 Spain formed the Council of the Indies to administer affairs in the new colonies. The laws made by the council were interpreted and carried out by the viceroys who ruled each territory. The viceroys' duties included revenue collection, defense, civil order, and appointment of subordinates.[15] When Spain moved into Alta California, New Spain's viceroy in Mexico City supervised both the missionaries and California's provincial governor. The California missionaries operated from each mission, and the governor held power from Monterey. Mission San Carlos served as headquarters for the mission system through most of the Spanish period of 1770–1803, and Mission La Purísima was the administrative center for the remainder of the mission period.

The remote location of Spain's overseas colonies contributed to a divide between the colonial administrations and the mother country. A further divide between the government in New Spain and the colony of California made their relationship problematic. Missionaries sent to previously unexplored regions were forced to perform their duties with little guidance, frequent delays in communications and supplies, and much determination.

The early years of Spanish California were marked by constant disagreement between civil and religious authorities. José de Gálvez, the visitador general who dispatched the first mission expedition to Alta California, tried to keep a tight rein on the Franciscans. Serra also butted heads with Governor Pedro Fages over the establishment of new missions and troop provisions. Fages delayed the building of Mission San Buenaventura for several years, claiming a lack of soldiers. He wrote that Serra's "vehement desire to establish missions additional to those of San Diego and Monterey was, in the dearth of troops, nothing less than the temptation of the evil one."[16]

Affairs ran more smoothly under the governor of Las Californias, Gaspar de Portolá. In 1772 Serra made the long journey to Mexico City to make clear his concerns about the new province's problems, including friction between the missionaries and military commander as well as the dearth of supplies and settlers. The meeting with Viceroy Antonio Bucareli, with whom he corresponded regularly to manage affairs at the missions, was successful, and for a time food supply and distribution increased.

Confusion over points of authority and assigned duties slowed mission building. Officially, all projects needed approval from the visitador general.[17] Letters, petitions, and reports reveal bickering back and forth. There were arguments over division of authority, soldier behavior and punishment, supply shipments, materials for new missions, soldier and missionary pay, and time needed to turn the missions over to civil administration.

Communication on this and other issues was unreliable and slow. Supply problems were ongoing from the beginning. Delayed communication and frustrated efforts to get a response from the colonial bureaucracy made administering the missions according to regulation impossible at times. Letters and supplies arrived months, sometimes a year late, and occasionally never showed up at all. Serra's frustration was strong when a year would pass with no letter from the "Christian world": "Your Reverence should tell us any news that you would think to be of interest to us poor hermits cut off from all human society."[18]

Land tenure during the Spanish period was in royal hands and under the supervision of New Spain's colonial government. The Catholic Church and missionaries owned no land, despite their capacity as managers of the religious institutions. Though partially financed by the royal treasury, the missions were expected to become self-sufficient; many of them became rich establishments for a time through stock raising and farming. After a decade the missions were to be turned over to the parish clergy and the mission lands distributed among the Indians. Missionaries argued with colonial officials over the amount of time needed to "civilize" the local Indian population. The Franciscan consensus was that several generations were needed.[19]

For necessities as well as luxuries, missions and settlements relied on the two to four creaky transport ships that traveled north each year from San Blas to dock at San Diego and Monterey. These creaky ships carried necessities as well as luxuries from San Blas to the presidios and missions.[20] Occasionally land shipments would arrive as well, brought up the Camino Reál. Along with supplies, the ships also brought new diseases, which were spread through contact between their crews and mission settlers.

Junípero Serra was father-president of the missions for fifteen years and survived the terms of several governors and viceroys. Governor Felipe de Neve, the first governor of provincial Alta California, strongarmed the colonial administration with his distinctive ideas and policies. During his term and with the backing of the Spanish government, Neve increased Spanish presence in California via the mission system and helped bolster the network of defense, troop numbers, and civilian settlements.

Despite his contributions to this network, Neve was an outspoken opponent of the mission system. He suspected the missionaries profited from the missions so they could eventually accumulate livestock and crops to live on their own. Neve relegated control of all mission crops and products and towns to the viceroy, and in 1778 he tried to facilitate future Indian oversight of the missions by ordering special training of Indian leaders.[21] Despite opposition from friars like Serra on this and other policies, authorities in Mexico and Spain upheld Neve's orders. Neve and the mission leaders, particularly Serra, were constantly in conflict. Eventually Neve was transferred to Mexico City and was succeeded in 1782 by Pedro Fages.

During Neve's governorship, California's financial allotment was limited—the missions were barely supported by cattle supplies and scraped together from the Baja Peninsula missions. By this time the royal treasury had taken over the Pious Fund, but its money was not enough to finance the Alta California network. The Franciscans needed to convert the missions into self-contained settlements to remove their dependence on unreliable government funds and supplies.

# 5

## The Messengers of St. Francis

The men who implemented Spain's colonial policy in California were far removed from royal and colonial officials in Madrid and Mexico City. Missionaries bore the burden in South America, Mexico, California, and the American Southwest. Franciscan friars trained in Catholic doctrine were expected to map out new territory, plan for encounters with hostile forces, befriend strangers, and convince them to accept Christianity. Alta California's distance from Baja California added the additional risk of a journey far from the colonial base in Mexico City and its outlying mission posts.

Although an important reason why Spain began to explore the California coast in the late eighteenth century was to counter potential exploration or invasion by Russia and England, Spain's missionaries, far from their homeland, were more likely preoccupied with their immediate duty to convert the Indians. The Franciscan priests who traveled around the world to New Spain were driven by religious zeal, both their own and that of their country.

Although the Franciscans traveled north accompanied by soldiers and settlers, colonization of California by military force alone would have been fiscally unfeasible. Spain's funds and troops were employed in Europe and other territories.

Conversely, the missionaries could not have explored and settled California without soldiers to protect them. Like the Jesuits, Franciscans independently conducted expeditions in Baja and Alta California, with the help of Spanish soldiers.

## The Franciscan Order

Saint Francis of Assisi founded the humble "Order of Little Brothers" in 1209. Known as *religiosos,* or men bound by vows to religious order, Franciscan friars dedicated themselves to a life of service and poverty. Poverty, chastity, and obedience were central vows of Franciscan life. Extensive Franciscan mission duties, combined with their vows, made for an austere and backbreaking lifestyle. In many ways the Franciscan order was suited to the task of colonizing a territory untouched by modern civilization. Having already chosen a life of sacrifice, the friars may not have found the rugged frontier life as challenging as did other settlers from Europe. The Dominicans, or Black Friars, another mendicant order, were also founded in the thirteenth century with a mission to convert by training and scholarship. They too played a central role in colonizing New Spain and converting the Indians.

The Order of St. Francis of Assisi came to be known as the founding order of California's Spanish missions, also referred to as the Order of Friars Minor. The Franciscans could not have been more different in background from the Jesuits, the "Soldiers of God," who structured their missions in a military way. The Franciscan order was more localized and provincial than the Jesuits, harking back to medieval times in some of its practices. The peaceable Franciscans looked to Jesus Christ and to St. Francis as their models of humility, selflessness, and suffering. The friars strove to lead their Indian charges in the spirit of St. Francis, who saw himself and his followers as servants of all people: "Since I am the servant of all, I am obliged to serve them all and to communicate to them the fragrant words of my Lord."

Franciscans were the first missionaries in Mexico.[1] They landed with Cortés at La Paz in 1535, but efforts to set up missions there failed because of inhospitable soil and few supplies. More friars accompanied Sebastián Vizcaíno on his expedition in 1596, but hunger and hostility from the local Indians prevented any settlement. The Jesuits, as we have seen, then undertook the conquest, and after Spain ousted them from its overseas holdings, the Franciscans came to succeed them. These men, trained in the Spanish priesthood, left their homes to journey halfway around the world for a life of hardship and poverty.

Padres' church interior, La Purísima.

Franciscans trained at the College of San Fernando in Mexico City as frontier missionaries, taught to weather fatigue, deprivation, and danger in new territory. Each missionary then signed on for a minimum of ten years. They were usually sent to small missions in remote areas such as the mountains of Sierra Gorda in northeast Mexico. Franciscan missionaries in California followed standard practices to accomplish their duties. Their primary task was to convert populations of Indians and establish productive working communities.

With the help of their soldiers, the Franciscan friars established each mission with the resources at hand and improvised the rest. They learned the dialects and languages of resident tribes, disciplined soldiers and servants, and oversaw all aspects of mission production and behavior, religious and otherwise. Without the financial independence the Jesuits had enjoyed, the Franciscans had to make constant pleas to the provincial government and the viceroy in Mexico City for funds and supplies.

### Father Junípero Serra

Father Junípero Serra so transformed California's frontier culture that he overshadows most other players in the history of California in the mission period.

Serra's leadership in the establishment of Spanish missions in California was the driving force behind their development. He worked tirelessly to found nine missions during his lifetime, and envisioned a chain of missions stretching up to Alaska. Serra lived to see almost six thousand Indians converted at the missions.[2]

Born in 1713 in Petra, Majorca, the largest of the Balearic islands of Spain, Serra was renowned on his native island for his skills as a Catholic philosopher, teacher, and priest. In 1749, soon after the missions had become fixtures in New Spain, Serra left this work to serve at the Franciscan College of San Fernando in Mexico City. Serra quickly moved up the church hierarchy in Mexico. He founded a mission and led a religious revival in Mexico's Oaxaca region, and served in Sierra Gorda and various parts of central Mexico as pastor and missionary. After the Jesuit expulsion in 1767, Serra was appointed superior and father-president of the California missions. He led the religious arm of the first mission expedition to California, along with Inspector-General Gálvez, under Don Gaspar de Portolá's military lead and governorship.

A direct and principled man, Serra encountered opposition from frontier military and civil authorities as he tried to protect the interests of his missions. He was in constant conflict with provincial leaders over the behavior of soldiers at the presidios, fearing such scandals set a negative example for his Indian converts. Serra, while respectful of state authority, did not easily give way in his views of morality. His writings suggest profound concern for the spirituality and evangelization of the Indians. He described a journey from Loreto to San Diego, when he happened upon some Indian families as night was falling: "When I asked them what they were doing there, they answered, with much sorrow, that they belonged to the Guadalupe Mission, not to any particular rancheria, but to the principal village, and that the Father, for lack of food, had been forced to send them to the mountains to look for food, and . . . not being used to that way of life, they had . . . no success. They suffered very much, especially at seeing their babies starve and hearing them cry. I pitied them very much."[3] Serra shared all his corn with the families and assured them that supplies would soon arrive at their mission by boat.

Serra pleaded in many letters to the viceroys for funding and permission to found more missions. At age sixty he traveled on foot to Mexico City to meet with the viceroy and plead for improved conditions and funding at the missions. During Serra's visit to Mexico City he was able to gain approval of expansion of the mission system, exclusive missionary control over Indian welfare and actions, a redefinition of relations between presidio and mission, a proposed increase in supplies to the province, and encouragement of Mexican settlement in California. A petition that he presented in court, a "bill of rights" for California, was accepted and put into effect in January 1774. It served as Alta California's civil code until Mexican rule began in 1821.[4]

Serra's ascetic ways set an example of self-denial for other Franciscans. He used self-punishment to bring himself closer to God and the suffering of Jesus: under his clothing he wore a hair shirt and a belt with sharp hooks.[5] When Serra was seventy years old and in poor health, he would cover hundreds of miles by foot between the missions. In six years, he purportedly walked approximately two thousand miles. Working alongside the Indians, Serra, tucking up his habit, mixed straw and clay together with his bare feet, carried stones, mixed mortar, hewed timber, cut out diapers for Indian babies, and taught converts to sew.[6] California historian Hubert Bancroft called Serra "a great and remarkable man. . . . Limping from mission to mission with a lame foot that must never be cured, fasting much and passing sleepless nights, depriving himself of comfortable clothing and nutritious food, he felt that he was imitating the saints and martyrs who were the ideals of his sickly boyhood, and in the recompense of abstinence was happy."[7]

Serra has frequently been seen as a sympathetic figure in a Spanish colonial history dominated by noblemen, soldiers, and gold-seeking conquistadors. He has also been reviled for founding a chain of missions that depended on Indian labor and indoctrination. In 1934 Serra became a candidate for sainthood. In 1960 the Vatican made Mission San Carlos in Carmel a minor basilica due to the role it had played in Serra's life. In 1987 Pope John Paul II visited Mission San Carlos and prayed at Father Serra's grave, then proceeded to Phoenix, Arizona, and met with Indian groups to defend Serra's legacy. The pope acknowledged that there had been maltreatment of Indians during Serra's time, but upheld Serra as a great man who genuinely intended to protect the Indians from the soldiers. Finally, in 1988, despite Indian protests, Serra was canonized. A shrine to him in his native Petra instructs visitors to "Imitate his virtues."[8]

Serra's friend and disciple Father Francisco Palóu wrote Serra's biography, which some scholars have criticized as trying to glorify the missions under Serra's leadership. Palóu's friendship with Serra began in Majorca and continued for forty-five years, and after Serra died in 1784, Palóu took over for a short time as father-president. Father Palóu also wrote the first comprehensive history of colonial California.

Father Fermín Francisco de Lasuén assumed Serra's post in 1784 and remained until 1803. Before that, Lasuén had revitalized a decaying mission in Baja California, then increased the numbers of converts at the San Diego and San Gabriel

Silhouette of Serra and Campanario, San Miguel.

missions despite their problems with drawing Indian populations.[9] Serra has outshone Lasuén in the mission period and in subsequent histories, but Lasuén was also a very capable leader. When he appeared on the mission scene, nine missions were in operation. He founded nine more and increased the number of converts in California from six thousand to approximately twenty thousand.[10] Lasuén also jump-started the practices of animal husbandry and agriculture in the missions, and introduced the now-famous mission style of architecture, using tile, stone, and adobe.[11] The missions reached their greatest prosperity and number of conversions during Lasuén's term.

## The Franciscan Perspective on Indians and Missionary Work

Father Serra's faith and his belief in the Spanish mission institution shone through in his correspondence with colonial officials and other priests and set an example for his peers and for future mission leaders. He wrote: "I trust confidently in the Divine Majesty that the God-inspired ambitions . . . the upbuilding of new establishments and the discovery of new territories will meet with the success they deserve. They will shed a light of glory on you and your family and will aid in the propagation of our Holy Catholic Faith, and contribute to the greater glory of God."

During his first journey to Alta California, Serra saw the governor and another priest; he and they were all "as happy as possible to see each other, all eager to start on our new venture across the desert land, for a country peopled by pagans in great numbers." In early 1775 Serra spoke of the eagerness of unassigned missionaries to work in the new missions. Sometimes there were even too many missionaries for the job. Serra asked, "Can there be a greater happiness than to live in a land which God and our Seraphic Father, Saint Francis, have taken so much to their hearts?"[12]

In his drive to gain converts in San Diego, Serra offered to send another priest his diary of the expedition so that "it may help to have a knowledge of these lands that had never before been trodden by a Christian foot. It will show how rich is the harvest of souls that might easily be gathered into the bosom of our holy Mother the Church."[13] Serra was encouraging in March 1774: "Coming to the spiritual side, the Indians in all the missions are still as nicely behaved and tractable as ever—without anything untoward happening anywhere." In May of that year he reported back to Mexico City: "On my trip from San Diego . . . which lasted a month and five days, I saw all the missions and stayed a few days in each one of them. In the case of every one . . . I was delighted and in admiration at the sight of the progress they had made both spiritually and temporally, in spite of the scarcity of food."

Serra presided over mass on a Monday of Pentecost, in part to "encourage them [his missionaries], as far as I could, to put their shoulders into the new undertaking they were on the point of launching . . . [and] how happy they should all consider themselves who had a part in the enterprise, even if it were only to scrub the decks. Nor did I conceal from them the envy I felt that I was not allowed to accompany them, and the ardent desire I had to place the Sign of the Cross on the forehead." Serra prayed that "the Name of Jesus Christ be known, praised and sung among these far-off and barbarian nations." He was "anxious for the number of our mission foundations to be multiplied, when the field is so large and uncultivated."[14]

Not all Franciscans viewed the Indians with the same compassion as Father Serra did, or as their admired Saint Francis of Assisi would have. Father Pedro Font, another prominent Franciscan, served as diarist of Captain Juan Bautista de Anza's expedition to Monterey in 1775–76. He questioned the spiritual health of the Indians and made an observation that many early Spanish settlers of California would have concurred with:

> One might inquire what sin was committed by these Indians and their ances-
> tors that they should grow up in these remote lands of the north with such in-
> felicity and unhappiness, in such nakedness and misery, and above all with such
> blind ignorance of everything that they do not even know the transitory con-
> veniences of the earth in order to obtain them; nor . . . do they have any knowl-
> edge of the existence of God, but live like beasts, without making use of rea-
> son or discourse, and being distinguished from beasts only by possessing the
> bodily or human form, but not from their deeds.[15]

In this common colonial view, Indians were barbaric, lacked reason, and were ignorant, through some fault of their own, of the grace of their God. To the missionaries these shortcomings made the Indians all the more in need of conversion. Mission documents demonstrate both viewpoints, with priests parentally caring for the Indians, guiding them, and keeping them from non-Christian ways and ultimately from hell. Like Serra, Father Lasuén believed that he and other Franciscans were trying to accomplish the task of transforming the Indians "into a society that is . . . Christian, civil, and industrious . . . successfully by means of patience, and by an unrelenting effort to make them realize that they are men."

## Challenges of Mission Work in California

Serra's writings provide insight into the difficulty of establishing settlements in a foreign land: "Among the religious I know of none who are sick or discouraged, although, in one direction and another, brambles and thorns are not wanting; and they are not small ones: for instance our ignorance of the language, the lack of interpreters . . . and all the inconveniences that arise." His frequent letters to the viceroy of New Spain make clear the frustration of waiting years for a reply for supplies requested and answers to questions: "[A]ll the religious feel quite discouraged . . . asking, 'What are we doing here, if it is apparent that this man will never begin a new mission?'" and "How can we make progress in spiritual matters if fornications are not corrected by the measures, so fitted to correct them . . . and what progress can we make in temporal matters, if we are not allowed to have a man to superintend labor, animals, and all mission business?" In communiqués to his superiors in the colonial government of New Spain, Serra emphasized the collective benefit of cooperation between missionaries and government "for the progress and propagation of our holy Faith, and for the salvation of these souls that are united to their poverty-stricken and starving bodies."

A letter to a superior illustrates the trying lifestyle of mission work:

[T]hose who come here as ministers should not imagine that they come for any other purpose than to put up with hardships for the love of God and the salvation of souls. In a desert like this it is impossible for the old missions to come to the help of the new ones. The distances are great and the intervening spaces are peopled by gentiles. In addition to this, the almost complete lack of communication by sea makes it necessary that they endure, especially at the beginning, many and dire hardships. But to a willing heart all is sweet, *amante suave est.*

Father-President Serra also wrote of his excitement at the results of conversion: "Just to see a hundred boys and girls of about the same size, to hear them pray, and answer questions—being well-versed in all the questions and answers of Christian Doctrine; to hear them sing, to see them all dressed in worsted clothes and woolens; to see how happy they are at play, and how they run up to the Father, as if they had known him all their lives—all of this gladdens the heart." Serra was confident that the Indians believed "that we did not come here in search of riches, but to work for their happiness."[16]

European visitors also wrote their observations of the Spanish missionaries in California. Russian visitor Nikolai Rezanov, who visited the missions in 1806, admired the work and dedication of the padres. Rezanov, one of the founders of the Russian-American Company, sailed to the coast of California with German naturalist Georg von Langsdorff. Their visit to the missions at San José and San Francisco was unplanned; the expedition was forced to divert from Alaska when food and supplies became depleted. The visit came at the beginning of the worst

Missionary quarters, La Purísima.

measles epidemic of the Spanish period, which killed one-third of the mission Indian population between 1806 and 1818.[17] Noted Rezanov:

> When one considers that in this way two or three missionary padres take upon themselves such a sort of voluntary exile from their country, only to spread Christianity, and to civilize a wild and uncultivated race of men, to teach them husbandry and various useful arts, cherishing and instructing them as if they were their own children, providing them with dwellings, food, and clothing, with the utmost order and regularity of conduct—when all these particulars, I say, are considered, one cannot sufficiently admire the zeal and activity that carry them through labors so arduous, nor forbear to wish the most complete success to their undertaking.[18]

The colonial system and missionary motives and practices have been criticized since the missions were first planted in California. In 1839, Englishman Alexander Forbes admired the work of missionaries but opposed the missions as tools of colonization. He believed that "the missionaries are honest men; that they pursue with assiduity what they believe to be their duty; that they labor in their vocation with zeal; but we entirely condemn their system, and lament its results."[19] Sixty years later, historian and mission priest Father Engelhardt reflected on the history of California's missions: "The men who presumed to guide the destinies of Spain cared not for the success of religion or the welfare of its ministers except insofar as both could be used to promote political schemes."[20] These observations contradict the founding goals of the Franciscan order and the tasks expected of missionaries in Alta California. Analysis of mission history and the roles of leading Franciscans can help readers decide for themselves whether the mission system was an instrument of slavery and indoctrination and to what extent it was a product of its time and its origin in Spanish colonial doctrine.

# 6

# Conversion and Mission Life

Once missionaries were able to convince an Indian community to join a mission, their next goal was to steep the Indians in the tenets of Catholic religion. Baptism and basic Catholic indoctrination were the first steps to conversion. After the formality of baptism, Indians were officially subjects of missionary supervision and were immediately assigned work.

Attracting Indians to the new settlements and missions was the initial challenge for missionaries and their military entourage. When large numbers of Indians were ready to become Christians and educated to the satisfaction of their missionaries (a qualification often overlooked to facilitate instantaneous conversion), mass baptisms expedited the process. Acceptance of baptism was central to achieving of missionary goals; it signified a rejection of all pagan beliefs and practices. In earlier years, most baptisms were issued before indoctrination took place. Later, prospective converts, or neophytes, were expected to learn basic beliefs, practices, and recitations before receiving baptism and officially entering the church. Babies, small children, and ill adults received baptism immediately.[1]

English observer Frederick W. Beechey outlined his own encounters with the mission culture in California from 1825 to 1828. He described the process of converting Indians and the consequences for Indians who resisted conversion:

> In a few days a willing Indian becomes proficient in these mysteries [the doc-
> trine of the Church], and suffers himself to be baptized, and duly initiated in to
> the church. If, however, as it not infrequently happens, any of the captured In-
> dians show a repugnance to conversion, it is the practice to imprison them for a
> few days, and then allow them to breathe a little fresh air in a walk round the
> mission, to observe the happy mode of life of their converted country men;
> after which they are again shut up, and thus continue to be incarcerated until
> they declare their readiness to renounce the religion of their forefathers.[2]

Although missionized Indians have been referred to as "converts," the term
is misleading. A convert is usually an individual who independently seeks and
adopts a particular faith. At the missions, though some of the converted Indians
may have accepted church doctrine, as a whole they were persuaded by the
missionaries, hurried through the rites, and immediately put to work under the
supervision of the missionaries and the soldiers. Thus, "converts" was more an
administrative category than the reflection of a spiritual choice.

Indians brought into the missions had to adjust rapidly from their traditional
ways of life to a hierarchical world of rigorous rules and regulations based in a
radically different ideology and social mores. Each mission resident was responsible for completing assigned tasks according to the daily schedule. Those who
resisted faced solitary confinement, imprisonment, and beatings. Both Catholic
doctrine and the labor system shaped this environment.

## Role Models

To encourage the Indians to live peacefully, complete mission tasks, and obey
Christian laws, missionaries relied on visual symbols. For example, at the time of
Juan Bautista de Anza's expedition (1775–76), New Spain chose the Virgin Mary
as patron saint of Spain's colonization effort in California.[3] Indians of the missions came to know Mary, the mother of Jesus Christ, through daily recitations
and prayers and from her image inside the church. For both missionaries and
Indians, her image symbolized Christian purity, but for the Indians it also symbolized either colonial domination or protective sympathy.

Along with the Virgin Mary, Jesus on the cross came to symbolize a new California culture, as it did worldwide in Catholic dominions. Statues of the cruci-
fixion hung above the altars, and crucifixes appeared in most rooms.

Crucifix, Mission San Francisco. © iStockphoto.com/Jeffrey Staley.

Called "Father," the Franciscans were patriarchal figures whose personalities set the tone at each residence. Priests were expected to serve as fathers in all senses of the word, as spiritual leaders, paternal role models, and taskmasters. The comparison of a priest to one's father could also signal affection, as it did for Father Serra, who was reputed to have great fondness for the Indian children of the missions.

Another salient feature of this imported patriarchal society was the wide social gap between priest and Indian. Mission Indian Pablo Tac described the

"Fernandino Father" as "like a king . . . he has pages, *alcaldes* [Indian leaders], *majordomos* [mission foremen], musicians, soldiers, gardens, ranchos, livestock, horses by the thousand, cows, bulls by the thousand, oxen, mules . . . etc."[4]

Compared with the Indians, who lived in tight quarters, the Franciscans and Spanish leaders lived in relative comfort, to the extent that was possible on the frontier. They slept in individual rooms sometimes outfitted with fireplaces. Except for Serra himself, who slept on a board, missionaries slept on crude four-poster beds with rawhide straps and wool mattresses. Everyone else at the mission—converts and soldiers—slept on straw pallets.[5]

Differences in status and freedom were evident in all aspects of mission life. The Franciscans, although operating under provincial governorship, were in effect the rulers of the frontier. In their function, the missionaries replaced tribal elders as leaders of converted California Indian society, albeit with an entirely different system of values and expectations.

## The Reality of Conversion

Missionary success could be measured by the numbers of converted Indians. Converting Indians and convincing them to remain on mission grounds was a primary colonial goal of Spain. More converts meant more subjects of Spain. Conversion made only slow progress in California, however. Setbacks such as disease, drought, floods, earthquakes, famine, desertion, and declining birth rates occurred throughout the mission period, making conversion integral to the maintenance of a colonial population.

Conversion at the first missions was slow. In 1773 there were 491 recorded baptisms and 62 recorded marriages in the existing five missions.[6] Despite gifts, clothing, and food from the missionaries, Indians living near San Diego and San Gabriel consistently resisted conversion, so Christianity took hold there very slowly.[7] In the first five years, less than one hundred converts were listed at San Diego.

During the entire mission period, 83,407 baptisms were recorded.[8] Another set of records shows that between 1769 and 1834, 53,600 Indians converted to Roman Catholicism.[9]

Father Palóu observed distinctive characteristics of the first Indians at the San Diego mission: "In the beginning the Indians of this port showed themselves to be very bold and arrogant, even daring to attack the camp, seeing that there was but a small number of soldiers and most of them sick, when the expedition left to look for the harbor of Monterey."[10]

Baptismal font, La Purísima.

Part of the difficulty in attracting converts was the sluggish production of food at all the missions in those early years. Gradually growth in agricultural production paralleled an increase in the number of Indians taken into each mission. As years passed and the missions became more productive, some tribes and groups entered the missions in large numbers, such as the Miwok and Ohlone of the San Francisco Bay area in 1794 and 1795 and the Chumash of the central coast in 1803.[11] San José, forty-eight miles from San Francisco, attracted more converts than any northern mission.

## Keeping Converts and Building a Settlement

In his correspondence with provincial governor Felipe de Neve in 1779, Father Lasuén gave his perspective on the motivation and process of Indian conversion. He explained the missionaries' role in Spain's colonial policy, under which the missions would, in theory, become Catholic communities no longer in need of Franciscan leadership:

> We are apostolic missionaries bound by papal bulls [official documents with a round leaden papal seal] to depart from the missions as soon as we recognize that the neophytes, whom we have brought together by our missionary efforts, are sufficiently instructed in the divine law, and sufficiently competent to care for the economic welfare of their families and for the political government of their pueblos. When that stage is reached, they may then come under the jurisdiction of the parish priests sent by the bishops to whose care they are to be entrusted. As for us, we then return to our college; or we look for other Indians to take under instruction.[12]

Religion was the structural basis of each day at the mission, with services and prayers several times a day. Church obligations included memorization and daily recitation of catechism, or *doctrina,* regular attendance at mass, and fulfillment of the stages leading to baptism and confirmation. Assigned work duties were also central to the daily expectation that all mission residents serve God.

Acceptance of Christianity, whether coerced or voluntary, did not eliminate the native religions completely. Some Indian ceremonies continued alongside Catholic traditions at the California missions, tolerated by some priests as secular events. To the extent possible, many rituals were practiced in secrecy. The mission Indians were also permitted periodic recreation such as hoop-and-ball games, some gambling, and traditional dancing around a fire.

The Franciscans tried to maintain interest and participation among the Indians in various ways, mainly in connection with the church calendar. Celebration of regular feast days broke the daily routine of work and study with processions, fiestas, and games. Many of the missions allowed a two-week leave period for Indians to visit their ancestral villages and relatives several times each year, during the summer and after the fall harvest.[13] During times of the year when they were not needed to tend the mission crops, some Indians were also granted leave to bring back converts from outside mission territory.

Part of both church tradition and Hispanic culture, fiestas, saints' celebratory days, and other activities filled the calendar, providing routine and a sense of community. Saints' days, especially the day of the mission's titular saint, and important holidays such as Christmas, Easter, and Holy Week were recognized with feasting and singing. Celebrations were not always treated as entertainment, as the word suggests today. They recognized church days that honored a phase in the Christian calendar, an important saint's birthday, or a holy day. As in Catholic communities worldwide, local elements were incorporated into the religious celebrations.[14] For example, some missionaries approved the inclusion of certain games or dances traditional to the Indian culture of the mission.

The entire mission community prayed, ate, and slept at designated times under priestly supervision. The friars directed all Indian work and recreation. With the help of artisans brought in from Mexico when funds allowed, friars and soldiers worked with the Indians and supervised their progress. Some soldiers were detailed to assist a specific site, usually six men to a mission. One soldier or Indian was the master of works and responsible for teaching and supervising the population.[15] Work and prayer filled the days, leaving little time for rest and recreation. About ninety-two days of the Catholic calendar were either Sundays or religious holidays, which were also days to rest from work.

The sound of church bells was ubiquitous in mission life. Mission bells called people to meals, work, and church. Bells like those at Mission La Purísima were cast in Lima, Peru, the "city of bells," and sent by ship to New Spain and California. Made from bronze and inscribed with their place of origin and the mission name, they were tuned to create a variety of tones. The sunrise bell announced the first meal of the day, usually *atole* (porridge), *oraciones* (morning prayers), and Christian instruction. Pablo Tac described the mornings at San Luis Rey: "When the sun rises and the stars and moon go down . . . the old man of the house wakens everyone," and they eat breakfast.[16]

Married Indians ate in their quarters, and the unmarried ate in a common area. Soldiers, missionaries, and Indian alcaldes assigned tasks for the morning. The women served a second meal at midday, usually meat cooked with corn or beans. In the afternoon, boys and catechumens received more instruction, and another meal of atole was consumed in the evening. Work was concluded by sunset to leave time for evening prayer.

## Language

Since 1550, as a way of maintaining control of its colonies, Spain had required that its New World citizens be taught Spanish. Just as Catholicism was meant to supplant Indian religions and beliefs, the Spanish language was meant to supplant the multiple native languages of the mission's inhabitants. In 1770 King Charles III issued a language policy that prohibited the use of Amerindian languages and customs and promoted Spanish culture in all its forms.

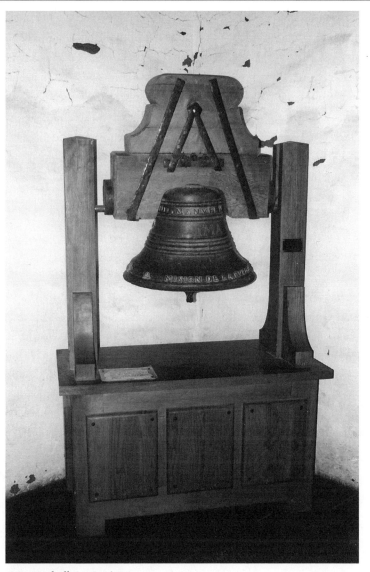

Mission bell, La Purísima.

Nevertheless, Indian languages coexisted with Spanish at all of the California missions.[17] Jesuits working in the colonies had compiled grammars and dictionaries of tribal languages to help new missionaries in the field.[18] Father Serra saw the need for missionaries to learn local languages as they evangelized. All missions, though without official approval, kept copies of the catechism in indigenous languages.

Father Buenaventura Sitjar, the head Franciscan at Mission San Antonio, mastered the foreign guttural idioms of the local Indian population and compiled a vocabulary of the local Telame language. Father Arroyo de la Cuesta of Mission San Juan Bautista compiled a grammar and a phrase book of the Mutsun language.[19] In some places missionaries tried to teach the Indians in their native idiom, resorting to Spanish when the variety of languages and dialects became too overwhelming. Father Serra recalled how at Monterey the friars used an interpreter, a "California Indian, who came at the start as a child, [with] a good knowledge of the language and speaks Spanish with great facility." By use of translators "the religious missionaries are beginning to understand the various languages . . . in none of the five missions . . . are there any two where you will find the same language spoken."[20]

In the missions, speakers of Spanish and of the Indian languages got through daily life by learning a bit of the other's tongue. The Indian languages incorporated Spanish words, especially for such things as firearms, crops, animals, mission leaders, and religious customs and items.

Indian servants in Mexican and Spanish families learned more than converts who stayed at the missions. Those who spoke suitable Spanish worked as interpreters for the padres in the field and for neophytes brought to the missions. Known as *ladinos,* they adopted Hispanic ways and dress. By the 1820s greater numbers of Indians spoke Spanish, particularly those born at the missions and raised in a Spanish-speaking environment. Missionized Indians brought Spanish to the San Joaquin Valley in the 1830s and 1840s.

Within a few generations native languages were almost forgotten. By the time efforts were made to record them in the late 1800s and early 1900s, much had been lost. Some California tribes today are striving to revive their traditional languages.

## Music

Music, for centuries a core element of the Catholic mass, was also central to life and acculturation at the Franciscan missions. European religious music and sung sections of the liturgy encouraged interest and participation and reinforced a routine of worship. Indians learned choral music, songs, and chants, participated in group repetitions of musical or chanted passages, and memorized the responses to be used during mass and other ceremonies. In the church, men and boys of the choir stood in the back with the musicians in the loft.

Mission San Antonio was praised for its fine orchestra of Salinan musicians. The orchestra formed around 1803 under the direction of mission pastor Juan

Bautista Sancho, an educated, talented musician and composer skilled on the harpsichord and organ. Mission San José was famous for its excellent and distinctive music, as was San Juan Bautista, where resident friar Esteban Tápis taught and led a fine Indian choir. Indian musicians performed on holy days, Sundays, and holidays. San Luis Obispo Indians played a native wind instrument made from the branch of an elder tree,[21] and Indians at all the missions learned to play the violin, flute, guitar, bass violin, and percussion instruments such as drums, the triangle, and cymbals.

A Mexican landowner from the later mission period remembered the musical atmosphere in the missions: "Many young Indians had good voices, and these were selected with great care to be trained in singing for the church choir. It was thought such an honor to sing in church that, the Indian families were all very anxious to be represented. Some were taught to play on the violin and other stringed instruments. . . . Every prominent mission had fathers who paid great attention to training the Indians in music."[22]

A museum display at Mission San Antonio de Padua shows a chart, in the form of a drawing of a hand, listing the basics of music and the names for notes and major and minor keys. Each note and key is written in a particular place on the hand and numbered.

## Moral Obligations

To keep order and regulate the behavior of Indians living at the missions, the Franciscans followed a moral system founded in church doctrine. In general, traditional Indian behaviors and practices clashed with missionary expectations of how Catholics should live, and a list of prohibited behaviors became commonplace. Practices such as body piercing, tattooing, and use of plant drugs were unacceptable to the Franciscans.[23] In the early mission years, the friars tried to suppress dances and assemblies, but eventually changed their policy to allow the Indians entertainment.[24] Other Indian practices seen as inappropriate in the framework of Christian society were denounced as sorcery and works of *el Demonio* (the devil).

Concepts of sex, gender, courtship, and marriage roles differed between the two cultures. Scandalized by adultery, polygamy, barter of wives, casual marital bonds, abortion, and infanticide, Franciscans expressly prohibited such practices. Catholic codes of sexual behavior insisted on chastity and monogamy and allowed sexual activity only within the sacrament of marriage. Priests tried to reform Indian sexual behavior during the conversion process, and Franciscan writings criticized what they saw as the sexual vices of the native populations.[25] The frequency of venereal disease in the missions fueled the belief that Indians were involved in immoral sexual relations.

Missionaries worried that the soldiers living in the mission and at the neighboring presidio would taint the converts with their behavior, including drinking, gambling, and illicit sexual relations. Mission Santa Cruz, founded in 1791, was further hampered by an adjoining pueblo housed by convicts. In 1812 mission priests, responding to a questionnaire from the government in Mexico City, named "licentiousness and debauchery" as the two biggest problems facing the missions.[26] In a letter to his senior father, Serra said he had written to the viceroy to inform him of "news about the married soldiers and the crimes of rape . . . and I will be most insistent . . . that serious measures be taken to stop such awful outbreaks of debauchery."[27] Indians were not allowed to associate with the soldiers and guards, and soldiers could not gamble or communicate with the Indians.

Early in the mission years, eligible women, either for marriage or unlawful relations, were limited in numbers. Unmarried men and women slept in separate quarters and worked in different areas during the day. Unmarried girls and women were guarded and kept under lock and key. Married couples had their own quarters, but shared meals with other mission residents in a communal kitchen when living at a mission.[28]

Another area of conflict was clothing. Traditionally, Indians wore little clothing, which offended the missionaries, for whom modesty and humility required covering one's body. Indian women in San Diego were given European-style clothing—chemises, gowns, and ribbons—and then taught to spin and weave their own clothes. The men were made to wear overalls and dark, broad-brimmed hats worn low on the forehead. At Mission San Luis Rey, males received a new shirt and pair of breeches every six months, and women a new chemise and skirt.[29]

Serra was dismayed by Indian nudity:

> [T]o cover in some fashion the nakedness of so many girls and boys, men and women, not so much against the cold . . . as for the sake of decency and modesty, especially with the gentler sex; that appears to me an almost impossible task. . . . Today . . . when I look at my audience in church, I can scarcely see anything else than animal pelts, which the gentiles use, and which our Christian had thrown away when they received Holy Baptism. . . . We are living in the midst of a countless number of naked people.[30]

Covering nakedness was the missionaries' way of bringing the California Indians one step closer to the grace of the Christian God.

## Cycle of Work

Work for its own sake was intended to provide moral enrichment and discipline and enhance both the civil and spiritual aspects of life. Assigned tasks were also necessary for the mission's survival. Between shipments, supplies often dwindled. In July 1774 families of blacksmiths, carpenters, and other craftsmen in San Diego found their resources stretched. Serra told them that "they would find the doors of the royal warehouses open for them to buy what they needed . . . but government regulations did not allow for more than a small portion of corn. . . . Neither has anyone, until now, been able to lay his hand on a frying pan or any grinding stone for making tortillas, or on a piece of linen to cover his nakedness. The storekeeper is willing to give credit, but he has strict orders not to do so. We do not know how long this state of affairs may last."[31] This need to maintain self-sufficiency would be the Franciscan missions' raison d'être for the duration of the mission period.

Franciscans worked alongside their Indian charges. "The missionary fathers are the foremen of the work and the neophytes the workmen," wrote Father Palóu in 1774.[32] Everyone followed a rigid timetable to complete duties that helped the mission remain productive. Men and women performed piecework labor, such as grinding a certain amount of grain daily or making a specific number of adobe bricks. Their work varied with the needs of the season and supplies. No wages were given, but everyone living at the mission received food, housing, religious instruction, and clothing.

Young children were given simple and less taxing chores like weeding. At puberty children were considered adults and were ready to take part in the true labor, including tanning hides, firing clay tiles, and weaving. Mission Indian Pablo Tac remembered:

> Daughters and mothers make shirts while sons attend school and learn catechism and the alphabet. Those in the choir work all week in their respective jobs, then sing on Sunday, but without a book, because the teacher teaches them by memory. . . . The daughter joins with the single girls who all spin . . . blankets for the San Luiseños and for the robe of the Fernandiño Father. . . . At noon they all share a meal from cups of clay [and] vessels of well-woven fiber which water cannot leak out of . . . seated around the fire . . . talking and eating.[33]

Selected Indian males, known as alcaldes and *regidors,* served as supervisors. Pages assisted the missionary father-in-charge and hosted European and American travelers passing through the Spanish settlements. Some young men and boys were called upon to complete religious duties. They worked as pages, acolytes, and sacristans (persons in charge of the sacristy, where sacred vessels and vestments were stored).[34] A mission Indian or soldier was placed in charge at each mission when the lead missionary was absent on recruitment trips or establishing a new mission.

Russian visitor Nikolai Rezanov saw nothing inappropriate in the Indian life of work and instruction he witnessed: "The government has not, nor have the padres, anything in view other than the propagation of the Christian religion. Hence it may be supposed that the Indians, to whose maintenance and instruction all their efforts are devoted, must be much happier in their condition of comparative civilization than they were before, since they are permitted to retain their former habits and customs not interdicted by the missionaries."[35]

The presidios, like the missions, were centers of Indian labor. Indian convicts were sometimes sentenced to labor at the presidios, although Franciscans condemned this practice, saying it was too convenient to arrest Indians on any pretense. Despite missionary hesitation about Indian interaction with soldiers, some Indian contract labor was sent to the presidios, bringing more money to the mission treasury, along with higher wages for skilled artisans and masons. Some Indians left the missions to work at the presidios on Sundays and during summer leave.

Indian tasks at the presidios included cooking meals for the soldiers and maintaining the grounds and buildings. Nonbaptized Indians from outside the missions worked for a month at a time on projects such as construction and building maintenance. Aside from their daily food rations, these workers were paid very little or were simply given a blanket or some other European good for their work. Informal Indian labor also took place at the presidios, without the knowledge of the missionaries. In exchange for additional tasks such as gathering wood, grinding corn, and washing clothes, soldiers paid Indians directly with items such as corn and leather. Indians thus acquired more food and trade goods for their own use.[36]

Religious instruction, labor, meals, and the church calendar all regulated life on the mission frontier. Each mission ran like a small factory where everyone was assigned a specialized task and expected to fulfill his or her obligation to the operation as a whole. Each person's role in the mission was clearly defined. Missionaries implemented the system and soldiers enforced the rules. Through religious education and indoctrination, required changes in behavior and appearance, and the imposition of a work ethic, the missionaries strove to convert the California Indians and transform them into productive residents of a Spanish colony.

# 7

## The Women of Mission California

Historians and anthropologists have studied the roles of Indian women of the Spanish missions in California, Mexico, and South America in Spain's territorial and political conquest of new lands and cultures. Assimilation of local women in newly conquered lands as a means to cultural domination has been addressed in academic studies. The Catholic Church's prescribed role for women in society, its incorporation of the Virgin Mary as an ideal, and the goal of increasing colonial populations defined the place of females.

At the California missions, marriage between Indian women and Spanish men was encouraged as a way to increase the population and spread Spanish power. Another means to that end, however, was rape and violence. In a patriarchal colonial society, women, especially Indian women, were vulnerable. Rape of Indian women by Spanish soldiers and settlers was a major concern of the Franciscan missionaries, who worked hard to curb this and other violent behavior.

Officially the kingdom of Spain discouraged violence toward women. Prior to mission settlement in California, official royal documents from Spain held both explorers and captains of Spanish ships responsible for the behavior of their subordinates toward Indian women. Unfortunately, reality did not always correlate with expectations. For example, Cabrillo reputedly enlisted gangs of men to gather dozens of Indian women and girls to serve the men in a seaport village in Guatemala where he was stationed prior to traveling to Alta California.

Once the religious orders assumed leadership of the colonization effort, treatment of women became a more prominent issue. Missionary records and letters to superiors in Mexico City clearly document the rapes of Indian women by Spanish and later Mexican soldiers and settlers. In their correspondence with viceroys, missionaries identified both rape and extramarital sex between Spanish men and Indian women as ongoing problems at San Diego, San Gabriel, and San Luis Obispo.[1]

In 1772 Serra notified the College of San Fernando in Mexico that soldiers at the new mission at San Gabriel were "guilty of the most heinous crimes, killing the [Indian] men to take their wives."[2] In 1773 Serra raised the rape of two Indian girls near the San Diego mission to oppose the governorship of Pedro Fages. He complained that these crimes had been ignored by the royal administration or handled with great delay. After Fages was removed from his post in 1774, Serra petitioned the government in Mexico City to instruct the next governor to replace "soldiers who give bad example, especially in matters of licentiousness."[3]

Although missionaries and the government of New Spain encouraged marriage between Spanish settlers and Indian women, missionaries tried to keep presidio soldiers separate from the Indian women living at the missions. Priests tried to protect their converts from soldiers by creating logistical and social barriers inside and outside mission walls. However, mission birth records and written complaints by priests show that efforts to prevent illicit relations and sexual violence sometimes failed.

To prevent illicit socializing between Indians and settlers at the pueblos, the military administration had strict guidelines. In Los Angeles after 1787, Indians were not permitted to enter the homes of settlers or live in the town. If they stayed overnight in the pueblo, a sentry had to keep watch over them at night.[4] Indian women were often not allowed to work in the homes of *pobladores,* the settlers of the pueblos.

In the eyes of the Catholic Church and Christian societies, sexuality was one of the most tangible representations of morality. This same perception held true in California with regard to women.

## The Colonial Female Ideal

Spain had kept the ideal of female honor from its medieval past. Morality, religion, and the family name were all esteemed, and the burden was often placed on women to uphold these ideals. Though the missionaries were sympathetic to the dangers a woman faced in a society dominated by men, including unruly soldiers, the Spanish Franciscan culture had high expectations of female behavior in the missions. Relations outside of marriage were outlawed and punishable, and all contact with the opposite sex was tightly scrutinized. Women were more severely punished than men when cases of adultery, premarital sex, or pregnancy outside of marriage were discovered.

The Indians' social customs sometimes baffled and shocked the Spanish. Pedro Fages observed that the Chumash Indians were "addicted to the unspeakable vice of sinning against nature," i.e., committing forbidden sexual acts.[5] Missionaries complained of scattered occurrences of polygamy, transvestitism, and extramarital relations in some Indian communities.

The Franciscans prohibited initiation dances and other traditional tribal ceremonies to mark the milestone of puberty for girls and boys. Mission leaders harshly punished abortion and infanticide among Indian women. A woman known to have obtained an abortion might be required to appear in church on Sunday carrying a *monigote,* a small wooden doll symbolizing the aborted child.[6]

According to the Franciscans and the colonial authorities, marriage was an antidote to the "heathen" condition of Indian life. Some California Indian groups were accustomed to more informal marital arrangements, yet within the new Catholic society they were forbidden to divorce or separate once married. As a result of this prescribed system of behavior, illegitimate births were unusual in the missions.

In Europe the Christian model of marriage was both a sacrament and a contract that often transferred property. Marriage was monogamous and a lifelong bond. Especially in Mediterranean countries like Spain, female virginity until marriage was highly prized. The church granted divorce only in unusual circumstances. Marriage, blessed by a priest, was the only appropriate place for sexual relations between a man and woman. In California, when Spanish Christian laws were applied, Indian couples already married in their own society prior to conversion remarried in the Catholic Church. A newly baptized Indian married to a non-Christian Indian would be permitted to take a new Christian spouse. An Indian man who had several wives could keep only the first one.

The ideal result of missionization was a Christian society defined by Spanish culture. Connections between Indian relatives and families through marriage served as an advantage to the Franciscans, helping in difficult times. Secure links of kinship with other groups could provide insurance during food shortages.[7]

Marriage accorded Indian families a small amount of freedom at some missions. Extended families lived elsewhere on mission property, in small adobe dwellings or straw houses. In some regions they lived in adjacent pueblos or rancherías incorporated by a particular mission. Sometimes women later returned to the rancherías with their husbands.

### The Bottom Rung

Because women living at the missions came from different social and ethnic backgrounds, there was a hierarchy within the female community. Indian women and girls living at the missions were accorded lower status than Spanish and Mexican women who settled in California. Women at the lowest rung of the Spanish class ladder, the laborers, ranked lower still than men of that class, as Indian women had no rights under colonial law.

Under civil law in Spain and Mexico, married Hispanic women, unlike married Indian women, possessed rights to property and wages and other legal individual rights.[8] Hispanic women oversaw Christian Indian women in chores and religious duties. Christian Indian women (*prioras*), in turn, oversaw Indian neophytes and new Indian female converts.[9] These women reported directly to the priest rather than a Hispanic intermediary. Women of mixed parentage fit somewhere in between.

In Spanish society a duenna was an elderly woman appointed to watch over the younger women. The mission duenna, usually the wife of a soldier, chaperoned the young women at the mission. The celibate lifestyle of missionaries made female supervisors necessary in some cases where a male supervisor would be inappropriate. Said Serra: "[T]he wives of the soldiers should devote themselves to instructing the women of the missions—a piece of work that presents obvious difficulties to the Fathers."[10]

### Under Lock and Key

Immersion in mission culture was a shock for Indian women. In their native societies these women were accustomed to greater power and influence. They lived more independently and sometimes served as shamans and healers. Under Spanish rule women lost all such status. On mission grounds they were constantly scrutinized by soldiers and missionaries. With the language barriers and culture imposed from within, the change for Indian women in the missions was dramatic and not always explained.

Younger, unmarried females slept in a firmly locked *monjerío* (dormitory). The monjerío at the San José mission was a large adobe building enclosed by high adobe walls.[11] The monjerío was one of the first structures built at each mission.[12] Any activities outside the mission, such as work or trips back to the ancestral homeland during free time, required a soldier, missionary, or trusted Indian man as chaperone. The Rezanov account describes this arrangement: "All the girls and women are closely guarded in separate houses—as though under lock and key—and kept at work. They are but seldom permitted to go out in the day, and never at night. As soon, however, as a girl marries, she is free, and, with her husband, lives in one of the Indian villages belonging to the mission." The missionaries hoped to bind the neophytes to the mission and ensure their faith with more ease and security.[13]

In the nearby rancherías Indian girls lived with their parents until age eleven, when they were brought to the monjerío to live with other unmarried girls and widows. These unattached women and girls were separated from their extended families and locked in together at night. A duenna guarded them and was sometimes entrusted with the key to the dormitory.[14] Frederick Beechey wrote, "The children and adults of both sexes, in all the missions, are carefully locked up every night in separate apartments, and the keys are delivered into the possession of the padre; and as, in the daytime, their occupations lead to distinct places, unless they form a matrimonial alliance they enjoy very little of each other's society. It, however, sometimes happens that they endeavor to evade the vigilance of their keepers and are locked up with the opposite sex; but severe corporeal punishment . . . is sure to ensue if they are discovered."[15]

The monjerío institution reflected Spanish beliefs about honor and female roles. It enabled the priests to regulate sexual behavior, protect women and girls from abuse, and uphold female virginity. Any who rebelled were whipped.


### Female Work Roles


Mission women filled traditional domestic positions. They cleaned, laundered, sewed, cared for the sick, and performed other duties prescribed by the missionaries, soldiers, and Indian leaders. Pregnant women washed wool or pulled weeds, and children helped with lighter tasks. Some women were sent, chaperoned, outside the mission to collect food or work as domestics in Spanish households.

Old keys from Valencia, Spain. © iStockphoto.com / José Delgado.

More typically, women were assigned to roles on-site, including domestic chores, gardening, and female-only crafts such as weaving and sewing. Rezanov observed some of these women at work: "Behind the residence of the padres there is a large courtyard, enclosed by houses. Here live the Indian women of the mission, who are employed under the immediate supervision of the padres in useful occupations, such as cleaning and combing wool, spinning, weaving, etc. Their principal business is the manufacture of a woolen cloth and blankets for the Indians' own use."[16]

In a culture where trades and skills were passed along to new members of the community and to girls old enough to learn a skill and make a contribution to the group's survival, there were limited opportunities for leadership in the female community. Some women held positions in the church, such as the *cantora,* an Indian woman trained to sing and lead other singers in mission church services. Very occasionally mission women were assigned greater responsibility, such as overseeing agricultural tasks and stocking the mission with supplies from the cargo ships and overland supply trips.[17]

As they did before Spanish settlement, Indian women ministered to the sick with teas and healing herbs, as directed by the missionaries. They were not,

Weaving room, La Purísima.

however, formally given the status they had held in Indian society as healers. Without medical supplies and doctors on the frontier, Hispanic women also helped with these activities. Women not born to such healing practices learned them from the indigenous healers.[18]

## Colonization through Reproduction

With its colonies, Spain wanted to create loyal and productive populations. Multiplication of resources and procreation were the keys to accomplishing this goal. Marriage and parenthood increased the population of colonial settlements at each mission and in theory solidified ties to the mission itself. The conjugal family unit helped create a sense of permanence in a colony where families were dependent on each mission for food and shelter. Intermarriage with local women created local ties, and the presence of married men and women guaranteed a growing population when disease did not slow that growth.

From the time of Cortés, marriage between natives and Spaniards was encouraged, resulting in a mixed-race group called mestizos. Marriage was also a way to reshape a society and teach Spanish customs to Indian women. Spanish ships brought women to the colonies before the settlement of Alta California, some as wives of colonists and others as slaves. From the sixteenth century on, Spain required settlers to travel to the New World with their wives and encouraged families to travel together.[19]

The colonial government recruited mixed soldier and settler families from New Spain to populate the newest colonial state. Serra also promoted marriage between Indian Christian women and soldiers.[20] The often restless soldiers, expected to protect the mission but faced with hours and days of either no work or nonmilitary duties, needed familial distraction. In 1775 Serra approved of new Spanish regulations that subsidized interracial marriages with a salary, rations, livestock, and land.[21]

Later New Spain, through a system of rewards, encouraged settlers to travel north and help populate California. Willing settlers received land and livestock in addition to a stipend. In the 1790s Spanish authorities in California and Mexico began formally recruiting settlers to help increase the population in the California colony. In 1797 the colonial government advised California governor Diego de Borica that volunteer soldiers could marry Christian Indian women to help increase the colonial resident population.[22] Borica responded to the viceroy in September 1797, requesting wives for the settlers and soldiers: "strong young spinsters, especially for criminal settlers, since the padres objected to the native women marrying such husbands. Besides good health the girls must bring good clothes, so that they may go to church and be improved. A *sine qua non* of a California female colonist must be a serge petticoat, a *rebozo coriente,* a linen jacket, two woolen shifts, a pair of stockings, and a pair of strong shoes."[23]

As described above, the Franciscans constantly regulated sexual behavior and interaction between men and women at each mission. Sexual orthodoxy was expected and encouraged, and women were forced to behave within the parameters of Christian morality. In their writings, the missionaries were preoccupied with ensuring traditional women's roles and preventing adultery and premarital relations.[24] Marriage was considered a Christian duty that brought order to colonial society.

# 8

# Spanish and Mexican Settlement

Spanish and Mexican settlement of California during the mission years was the first wave of Hispanic immigration to California. Though the numbers were relatively small, it laid the cornerstone of Spanish culture and established institutions that remain visible today. The study of Spanish colonialism in the Americas is thus necessary to an understanding of today's Californian and American history. These Hispanic roots also provide historical context for today's regular influx of Spanish-speaking residents into California and elsewhere in the United States.

Hispanic settlement of California during the mission period was encouraged and largely sponsored by the colonial governments of Spain and Mexico. In exchange for land and other benefits, settlers made the hard journey in small groups to start towns and prosperous farms and ranches. Along with the soldiers and their families at the first missions and presidios, these settlers were among the first ancestors of California's later elite rancho class.

From the first California mission in 1769 to the end of the Spanish period in 1821, New Spain tried to supplement output from the existing missions and presidios with more farmers. Hispanics from Mexico settled in pueblos, and experienced farmers helped jump-start California's agricultural production and lessen its dependence on supplies from San Blas. Farmers and tradesmen were sent to add weight to the colonial population and economy.

Junípero Serra, whose communiqués usually made plain any disagreement with the colonial government, agreed with New Spain's wish that settlers be brought to supplement mission production: "Without this regulation that these men remain as settlers . . . it will be utterly impossible for these missions and new establishments to make any progress."[1] Some Franciscan critics, however, complained to the first governors of California that the settler class was a threat to the mission Indians because of its relative independence and cause of discontent.[2] Indeed, enmity between missionaries and settlers continued through to the end of the Mexican period. The cause was economic; missionaries sat on but did not own land that yielded high production and brought profit from its products and the hide and tallow trade.

While the missions brought only a narrow population of select soldiers and Franciscan missionaries to California, later settlements introduced a broader variety of people from New Spain. Farmers and soldiers were common, as were people from other occupations needed to keep the colonies alive. New Spain's intent, in theory, was that settlers familiar with farming methods and other trades would help get the colonies off the ground until the Indians became productive colonial residents of its California province.

Serra suggested to the New Spain administration in 1773 that "respectable Spanish families" of mission soldiers be encouraged to settle in California to supplement the mission settlements already in progress. This suggestion was the first sign of the secular settlements to come, starting with San José and Los Angeles.[3]

For several years during the 1770s, Viceroy Bucareli brought settlers to California with free transportation as well as financial and other help.[4] After 1774, California's colonial officials sent recruiters south to bring soldiers, settlers, and artisans by land and supply ships from the northern Mexican provinces of Sonora and Guadalajara. In 1777 California governor Felipe de Neve chose fourteen families in the Mission Santa Clara locale to populate the first town. The colonists received goods and livestock in exchange for their labor, as well as lots where they could grow grain, beans, and vegetables and graze their cattle.

Governor Neve created his *Regulations for Governing the Province of the Californias* in 1779, with specific rules for settlements. In new towns, each settler would receive a plot of land of approximately eight acres, along with a lot for living quarters. Both the land and the house could be passed on to the settler's descendants. The settlers were also exempt from taxes for a period of five years.

Settlers would provide their own horses, guns, and other weapons and be ready to defend the district in an emergency if the governor ordered them to do so. These regulations continued until Mexico's assumption of the territory.[5]

Between three and seven thousand Hispanic and several thousand other settlers immigrated to California prior to 1821, the year of Mexican independence from Spain. Those numbers would increase dramatically after Mexican independence from Spain in 1821. In another example of government-sponsored colonization, colonial officials in New Spain sent a group of boys and girls to Alta California in 1800. These orphans or foundlings were placed with different families to help increase the population.[6] Between 1821 and the U.S. acquisition of California in 1848, while the missions languished, settlers came to California in increasing numbers to cultivate crops and tend livestock. Mexico's 1824 laws of colonization offered incentives for settlers to make the long trip. Between 1821 and 1846, eight hundred sections of property were granted, leading to a land rush and to rampant speculation in land and cattle.[7]

The Mexican government secularized the missions in 1834 and opened their lands to private farmers. That year the government sponsored the Híjar-Pádres expedition, a group of forty-two families, including teachers, artisans, and farmers. In addition to a per diem, each colonist was given, from former mission land, a plot of one hundred square yards in town and land outside town for livestock grazing.[8] Infighting back in Mexico City removed the funding once the colonists arrived, and this was to be one of the Mexican government's only colonization efforts.

After 1834, the ranchos, carved from mission lands, replaced the missions as California's primary land institutions. While Spanish settlers from Mexico had lived in the towns or in pueblos close to the missions, the new settlers set up outside the missions and became major farmers and livestock ranchers. The farmers followed the mission style of crop irrigation, and the ranchers raised cattle, sheep, goats, and horses.

In the Mexican period, people from areas other than Spanish America were more welcome to California than under Spanish rule. Non-Hispanics were allowed citizenship and land in exchange for adopting Catholicism. Later, descendants of the earliest Spanish settler families began to marry other European and Anglo settlers, whose numbers increased with the influx of merchants in the 1820s and trappers and traders in the 1830s.[9] California's ports and towns exploded with the growth of the hide and tallow industries begun by the missions. With the influx of these new settlers, California began to change yet again from a Hispanic and Indian region to one with American influence.

## Pueblos

Spain's 1681 Laws of the Indies made settlements important in its overseas colonies. Under royal order to produce agricultural food supplies and to encourage the building of Spanish colonial settlements, New Spain ordered the creation of pueblos in Alta California, of which three were built. Once the Indian population accepted Christianity and could support itself without outside assistance and supplies, frontier missions and presidios developed by then were expected to evolve into pueblos. Mission property would be divided among the Indians, and land, seeds, farming tools, and livestock would be provided. Parish churches would replace mission churches. In the words of Hubert Bancroft, a prominent historian of early California, "California was to be a country of towns and farms . . . a community of tribute-paying, God-fearing Spanish citizens."[10] As it turned out, California missions remained in Franciscan hands until they became secularized in the latter part of the Mexican period, and the pueblos developed by then remained mainly Hispanic settlements with Indian laborers. According to colonial plan, the pueblos would eventually relieve the missions and other Spanish settlements of the constant wait for supply ships.

Under Spanish rule pueblos were limited in size and importance. They rapidly grew during and after secularization as more settlers arrived and bought out the mission economy. Under Mexican rule, pueblos were run by a municipal government and administered thousands of acres of land owned by the town.

Pueblos were "free" towns, meaning they operated independently of the missions and presidios. They were a combination of private and government land. In their agricultural focus and military protection, pueblos resembled the missions. In other aspects they resembled small towns, with inhabitants going about various trades and raising their families. The pueblos provided New Spain's frontier military forces with supplies, especially food items like flour, corn, and beans. Settlers, food, and supplies from Mexico supplemented the colonial population and reinforced mission and presidio settlements.

The first settlers of pueblos in the Spanish Americas were Spanish or Creole soldiers who had retired from their service to the missions. Retirees could either return to their native Spain or Mexico or remain in the country.[11] In California the residents of many of the first settlements on the outskirts of mission grounds were retired military officers. Families and individuals who followed from Mexico received government grants of land for cultivation. Eventually, during the Mexican period, most ranches were run by private parties.

San José, the first official pueblo in California, was founded in 1777 near the mission of Santa Clara with sixty-six settlers.[12] California's largest pueblo was Nuestra Señora de los Angeles, eight miles from Mission San Gabriel. It was founded in 1781 with forty-six people from eleven families from Sonora and Sinaloa in Mexico.[13]

Indians and some Spaniards at the pueblos received stipends from the government of New Spain, along with a house, tract of land, and common land to share, all free of taxes and tithes. The people of Los Angeles soon built a town hall, barracks, guardhouse, and granary. These largely civilian settlements helped support nearby military and religious communities. Villa Branciforte, a military and civil settlement founded near present-day Santa Cruz in 1797, was another early California pueblo. Most Branciforte settlers at this time were bachelors—farmers, tailors, carpenters, merchants, miners, and engravers. Like the first mission settlers, many of Branciforte's residents raised small crops of maize, wheat, and beans.[14] Villa Branciforte was at odds with Mission Santa Cruz, and was an important contributor to the failure of the mission. It survived into the mid-nineteenth century, when it was absorbed into Santa Cruz.

Just as mission pueblos developed in association with the nearest mission, presidial pueblos were civilian settlements that grew up outside the presidios. For protection, each pueblo maintained its own small guard of active-duty soldiers who lived on-site. For soldiers who retired with their families, military commandants issued house lots and planting fields near the presidios.

In the early nineteenth century, once the pueblos were able to produce a surplus, they traded goods with supply ships.[15] Ultimately California's pueblos experienced more economic success than the Franciscan missions and became the basis for the new towns of Spanish, Mexican, and eventually American California.

### Ranchos

While pueblos were developed as urban and farming settlements to serve the missions and presidios, ranchos were more focused on cattle raising. Beginning in 1786, the first of over five hundred ranchos was granted to private owners. Tightly controlled under Spanish rule, the number of ranchos increased under Mexican oversight, and ranchos grew as symbols of Spanish and Mexican culture in California. By the time Commodore Sloat raised the American flag over Monterey Bay in 1846, the land area contained in these baronial estates exceeded the areas of Massachusetts, Delaware, and Rhode Island combined.[16]

Mission period breeds, La Purísima.

Ranchos were individually owned and dedicated to farming and stock raising. Some ranchos kept a few cattle belonging to the presidios. At the center of California's thriving hide and tallow trade in the first half of the nineteenth century, ranchos supplied hides to Eastern shoe manufacturers. Set up to sell these products for a profit, early ranchos produced just enough food and supplies to support their owners.[17]

Rancho communities worked mainly at their profitable trades, but also planted fruit, grapes, barley, corn, beans, wheat, onions, potatoes, and hemp. The wool trade also stimulated enterprise in California.

After the missions were taken from the Franciscans, ranch owners replaced the missionaries and soldiers as overseers of Indians on the estates. This work arrangement continued the tradition of Indian dependency, creating a new underclass.[18] As before, Indians, both conscripted and from the missions, performed the hardest labor on ranches, such as tilling the soil, pasturing the livestock, and constructing buildings. By 1840, several dozen large Mexican ranches maintained hundreds of Indian laborers.[19]

Vaqueros, who learned their trade at the missions, faced an easier change-over from mission to rancho. These invaluable ranch hands helped protect private land and stock from Indians looking to raid the ranchos, which were often located in isolated regions. Of Indian or Hispanic descent, vaqueros were seen everywhere in the settlements of California's provincial frontier.

### The Spanish Settler Class and Culture

The arrival of merchants, farmers, and newcomers of other occupations began to change California's society and economy as their settlements overshadowed the missions in both population and productivity.

Christian settlers of Spanish descent and Spanish-speaking Christians in the new colonies, as well as mixed-race Christians from both Mexico and California, were known as *gente de razón* (people of reason) to distinguish them from unconverted Indians, who were *sin razón* (without reason). The terms date from the Spanish Inquisition. Politically, gente de razón were in good favor with the Spanish crown and colonial governments. They were expected to set an example for mission Indians and to teach and mobilize them to achieve mission goals.[20] Military engineer and architect Miguel Constanzó wrote of their usefulness in New Spain in 1794: "Some missions have been for a hundred years in charge of friars and presidial guards. The remedy is to introduce *gente de razón* among the natives from the beginning. . . . They should be settled near the missions and mingle with the natives. Thus the missions will become towns in twenty-five years or thirty years."[21] This statement emphasizes the Spanish colonial view that settlers from Spain and Spanish dominions would help convert indigenous peoples living in territory assumed by Spain.

The Mexican and Hispanic upper class of California was descended from gente de razón who were handpicked by the Jesuits and brought to the Baja Peninsula and whose descendants received a large share of the land grants in California.[22] The settler families of California, legendary for their influence on the culture and place-names of their adopted country, enjoyed tremendous status and wealth in colonial society. Single families ruled miles of farm and ranch land, employed hundreds of Indians, and during the years of Mexican rule took over the wealth of the aging Franciscan missions, now emptying through disease and financial neglect.

Under Spanish rule the population of Hispanic settlers in the province was quite small relative to the size of the land, and Spain found it hard to attract new settlers to the region. By 1790 the Hispanic population of Alta California was only about 970, including settlers of mixed parentage. These people had arrived in California between 1769 and 1781.[23] By 1800 the number of settlers in California from New Spain had increased to about 1,200,[24] and by 1820 it was about 3,270.[25] In 1890 Spanish Californian Guadalupe Vallejo remembered, "When I was a child there were fewer than fifty Spanish families in the region about the bay of San Francisco, and these were closely connected by ties of blood or intermarriage." Vallejo mentioned how his father and uncle took part in "the revolution and conquest" of Spanish California, and his grandfather in "the exploration and settlement of the province."[26]

Although limited in number, settlers from New Spain formed the skeleton of society in Spain's frontier provinces. They worked as priests, soldiers, government officials, artisans, and farmers. In the minority during the Spanish and Mexican mission years, Spanish and Mexican settlers increased in numbers when Mexico secularized the missions, and occupied the first rung of the social and economic ladder until California became an American state in 1850.

Around the time the missions were secularized, Spanish and Mexican settlers started to mix with European and Anglo settlers. At the same time, the Indian populations of California hardly matched their original numbers. During the Mexican era, what was known as the *californio* population doubled while the Indian population sharply dropped.[27]

## Spanish Culture

Spaniards and Mexicans in California developed a distinctive californio culture by the early nineteenth century, a combination of Indian and Spanish ways. Physical manifestations of the Spanish frontier culture, the communities of californios, became more evident in the California landscape by the mid-nineteenth century as Mexican settlers increased in number. Ranchos and pueblos were the epicenters of californio culture. Haciendas (rural homes) sat adjacent to where sheep and cattle were raised.

Californios were well known for their exuberant celebrations at festivals, weddings, national holidays, and other special occasions, where they would dance the fandango and barrego, lively regional dances from Spain. Women at such occasions wore bright-colored gowns, while men wore elaborate embroidered trousers slashed to the knee and decorated with two rows of buttons. On nonfestive days women wore dresses made from silk, crepe, or calico, with a bright belt, satin or leather shoes, a necklace and earrings, long braids if unmarried, and hair in a high comb if wed. The *rebozo* (head drape) was worn inside and the *mantilla* outside. The men wore broad-brimmed hats, short jackets, open-necked

Traditional Mexican sombrero. © iStockphoto.com/Nat Girish.

shirts, waistcoats, knee breeches, white stockings, deerskin leggings and shoes, a red sash, and a serape.[28]

Still persisting in history and literature is the perception of californio families as a devout Catholic community steeped in the traditions and culture of Spain and old Mexico, combined with a dose of frontier pioneer spirit born of rustic conditions and adventure. Guadalupe Vallejo remembered this time: "Family life among the old Spanish pioneers was an affair of dignity and ceremony. . . . Each one of the old families taught their children the history of the family, and reverence toward religion. In these days of trade, bustle, and confusion, when many thousands of people live in the Californian valleys, which formerly were occupied by only a few Spanish families, the quiet and happy domestic life of the past seems like a dream."

Californios have been portrayed by some writers as old-fashioned and out of touch when the discovery of gold brought Americans flocking to California. Like the mission culture before it, the californio culture faded away. Guadalupe Vallejo reminisced: "We often talk together of the days when a few hundred large Spanish ranches and mission tracts occupied the whole country from the Pacific to the San Joaquin. No class of American citizens is more loyal than Spanish Californians, but we shall always be especially proud of the traditions and memories of the long pastoral age before 1840."[29] He also remembered proudly, "We were the pioneers of the Pacific coast, building towns and Missions while General Washington was carrying on the war of the Revolution."[30]

## An Ethnic Hodgepodge

Frontier California was a complex mingling of cultures and peoples. A caste system, already well established in South America and the Caribbean, organized people by race and social class, with *peninsulares* (Spaniards) at the top, followed by Creoles or *españoles* (Spaniards born in the Americas), then by mestizos (people of mixed Spanish, African, and Indian ancestry), and finally, on the bottom, by Indians and Africans. (In Spain, people of mixed race were allowed to buy certificates of racial purity.)[31]

Most of the missionaries were Spanish, as were most of the military officers, who came from the upper class. The soldiers, most of them from the Mexican lower classes, were mestizos,[32] as were many of the first settlers, reflecting the mestizo culture that prevailed in Mexico. At the first pueblo settlement in Los Angeles, the 1781 census listed only two of the forty-seven inhabitants as claiming pure Spanish blood.[33]

Spanish policy encouraged all single settlers and soldiers to marry, and they usually did so as soon as marriageable women were available, usually starting at the age of twelve. Archeological research confirms that Indians and soldiers interacted and mingled in the daily activities at the presidios,[34] and marriages between Spanish soldiers and native women were common. Extensive racial records maintained at the San Carlos, Santa Clara, and San Juan Bautista missions, however, show that marriages between colonists and Indians in these missions during the Spanish period made up only 4 percent of all marriages, despite Indians outnumbering the Spanish-Mexican population. Spanish and Creole men seemed to prefer to marry women from their own caste, class, and race.[35] Marriages between Indian men and Spanish or Mexican women were rare or unknown.

Demographically, colonization of California was quite different from that of the East Coast of North America. California's social institutions were based in Catholic Spanish culture and governed by a rigid patriarchy that did not loosen until the United States took possession. California, with its diverse racial makeup, caste system, and use of indentured labor, had more in common with the southern plantation colonies.

# 9

## Colonial Soldiers and the Presidio

As the Yuma massacre of 1781 made plain, the colonial military played an essential role in the colonization of California. The mission and pueblo settlements were small and isolated, and the missions, at least until the area had been explored and relations with the local populations had been established, needed protection to survive.

When New Spain sent military forces to California, resources, finances, and supplies were limited. Still, Spanish soldiers, with their guns and leather armor, outmatched their Indian opponents. Horses, also new to California, added the advantages of speed and intimidation. Mission Indian Pablo Tac observed that soldiers were needed on expeditions "so that nobody [did] injury to Spaniard or to Indian; there are ten of them and they go on horseback."[1]

Colonial soldiers protected Spain's territory and enforced royal colonial policy.[2] They were invaluable during exploration and helped chart new territory and defend both people and resources from intruders. Spanish soldiers manned the presidios and guarded mission buildings throughout the California settlements. The presidios, each of which guarded one or more missions, were the center of military administration for the missions, and soldiers for missionary use were trained and housed in them. Soldiers also oversaw the building and guarding of pueblos and performed administrative services for officials such as the viceroy of New Spain and provincial governors.

Felipe de Neve, governor of the province of Alta California, evaluated the coast along the Santa Barbara channel as he traveled to his post in Monterey in 1776–77. He estimated that eight thousand Chumash Indians lived in some two dozen villages on coastal lands between the cliffs[3] and suggested that a presidio would be essential to protect new settlements in the area against the Indians. One was subsequently built. The Chumash were later recorded to be cooperative and friendly, but the presidio remained.

## Presidios

Presidios had been tools of colonization and protection for Spain since the late sixteenth century, helping control land as well as gold and silver deposits in New Spain. They may have been patterned after the fortresses that protected the borders of the Roman empire from barbarian tribes. By the late seventeenth century, military posts and missions dotted both sides of the Rio Grande.

California's four presidios, while small, announced Spain's claim to the California coast. The San Diego and Monterey presidios appeared in 1769 and 1770, and the San Francisco presidio followed in 1776 to safeguard the northern coastline. The Santa Barbara presidio completed a defensive line of military settlements in 1782. Other small fortifications and pueblo districts with military personnel supplemented the presidios.

Each presidio sat about a mile from the coastline, out of reach of cannon fire from warships. Nearby, usually within a mile, was a *castillo* (fort), equipped with its own cannons. In 1770 the San Diego presidio was a crude stockade with two bronze cannons, one pointed out to sea, the other at the neighboring Indian village.[4] In the vicinity of Presidio Hill and Old Town, at the site the Indians called *Cosoy*, lived the eighteen soldiers who formed the nucleus of the presidio.[5] The San Diego presidio defended not only the San Diego mission but the missions of San Gabriel and San Juan Capistrano. The Monterey presidio, which defended the missions of San Carlos, San Antonio de Padua, and San Luis Obispo, sat directly on Monterey Bay, offering immediate assistance to boats arriving there.[6] The Santa Barbara presidio protected the San Gabriel and Channel missions.

Each presidio sat on a central square of about one hundred yards on each side. Nearby was lodging for the military commandant and soldiers. Presidio construction was similar to mission construction, with barracks encircling a quadrangle. The missions of San Diego and Monterey were enclosed in their presidios.

California presidios were generally not well maintained. The Monterey presidio was a poor example of Spanish defense when a pirate vessel from Buenos Aires captured it in 1819, destroyed most of its guns, and pillaged the town.[7] In 1792 George Vancouver was unimpressed by the San Francisco presidio's display of Spanish might:

> The only object of human industry that presented itself was a square area, whose sides were about two hundred yards in length, enclosed by a mud wall. . . . Above this wall, the thatched roofs of their low, small houses just made their appearance. On entering the presidio, we found one of its sides still unenclosed by the wall and very indifferently fenced in by a few bushes here and there, fastened to stakes in the ground. . . .
>
> . . . [The floor of] the commandant's house . . . was of the native soil, raised about three feet from its original level, without being boarded, paved, or even reduced to an even surface. The roof was covered in with flags and rushed; the walls on the inside had once been whitewashed; the furniture consisted of a very sparing assortment of the most indispensable articles, of the rudest fashion and of the meanest kind; and ill-accorded with the ideas we had conceived of the sumptuous manner in which the Spaniards live on this side of the globe. . . .
>
> . . . Thus, at the expense of very little examination, though not without much disappointment, was our curiosity satisfied concerning the Spanish town and settlement of San Francisco. Instead of finding a country tolerably well-inhabited and far advanced in cultivation—if we except its natural pastures, the flocks of sheep, and herds of cattle—there is not an object to indicate the most remote connection with any European or other civilized nation.
>
> This sketch will be sufficient, without further comment, to convey some idea of the inactive spirit of the people and the unprotected state of the establishment at this port, which I should conceive ought to be a principal object of the Spanish crown, as a key and barrier to their more southern and valuable settlements on the borders of the north Pacific.[8]

California historian Hubert Bancroft called the presidios "a kind of public works for the support of officials, and the drawing of money from royal coffers."[9] In his view the presidios were largely ineffective and were in fact not necessary for military defense, except in isolated instances. Instead, they served as extensions of the missions and the first settlements of colonial towns. Although

Soldiers' dining table in the *cuartel*.

modest in scale, the presidios contributed significantly to the initial settlements of the Spanish pioneer population in California. Once mission soldiers retired, they often settled on small plots granted to them near the mission or presidio,[10] unlike presidio captains, who usually lived and retired at the presidios with their families. After Mexico's independence from Spain, retired soldiers moved from the San Diego presidio into homes in the Old Town of today's San Diego.

### Soldier of All Trades

All presidio soldiers were royal employees, their appointments approved by the viceroy.[11] To enlist, soldiers needed to be at least sixteen years old, five feet tall or higher, Catholic, and in reasonably good health. Their presence in the vicinity of every mission site made colonization possible. Although Spain's military representation in California was paltry, it did act as a bulwark against Indians and an instrument of control. During the founding of the first mission, there was constant fear of Indian uprisings until military reinforcements arrived from Baja California and Anza came with more soldiers and settlers for the San Francisco Bay region.[12]

The life of a soldier on the frontier was one of uncertainty and hard labor. Soldiers and missionaries would often have to travel great distances in desert conditions with scant water and food. Like the first Franciscans in California, the earliest soldiers had had experience serving in the Baja Peninsula during the Jesuit years.[13] Some were second-generation Baja Californians; others were experienced lower- and middle-class soldiers from the presidios of Mexico and Baja California.[14] Some were recruited from Mexican ranches and villages or from the lower Spanish classes or were convicts serving out their prison terms as soldiers. Half or more of the forces at the Loreto mission settlement had served in the northern part of the Baja Peninsula, guarding the missions then run by Dominicans and overseeing supply trains to new missions in Alta California.

Soldiers protected the missionaries and missionized Indians and managed the Indian workforce, enforcing discipline and guarding against escape. A corporal's guard of five or six soldiers assigned to each mission helped to chase and return runaways. When needed, more troops would be sent on horseback from the nearest presidio. Soldiers provided protection outside the missions as well. "By a royal command, it is not permissible for the *misioneros* to go any distance without military protection. As they carry only the Bible and the cross as their personal protection, a military escort accompanies them at all times," wrote Nikolai Rezanov in 1806.[15] In return for these services, the missionaries provided food, shelter, supplies, and workers for the troops housed at the missions and presidios.

During expeditions beyond mission territory, clergy and soldiers used Indians as auxiliaries to capture runaways.[16] Presidio and mission soldiers led military raids to the interior in search of more Indians to bring to the missions. Mission San José served as a military base for punitive campaigns against tribes living in the marshlands of the San Joaquin River, who attacked the Christian Indians at the missions and offered refuge to runaways from the San Francisco Bay area.[17]

Soldiers provided order at ceremonies, services, and all other activities at the missions and presidios. Their other duties extended beyond traditional military tasks, for which they were often poorly trained. Serra wrote that soldiers of Monterey were more suited to work outside the military: "These men . . . have in mind to establish their homes, to work in the fields, and on their land, as they are accustomed to do in their native country. . . . That really is their chief calling in life, and not to be soldiers in this kind of service. Some of them do not even know how to put on a saddle properly."[18] The extent of soldiers' nonmilitary duties depended on the mission's needs. In the exploratory period, soldiers constructed graded trails for pack and riding animals. Some soldiers were experienced mule drivers who loaded and unloaded the animals for each journey. They transported supplies, helped construct mission buildings, furniture, and corrals for livestock, cleared fields and prepared soil for planting, and dug wells and irrigation ditches.[19] On occasion presidio soldiers worked their own fields or grazed herds using Indian labor from nearby missions.

A soldier at each mission acted as majordomo to the lead missionary. He secured and inventoried all mission food supplies and tools, trained and supervised Indians in agriculture and herding, and managed distribution of tools and craft materials.

## Military Bearing and Gear

The first soldiers to arrive from New Spain came from stations in Sonora and were nicknamed *soldados de cueras* (hide companies) in reference to the thick hides they wore to protect them from Indian arrows. Their heavy (seventeen-pound) sleeveless coats were made from several layers of tanned buckskin.

While not strictly enforced, 1772 uniform regulations specified a short jacket of blue woolen cloth with small red cuffs and a red collar, blue breeches, a blue cloth cap, a black neckerchief, boots, and an antelope-hide bandolier (a strip across the chest for carrying ammunition) with the name of the presidio tooled into it. The dress actually worn in the field varied, each soldier outfitting himself with available clothing at his own cost. Rezanov described how the soldiers were outfitted when they served as missionary escorts: "Each of the padres has several horses for his own use, and when one starts out on an expedition for finding prospective *neófitos,* he is always escorted by one or more soldiers, who precede him on the way. At such times the soldiers commonly throw over their breast and shoulders a deerskin mantle, which is intended as a protection against the arrows of the Indians, these being incapable of piercing leather. This mantle is worn on other occasions, also, as on dress parade, and when approaching a presidio or mission." A soldier's weapons included a musket kept in a deerskin case, a broadsword, sometimes a muzzle-loaded pistol, and a lance, which he used with great expertise.[20] In his left arm he carried a heart-shaped bullhide shield. Soldiers bought their own saddles, saddlebags, and wooden stirrups. For retirement money, a soldier could sell his gear to new recruits.

Although colonial soldiers answered to their superior officers, religion permeated military life. Mission administration and the provincial government required mission troops to recite the rosary regularly, adhere to nightly curfews, and avoid gambling and card playing. Nevertheless, soldiers had a reputation for irreverence, and secret card games were common. Missionaries were allowed to send disobedient soldiers back to the presidio for punishment.[21]

Mission soldiers' riding gear, La Purísima.

Off-duty conduct of the soldiers and their effect on mission Indians was an ongoing point of dispute between governors and the missionaries. The soldiers' pursuit of Indian women was a constant problem, causing unrest and occasional armed conflict with the Indian men.[22] Officials argued over how and when the soldiers should be disciplined for these offenses. Serra went so far as to move the Monterey mission to a new site to distance his converts from the presidio soldiers. Missionary and presidio soldiers developed a reputation for spreading venereal disease and other diseases to the Indians living in the settlements.

## Forgotten Soldiers

Without stipends and supplies for their soldiers, mission settlements were crippled from the start. Both missions and presidios competed for government funds to satisfy basic needs. Extensive equipment was needed to outfit the soldiers: riding and pack items, saddles, stirrups, spurs, reins, bells, and saddlebags, as well as gunpowder, musket balls, and swords. The tighter funds became, the scarcer the items, and the more soldiers had to find their own equipment.

Poor pay, always a constant in military life, worsened as Spain's overseas attention and finances diminished. Adelbert von Chamisso, an exiled French aristocrat, was the chief naturalist of a Russian expedition that traveled around the world.

He and his company shared the feast of St. Francis on October 9, 1816, with the military leaders of the San Francisco presidio. His account provides insight into the declining conditions for frontier soldiers:

> [T]he captain was able to accustom the commandant and his officers to our table. We dined on land under the tent. . . . The misery in which they had been wallowing for six to seven years, forgotten and forsaken by Mexico, the motherland, did not permit them to be hosts, and the need to pour out their hearts in speech impelled them to approach us, as life was easy and pleasant with us. They spoke only with bitterness of the missionaries, who in the face of a deficiency in imported goods nonetheless enjoyed a superfluity of the products of the earth and would let them have nothing now that their money had run out, except in return for a promissory note—and, even so, only what is absolutely necessary to maintaining life, among which things bread and flour are not included. For years they had lived on maize, without seeing bread. Even the detachments of soldiers who are placed in every mission for their protection were only provided with absolute essentials against promissory notes.[23]

English traveler Frederick Beechey wrote of a visit in 1825, "Each soldier has nominally about three pounds a month, out of which he is obliged to purchase his provision. If the governor were active and the means were supplied, the country in the vicinity of the establishment might be made to yield enough wheat and vegetables for the troops, by which they would save that portion of their pay that now goes to the purchase of these necessary articles."[24]

Near the end of the Spanish period and through the Mexican period, the soldiers were afflicted by the same ills as the missionaries and Indians. During the last years of Spanish rule, many of California's settlements operated at a bare subsistence level. Some troops had not received pay since 1810.[25] At the time of Beechey's visit, four years after Mexican independence, morale was still extremely low. With no pay and the high duties imposed on goods from abroad and from Mexico, soldiers were impoverished at best. The privilege of retiring at the pueblos after ten years of service had also been removed. The soldiers could only keep their land and graze their cattle subject to the government's whim. Far from the capitals of Spain and Mexico, they were neglected and left to eke out an existence in the newly settled land of California.

# 10

## Style and Layout of Mission Buildings

Architecture and construction style in mission California—clay brick buildings with whitewashed walls, red tile roofs, asymmetrical features, patios, and thick walls with deep-set windows—brought a Mediterranean look to North America. The Spanish missionaries imported these features from the churches of Mexico and Spain. Architects and urban planners to this day continue to design prominent California buildings in emulation of this manner.

Architecture reflected the practical needs of the mission. The California mission was a center of worship, religious instruction, regimentation, and colonial administration. It was also set up for agriculture and product manufacture to sustain its residents as well as nearby rancherías and presidios. The mission was a barracks-style rectangular structure enclosing dozens of rooms, each dedicated to a trade or function. At a central location was the church, a defining element in the mission's activities and daily schedule. Many mission churches were reminiscent of old Spanish churches or convents.

Architectural details varied between churches. The *espadaña,* an ornamental false front used in Spain and the Netherlands to embellish a building and make it more imposing, appeared at Missions San Diego, San Luis Rey, and San Car-

Campanario, La Purísima.

los. More frequently, building façades were plain, contrasting with the more elaborate decorations inside the churches. Like churches in Spain and the other Spanish colonies, the mission churches were known for their bells, imported from Mexico or Peru. A *campanario* (bell tower) was incorporated into a wall with openings sized to accommodate the bells. It was freestanding or attached to the mission wall,[1] a feature seen across mission California. Other hallmarks of Spanish colonial style include restraining buttresses, construction around a courtyard, wrought-iron grilles, arched corridors, tiles, domed towers, and scalloped bell towers topped by a cross.[2]

Some missions featured their own mixture of styles. Mission San Carlos boasts Moorish features and sandstone construction. The columned façade of Mission Santa Barbara, the only mission with imposing twin bell towers, blends Roman, Greek, and mission architecture. Its sandstone walls are six feet thick, with nine-by-nine buttresses. The altars are finished in marble and the floor is red cement.

## Building and Construction

In the first months of settlement, the mission founders had no time to waste clearing land and building shelter. Mission buildings began as rude temporary structures whose construction was limited by available materials and the rudimentary skills of the builders. San Diego was built by Indians and sailors, and the building of Los Angeles was assisted by one mason, one carpenter, and one blacksmith.[3] Many buildings were made of sticks and mud, with thatched tule roofs; others incorporated local materials like stones, seashells, and reeds.[4] Historian Hubert Bancroft commented on California's early mission buildings: "It is a rude architecture, that of pre-pastoral California, being stockade or palisade structures, which were abandoned later in favor of adobe walls. At every mission a line of high strong posts, set in the ground close together, encloses the rectangular space which contains the simple wooden buildings serving as church and dwellings, the walls of which also in most instances take the stockade form."[5]

Before more permanent buildings were constructed at Mission San Diego, the missionaries lived in mud or wood buildings with tule roofs and the soldiers lived in huts or crude barracks.[6] Serra's original mission building in San Diego was a crude outbuilding of the presidio. San Diego's first buildings were made by planting timber poles vertically in the ground, laying more poles lengthwise across the top, and then filling the spaces with sticks and grasses.

Mission San Carlos began as a rough shelter of logs and evolved into an elegant masterpiece.[7] At the founding of Mission San Carlos in 1770, Serra wrote, "Here I am newly arrived, and busy with the job of building a small cabin of wood, for my abode, which at the same time has to be used as a storehouse or magazine for everything the boat brought for the church and the house, and for our provisions; and as a church where we say Mass. Add to that all the inconveniences that are unavoidable in the beginning of things."[8]

In San Diego, Father Fermín Francisco de Lasuén replaced Junípero Serra's stick-and-mud mission structures with adobe buildings and tile roofs arranged to form a quadrangle, creating the prototype for today's mission architecture.

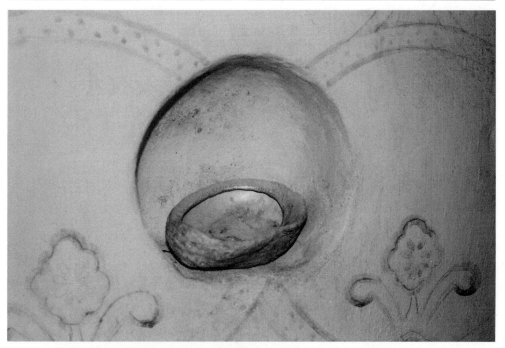

Shell in the wall of La Purísima church.

Shady arcades, supported by brick or heavy adobe pillars, lined the inner walls of the buildings. Arcades worked as outside hallways linking workshops and living spaces.

The palisade enclosed the main quadrangle along with its separate buildings and any adjoining ones, such as rancherías of huts or barracks where the married Indians lived.[9] Other villages were made up of open rows of streets lined with small adobe houses with tile roofs. When not enough such houses had yet been built to house the population, some missions kept traditional living structures, such as the domed reed huts inhabited by the Indians of Mission La Purísima or Mission San Diego.[10]

Like the presidios, the missions had massive fortified walls to protect them from danger outside and keep residents under control within. The walls enclosed a courtyard and were kept secure with heavy wooden and iron doors that were locked at night. The weight and thickness of adobe walls gave the impression of sturdy construction built to last for decades, although in truth they were quite vulnerable to the weather. Various mission compartments could be locked from the inside for additional protection from outside dangers and to control the residents.[11] A high stone or adobe wall also surrounded most mission villages.

Outdoor hallway, La Purísima.

Subsequent construction of missions, pueblos, presidios, and private ranchos reflected the typical mission building style, with single-story adobe buildings, whitewashed walls, red tile or asphalt roofs, and small barred windows. According to American traveler Henry Miller, Mission San Juan Bautista's ancient church stood "connected with a long somber looking building, in front of which is a porch formed by low clumsy arches. Windows are scarce and small, well provided with iron bars according to the Spanish style."[12]

The more richly ornamented missions, especially Missions San Carlos (Carmel), San Juan Capistrano, San Luis Rey, and San Buenaventura, had the benefit of skilled designers and artisans who lent their skills, creating a legacy of artisans from New Spain.[13] For instance, in the mid-1790s Indians worked under their direction on the church at Mission San Carlos and in the reconstruction of Monterey presidio.

Mission churches often took four or five years to construct.[14] Work and supply gathering were slow processes, and construction was interrupted by floods, earthquakes, and fires. All mission buildings also needed constant maintenance and preservation.

Plain, whitewashed clay adobe walls covered with plaster inside and out are the material most identified with California mission architecture. After 1778, adobe, valued for the accessibility of its materials, its ease of manufacture, and its resistance to fire, was used more and more. Adobe bricks were made by hand from local materials. Water, sand, and clay soil were mixed to form mud, and small amounts of straw were added to prevent the bricks from cracking as they dried. Stone or seashells were ground, and branches could also be used as a source of fiber. The mixture was then poured into wooden molds and left to dry. While still damp, but dry enough to hold their shape, the bricks were removed from the molds and left in the sun to finish drying. This allowed more bricks to be made from the same molds. The same mud mixture, without the straw, was used for mortar.

For building, adobe bricks were laid in rows and columns and with staggered joints.[15] When the walls had been raised, the mortar was allowed to settle for several days before a roof was added. Pillars, arches, and walls were weighted to the ground in solid proportions: to sustain their own weight and that of the tile roofs, adobe walls were four or five feet thick.[16] Even so, they could not be built too high; adobe buildings were usually low, with a single entrance secured by a strong gate. Wide eaves and roofed corridors protected the soluble walls from rain, and all exposed surfaces were plastered with lime stucco.

In some areas other materials were used. To construct the San Diego church in 1801, Indians hewed timber in nearby mountains and carried it to the missions. To construct Mission San Juan Capistrano, mission Indians transported large rocks from the quarries to the mission site.[17] Building beams came from pine logs and rafters from sycamore poles.

Mission San Luis Obispo was one of the first California buildings roofed with red tiles, said to have been used by the missionaries to deflect flaming arrows. Today this mission houses the oldest piece of clay roofing tile in California. Other missions followed, and these tiles have been used in various architectural revivals of mission and colonial style in states and towns with a Hispanic past, notably in Santa Barbara. The process of manufacturing roof tiles was experimental until perfected in the 1780s. Clay was mixed with water and poured into molds, then

Traditional Spanish tile roof. © iStockphoto.com/Bradley Mason.

fired in the mission kiln. Once ready for use, the tiles were placed on rough-hewn timbers tied together with rawhide.

Directed by a master builder and artisans from Mexico, San Juan Capistrano artisans designed elaborate arched doorways with stone facings. Its church was designed in the form of a Roman cross with six domes, the roof vaulted like the sky. Ceilings of tule were woven with rawhide strips, bound to rafters, and plastered.[18] At Mission Santa Clara de Asís, beams and rafters were made of redwood from the Santa Cruz Mountains. The paint used for the ceiling was made from rust-red cinnabar rock from fifteen miles away, mixed with cactus juice.[19] Timber from nearby forests was used to construct the beams of many of the missions, and clay for brick and tile was collected nearby.

At San Miguel, cedar timbers were used for the roof beams. The timbers were cut about forty miles away along the Pacific coast near the present town of Cambria, then hauled by oxcart across the Santa Lucía Mountains.[20] San Miguel was close to a good source of limestone, which when mixed with sand and water made a white mortar plaster for the stucco layer on adobe walls.

Missionaries and soldiers also added features that helped in the mission's defense. Remembered Guadalupe Vallejo: "Sometimes low adobe walls were made high and safe by a row of the skulls of Spanish cattle, with the long curving horns attached. These came from the *matanzas,* or slaughtercorrals, where there were thousands of them lying in piles, and they could be so used to make one of the strongest and most effective of barriers against man or beast. Set close and deep, at various angles, about the gateways and corral walls, these cattle horns helped to protect the enclosure from horse-thieves."

At every mission, earthquakes and deterioration from the elements made building and rebuilding constants. The earthquakes of 1812 and 1813 shook nearly every mission to its foundation and sometimes to the ground. Though heavy buttresses and thick walls have helped withstand tremors, earthquakes have been the single greatest cause for destruction of mission buildings. In late 2003 Mission San Miguel was closed permanently to the public after extensive damage from the magnitude 6.5 Paso Robles earthquake.

## Irrigation, Water Structures, and Roads

Water was integral to the success of each mission: it nourished the missions' animal and human populations, irrigated crops, facilitated laundry and cooking, and made it possible to grind grain and mill lumber. As such, it was a community responsibility and concern. As the Indian population's traditional lifestyle of hunting, gathering, and controlled burning was abandoned, it could only be supported by irrigated agriculture. Local *ayuntamiento* (civil) regulations outlawed wasting of water, irrigation overflow, and any damage of roads and property.[21] Hispanic colonists, experienced in building waterworks, initiated the widespread use of hydraulic systems in California, giving colonists a stable environment for setting up orchards, vineyards, and gardens.[22] For example, Mission San Antonio de Padua kept an extensive dam reservoir system that helped maintain its high farming output until 1808.

One of the first tasks of settlement was to locate a reliable water source, after which Indians, missionaries, and soldiers would construct a hydraulic system for the mission. This process was often the first full-scale mobilization of labor. Deep, narrow artesian wells were made by boring a hole into the soil. When water was struck, the pressure would make a fountain come spouting out.

To irrigate the land, missionaries and their charges turned over the soil and cut irrigation canals from the water source with a plow. Indians hauled rock for dams, dredged channels for the water, and cleared them of weeds and silt.[23] They released water into the trenches, then sowed fields for planting. Brush dams at small tributaries forced water into gardens and crops. Flumes of stone and mortar carried water from springs to small fields. The stones cleared from the fields were used to construct dams.[24]

Water from nearby streams and reservoirs flowed into a springhouse, where it was filtered through sand, then continued underground through clay pipes to the garden fountain in the center of each mission courtyard. The fountain was essential in arid environments like those at Missions San Diego and San Miguel. Residents used the fountain water for cooking and drinking. Remaining water flowed to the *lavandería* fountain for washing clothing and dishes. Excess soapy water then flowed into a cistern and was used to water the mission garden and crops.

Because Mission San Diego lacked access to abundant water and arable land to support a resident Indian population, mission Indians were allowed living quarters in their own villages and commuted to the mission for work and religious services. To solve this problem, at least partially, San Diego mission workers built a dam two hundred feet long with a gateway twelve feet high.[25] An aqueduct cut through gulches usually impassable on horseback, bringing water to the mission through cement flumes.

Other missions suffered from an excess of water. In the early months of Mission Santa Cruz, the nearby river rose, forcing the mission fathers to build their church on higher ground. When half the planting was completed in 1797, floods swept over the land and dozens of livestock died.[26]

Once rudimentary buildings were erected and a water source was located, road building for the transportation of supplies was the next task at hand. Eventually all mission roads led to *el Camino Reál,* the trail that would link all the California missions. The roads connecting the mission network followed the terrain, avoiding extremely rocky sections. Other trails were added to connect each mission to its pueblos. Workers, usually Indians, laid out new roads with stakes, cleared larger stones out of the way, and added borders to each side. They leveled the paths, filled holes with dirt, and moved rocks using iron bars or tree trunks.[27] Switchback trails zigzagged up hillsides, skirting large rocks. Roads had to be constantly maintained, especially after rain and storms.

### Human Handiwork

Architectural features of each mission vary with the inspiration and skills of individual builders. Asymmetry is a recurring architectural theme of the missions.

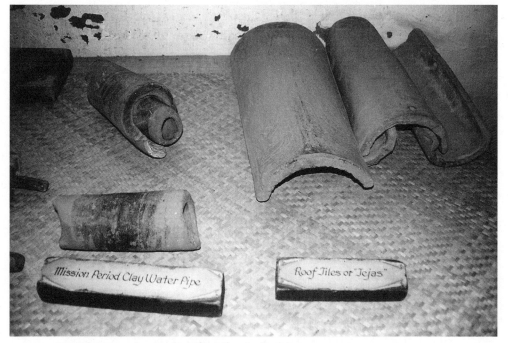

Spanish water pipes and roofing tiles, La Purísima.

Arches on arcades differ in width of span and design. Creative decorations on windows and doorways and uneven textures on walls and roofs are all evidence of the human touch. The unique church of Mission San Juan Bautista, the inland settlement that completed the ring of missions around Monterey by 1797, is styled with three naves.

Junípero Serra's input is evident at the second church of Mission San Carlos (Carmel), which resembles one he built in Mexico's Sierra Gorda region. The style of the church, also seen in the buttresses of Mission San Gabriel, is Moorish-Gothic, similar to those seen in the Alhambra in Granada, Spain.[28] Serra likely planned Carmel's star window, columns, arches, and Moorish tower, mismatched with the other bell tower. A master stone mason brought in from Spain constructed the mission's brown sandstone church, deviating from the typical white adobe style.

Mission building design incorporates both Spanish and Indian motifs, which adorn walls, ceilings, beams, pillars, and arches. Some wall design elements even come from traditions of Indian basketry, especially at Mission Santa Barbara.[29] Other designs were inspired by altarpieces from New Spain. Along with the painted decorations that suggest elegant church architecture, Indians painted or scratched native designs onto the walls. Some of these were whitewashed over

Intricate wallwork, La Purísima.

by the priests. Mission San Juan Capistrano has two symbols of a human figure wearing a headdress and skirt, thought to be a depiction of the primary Juaneño god.[30]

San Miguel's original twelve arches forming the colonnade were each meant to commemorate one of the twelve Apostles. Also, San Miguel is famous for its frescoes, painted in 1820 by Spanish artist Esteban Munras and his Indian assistants, whom he instructed in the art of fresco painting. Many of San Miguel's decorations, including the "eye of God" painting, are the work of Munras. Vegetable colors from berries, lichens, and mosses were mixed with cactus juice and glue from bones. Stones from the seashore were used for red, and nightshade for blue.[31] The San Miguel frescoes have survived the years in good condition.[32]

Indians carved fonts, altar rails, and statues and made musical instruments for use during church services. They also painted façades, altar screens, and dadoes (lower sections of wall panels) and carved and painted the icons.

Church interiors in the California missions were not sumptuous in the tradition of Gothic and Baroque Roman Catholic churches seen in Europe. Their modest but striking ornamentation, as in the ceiling of the San Francisco de Asís church,[33] uses the vivid plant dyes and authentic images of American Indian art. Without fuss and often without the help of trained artists, Indian painters and missionaries applied bold shapes and colors over doorways and windows, on bell towers, and throughout room interiors.

Ornamentation of window openings originated from the Moorish custom of embellishing deep-set openings in windows and doors.[34] Imitating European styles, painters added architectural features on interior church walls to give the illusion of ornate construction and depth. Frescoed walls, wood carvings, stonework, and forged iron, common in churches, were seen in residential and work rooms as well as the churches.

Priests, untrained artisans themselves, helped Indians paint imitation marble on the walls and added perspective by painting altars, alcoves, doors, pillars, balconies, and corridors. The tabernacle (container for the host or communion wafers) colors often matched the marble and floral tapestries from cathedrals in native Spain. These features are most evident at Missions Santa Barbara, San Miguel, and Santa Inés.[35]

Most of the building elements were made from local materials. Mission floors were earthen, later covered with unglazed terra-cotta tile. While adobe was made of unbaked clay held together by straw or gravel, terra-cotta ("baked earth") was made from clay only, fired in a pit to make it hard and durable.[36]

Windows in the San Miguel church were lined with oiled parchment, made from lamb or goatskin, rather than glass. Stonemasons chipped local granite into baptismal fonts. Smiths forged iron on-site and shaped it into bars for gates, window gratings, windows, grilles, and crosses. Masons, smiths, and artisans brought from New Spain helped Indians with painting, carving, and iron-forging designs. Wood carvings decorated benches, tables, chairs, pulpits, and confessionals.

Priest's pulpit (imitation marble), La Purísima.

## Outfitting the Church Interior

In a largely non-Spanish population, paintings and drawings helped the missionaries teach Catholic doctrine. A canvas of the Last Judgment hung in the church of Santa Barbara. Church artwork included images of the stations of the cross, as well as paintings and statues of the saints, Jesus, and the Madonna. At San Antonio a large hand was painted on the wall, a replication of the diagram used by the friars to teach hymns.

Even in the rugged frontier environment, churches, in keeping with Spanish tradition, were decorated as richly as funds would allow. Father Serra gave a lengthy inventory of items to be picked up in Loreto for the establishment of the first mission in San Diego: "oilstocks, censers, incense holders, chalices, cruets [small glass bottles for holy water or sacramental wine], all silverware, chasubles [sleeveless vestments], antependia [decorative hangings for the altar], albs [white linen robes worn by priests], amices [white linen vestments worn under the albs], cinctures [vestment sashes], purificators, a large bell and various other articles."[37] Elegant items were part of the church's role as a place of worship. Other items that had to be imported included altar vessels of gold and silver, an organ, tabernacles, a holy-water basin, chrisms, linens, carpets leading to the altar, cedar chests for vestments, bells to ring at mass, a large bell for the bell tower, crucifixes, incense, a missal, cassocks, robes for the choir and acolytes, and, of course, an altar gilded with gold leaf.

Pack trains and ships brought church and sacramental supplies (*sacramentos*) from existing or defunct missions in Baja California and elsewhere in Mexico. Hand-carved altars and redwood statues came from Mexico in 1780 for the church of San Luis Obispo.[38] Church furniture was basic and manufactured in the mission carpenter's shop. Even the impoverished Santa Maria gave a set of silver chrismatories, a silver shell for baptizing, an iron for making hosts, and three pounds of Castilian wax. The scarcity of funds and supplies is suggested by Serra's request to the viceroy whether "Your Reverence might see whether some paintings can be sent—so that the churches will have more than a single cross."[39]

### A Layout for Production and Daily Life

The church, the centerpiece of the mission complex, was usually built in the northeast corner of the quadrangle. The courtyard served as an outdoor workplace, stockade, and recreation area for mission residents. In the usually temperate weather, all kinds of trade activities took place there.

Missionary apartments, called the *convento,* were slightly more spacious than the quarters occupied by soldiers and Indian leaders. Unmarried Indians and younger residents lived in *dormitorio* rooms. Married Indians and their young children lived on the outskirts of the mission in brick homes or rooms, or sometimes in family dwellings constructed in the manner of traditional pre-mission Indian homes. When these decayed, they were burned and replaced.

The *camposanto* (cemetery) was situated next to the church. Those that remain today provide information to researchers about mission residents, such as the numbers of dead from certain years and Indian burial practices. In keeping with

the Indians' status in mission and Spanish culture, graves were often unmarked
or marked only with a simple cross.

The compound would also contain priests' quarters, a storehouse, stables, and
a guardhouse. Within the quadrangle there would be a granary, a tannery, a pottery, a flour mill, a soap factory, and a weaving room. In 1783 San Diego's mission land housed two priests' dwellings, a guardhouse, a granary, a storehouse,
an infirmary, a nunnery, a woodshed, a larder, a kitchen, and an oven.[40] A 1935
excavation of the San Gabriel courtyard uncovered old bake ovens, kilns for firing
floor tile, and the ruins of a smithy, a tannery, wine vats, a soap works, the foundations of original buildings, and intact water jars and urns.[41] Open-style wine
vats were commonly seen indoors.

A *sala* (room) was built for the lead missionary, where he sat at his Spanish in-
laid desk for meetings, record keeping, and letter writing. In very cold weather,
the rooms without fireplaces may have been heated with charcoal braziers.

San Luis Rey had a storage area where the stonemasons kept lime and mortar; a storehouse for wine with "two hundred casks of wine, brandy and white
wine . . . for Mass," and alcohol for "the Spanish and English travelers who often
come to the mission to sell cloth, linen, cotton and whatever they bring from
Boston—and not for the neophytes . . . because they easily get drunk."

Visitors, such as civil administrators, European travelers, other missionaries,
and traders, were common. Each mission had a room for "the General of California when he comes to the Mission," as well as four rooms for travelers. Tac
described a reception room decorated with portraits of "Louis King of France,
the Good Shepard [*sic*], and the Virgin of Guadalupe."[42] Important rooms such
as these were kept whitewashed with lime.[43]

Roof and floor tiles were molded and fired in the pottery shop, along with
water pipes, cups, bowls, and plates. Blacksmiths and locksmiths worked in the
smithy. To extract usable tallow, large vats in the courtyard sat on fires and rendered pounds of beef fat as it melted for soap and candles. At the tannery, which
was kept some distance away from other buildings due to its offensive odor,[44]
dried cowhides were made into leather. Mission Santa Inés housed a large tannery made from river boulders and covered with cement.[45]

Mules and horses supplied power to grain mills that sat in the courtyard. The
missionaries built water-powered flour mills early in the nineteenth century at
Missions Santa Cruz, San Luis Obispo, San José, and San Gabriel.[46]

Pablo Tac's accounts of San Luis Rey paint a picture of the typical mission
complex: "There is a small door for the missionary to get out easily in case of
earthquakes." He mentions six "houses for the *majordomos* of the Mission . . . an

enclosure for the lambs . . . house of the Shepard [*sic*] . . . place for the horses of the missionary and . . . the travelers and . . . the sacks of fodder," as well as a place where the *posole* and *atole* (grain dishes) were made. He describes a gateway at the entrance with "three thick timbers . . . placed in order not to let in the bulls and horses, spirited when there is bullfighting, though they come in often and frighten the old women who wash their clothes here."[47]

These details of design and construction, along with items of daily use seen in mission museums, are visual symbols of California history. The missions are studied each year in every fourth-grade public school classroom in California. Students construct models of a chosen mission with materials from home. Architectural features are studied and easily identified with the colonial period.

In 1941 the Ambassador Hotel in Los Angeles displayed a model of Mission San Diego. Thousands of miniature terra-cotta tiles covered the roofs, and the redwood walls were carved and whitewashed to represent the uneven plaster surfaces of mission buildings. The display recreated mission scenes and festivals with miniature figures, and furniture and tools were made to scale.[48] Today the missions that operate as tourist destinations try, to a degree, to recreate the atmosphere of mission life. A visitor in 1938 described his visit to some of the rooms of Mission San Luis Obispo: "The Mission atmosphere survives in the adobe building once used as barracks, now occupied by the pastor. Here are large cool rooms with deep-recessed windows and high ceilings. Upstairs in the museum is the oldest roof tile in California, clappers of recast bells, wooden bells used during Holy Week, shining copper kettles, Indian corn grinders. There is a chair with arms worn from long use by Indian lace makers. Highly treasured are the copper baptismal font and the original vestment case. The redwood crucifix was carved by the Indians."[49]

Each mission church had its own unique features, some of which survive today as tokens of a complex past. For many, visits to the remaining mission buildings and replicas are their only connections to California's (and America's) colonial history. What remains today of the original settlements are architectural and stylistic elements that suggest what was important to the missionaries as they built their Christian settlements.

# 11

## Farming

Dietary habits, building technology, Mediterranean methods of agriculture, irrigation practices, and water laws were all components of a transplanted European civilization. Invading settlers not only brought a new religion and lifestyle to California, but also introduced plants, livestock, and farming techniques. Farming and livestock raising were primary occupations of the Franciscans and the missionized Indians.

Compared to other missions of the American Southwest, Mexico, South America, and Florida, California's were arguably the most complex farming settlements. Each mission site, despite a typical lack of arable land and water, worked to sustain itself and provide enough food for its inhabitants.

The first question asked when missionaries evaluated a potential site was whether the location could sustain the necessary agriculture to survive. Food was needed for daily supplies as well as for church festivals and visitors. Each mission was allotted fifteen square miles of land to be used for trade, shelter, and farming.[1] Grassland was either used for grazing or plowed and farmed.

The missions farmed not only for sustenance, but to support the presidios. Wrote Frederick Beechey, "The plan on which the presidio stands is well adapted

Chicken coop, La Purísima.

to cultivation, but it is scarcely ever touched by the plow, and the garrison is entirely beholden to the missions for its resources."[2] As outgrowths of the missions, presidios, pueblos, and ranches had few supplies in-house.

Trade of surplus items was a source of extra income for the mission. After local needs were satisfied, certain items left the province bound for Mexico and elsewhere. Under Spanish rule, California's missions yielded about 2.5 million pounds of wheat and other crops. At the peak of their prosperity, between 1782 and 1832, missions harvested millions of bushels of grain and produce and more than 300,000 animals.[3] By 1805 there had been a thirty-fold increase in output over three decades.[4] Prior to secularization in 1834, the Indians at the twenty-one missions herded 396,000 cattle, 62,000 horses, and 321,000 hogs, sheep, and goats, and harvested 123,000 bushels of grain.[5] The coastal missions and pueblos peaked at around ten thousand acres before 1834.[6]

Mission San Miguel housed up to six thousand domesticated animals, produced thirteen thousand bushels of grain annually, and had a population of three thousand Indians.[7] In the early 1800s, Missions San Gabriel and San Juan Capistrano led in wheat production.[8] San Gabriel also had the largest winery for a time, established with grapes brought from Spain by Father Serra. Agricultural production at San Gabriel surpassed that of all other missions in 1832; the mission's livestock corral was second in size only to that of San Luis Rey.[9] San Juan Capistrano was the most productive mission in cattle and grain, with 31,263 cattle in 1819 and 14,662 bushels of grain harvested.[10]

## Farming Methods

Farming and livestock management were accomplished with antiquated methods and equipment. Oxen drew crude carts, and in the grist mills burros or horses turned the wheels to grind wheat and barley. Frederick Beechey observed, "Their plows appear to have descended from the patriarchal ages" and that mission animal husbandry was "still in a very backward state, and it is fortunate that the soil is so fertile and that there are abundance of laborers to perform the work, or . . . the people would be contented to live upon acorns."[11] Plowing, said Rezanov, was "done by oxen. Horses are kept principally for military service and for the use of the missionaries, and for the transportation of goods and provisions from one establishment to another one. Mules are also employed for similar transportation. The carts and wagons are of rough construction. Here, as in Spain and Portugal, block-wheels are in use, and they are generally very far from being perfectly round."[12]

## Livestock

Colonists from New Spain brought horses to California, along with other Old World animals such as sheep, goats, pigs, mules, cattle, and poultry. These early herds were the ancestors of the herds on the missions and the great ranches. As livestock reproduced and more continued to be imported, they spread throughout California. There was sometimes even a surplus. Mission Indian Guadalupe Vallejo described how the overpopulation of horses in the valleys around San José in 1806 was dealt with: "[S]even or eight thousand were killed. Nearly as many were driven into the sea at Santa Barbara . . . and Monterey. . . . Horses were given to runaway sailors, and to trappers and hunters."

By the 1820s many Indians had their own horses and livestock, especially Central Valley Indian groups outside the mission populations. After 1831 Mexican and Spanish settlers began to obtain stock animals such as horses and mules from interior Indians. Cattle, which numbered in the hundreds of thousands by 1840, shaped the economy and culture of provincial California.[13] To increase the

Original list of mission cattle brands.

cattle population, missionaries waited until the bulls were three or four years of age before castrating them.[14]

By the end of the mission period, the missions housed more than 308,000 head of cattle, sheep, mules, horses, and hogs.[15] Following secularization in 1834, the number of private ranches rose and the numbers of horses and cattle in California continued to multiply, leading to the increased slaughter of surplus animals, especially horses, whose large herds roamed the former mission pastures.[16]

The ongoing need for clothing, blankets, and meat made raising sheep one of the most important agricultural activities of the missions. An original passageway to the protected work area of the internal quadrangle courtyard has a gated entrance for the sheep flocks of San Miguel. Products of sheep farming were traded with the other missions for items that could not be obtained locally.

Horses, mules, and oxen transported both humans and supplies. Pablo Tac recalled a pasture near the garden of Mission San Luis Rey "for the horses of the Fernandino Father and for those of the Anglo-American travelers."[17] Guadalupe Vallejo recorded how "the fathers of the Mission sometimes rode on horseback, but they generally had a somewhat modern carriage called a *volante*. It was always drawn by mules, of which there were hundreds in the Mission pastures, and white was the color often preferred."[18]

Mission San Antonio de Padua was a center for Salinan Indians and a prosperous cattle and sheep ranch until the Mexican period. A wide range of Indian and Spanish-Mexican artifacts discovered adjacent to the mission in a possible Salinan ranchería indicate the use of European livestock imports such as pigs, cattle, and sheep. Clay figurines of a dog have also been found.[19]

Grazing animals, which were kept in fenced pasture areas until needed, were relatively simple to maintain. Rezanov observed, "The cattle, horses, and sheep do not require any particular attention. The herds are left in the open the whole year through. Only a sufficient number are kept in the neighborhood of the establishment to serve immediate wants. When a supply of cattle is wanted, some of the neophytes and soldiers are sent out to the pastures on horseback, and with *riatas* [lassos], which they throw very dexterously, catch by the horns the number required."[20]

## Crops

The mission croplands faced soil depletion, inefficient fertilization, insects, weeds, and drought. During the late 1770s, supplies from New Spain dwindled. To avoid starvation the missions planted wheat, barley, and beans. The missions also relied on Indians and their traditional hunting and gathering methods for food when supplies were low. Days of famine tried the spirits and bodies of everyone living at the missions. Father Serra remembered "[t]he hunger while waiting for supplies to arrive, starting the missions from scratch, without a stick of chocolate and most likely without a single tortilla to offer." In a letter Serra mentioned his appeal to Pedro Fages for more supplies during a famine: "If only people could get hold of some food by paying out money from their salaries. . . . My Mexican blacksmiths are practically naked: they have already paid back the money that was given them in advance, and they have not succeeded in providing themselves with breeches, pots, frying pans, ladles, grinding stones—of all these necessities they were given nothing. These families have to make their tortillas, and cook their beans, all with grinding stones and pots lent by the mission."

His news from Monterey was more positive. "Our new Christians here are content and well fed. Besides their daily *atole* and *pozole,* they are now busy in catching sardines which, for a week now, have been coming in schools to the beach. . . . The lentils, chick peas, lima beans and common beans look splendid; the garden has for many months already provided most generously two or three sacks for greens for the *pozole,* and for our kitchen."[21]

Mission agriculture employed a mix of Spanish and New World crops. Domesticated plants that thrived in the Mediterranean part of Spain, where rainfall and rivers were limited, also grew in California's semi-arid climate, made fruitful with irrigation systems.[22] Crop cultivation differed somewhat at each mission, depending on the climate and soil in each region.

The farms of Missions San Gabriel and San Luis Obispo each began with a group of Indian Christian families from the south. Already familiar with farming practices, the families were able to grow crops in the favorable soil. These two missions supplied grain to other missions and helped remove the dependence on shipments from San Blas, Mexico.

Corn (maize) was the most common staple, and most missions also grew wheat. Mission Indian Guadalupe Vallejo described how cows and horses were kept from eating the precious crop at Mission San José: "It was fenced in with a ditch, dug by the Indians with sharp sticks and with their hands in the rainy season, and it was so deep and wide that cattle and horses never crossed it. In other places stone or adobe walls, or hedges of the prickly pear cactus, were used about the wheat fields. . . . Sometimes low adobe walls were made high and safe by a row of the skulls of Spanish cattle, with the long curving horns attached."[23]

Barley was another staple, not only for people but for horses. Other crops included flax, chickpeas, and *frijoles* (beans). Mission San Diego's storehouses were filled with pumpkins, corn, wheat, and beans, and in its vineyards were six thousand grapevines for wine.[24] Crops at Monterey included white beans, barley, white wheat, and lentils.[25]

In the earlier years of the missions, hemp was grown as an export commodity that helped bring money to the colonial economy. Hemp, a tough, coarse fiber, usually of the cannabis plant, was used to make cordage for the mining and shipping industries, along with New Spain's navy. Not enough hemp was produced in New Spain for domestic needs, so the government promoted its cultivation in Alta California.

California's vineyards. © iStockphoto.com / Alessandro Bolis.

Orchards filled with fruit and rows of grapevines were typical sights at the missions. Henry Miller called Mission San Fernando "a fine property," with vineyards and orchards bursting with pears, apricots, pomegranates, oranges, quinces, and other fruits: "the church and mission orchards were planted with several hundred large pear trees, loaded with fruit."[26] Figs, apricots, pomegranates, apples, and peaches flourished at Mission San Francisco de Asís. In addition to the usual fruits, Mission San Buenaventura grew coconuts, kitchen herbs, indigo, sugarcane, and bananas. Peaches, quinces, and nectarines filled the groves at Mission San Juan Capistrano, and the mission's grapes were made into sparkling wine.[27]

Grape harvesting, wine manufacturing, and distilled spirits were sources of extra income. Raisins, along with grapes and wine, were consumable products of the vineyards. Father Zalvidéa of Mission San Gabriel was the father of viticulture and California's wine industry. San Gabriel was a viticultural jewel in the mission chain; its large vineyard was the *viña madre* of Spanish California.[28] The missionaries of San Miguel made red wine from mission grapes, a variety that they had brought to California, and they traded wine with the other missions in the chain. San Miguel missionaries established a commercial wine industry in San Luis Obispo County some time in the early 1800s.[29]

Olive tree. © iStockphoto.com/Victoria Wren.

## Gardens

Mission gardens were maintained to provide food for immediate consumption by mission residents. Vegetables and herbs supplied kitchens and infirmaries, and along with flowers helped to beautify the mission grounds. Typical mission-era plants include the Castilian rose, still seen today at many of the sites, along with bougainvillea and olive trees. The central fountain at Mission San Miguel is still surrounded by a garden of over thirty varieties of cacti, roses, and olive trees.[30]

Father Palóu brought experienced workers to Mission San Gabriel to teach Indians to plant wheat, corn, and beans in 1773. A talented and enthusiastic gardener,

Palóu excelled at growing vegetables. San Gabriel had the first vegetable garden in the vicinity of today's Los Angeles.[31]

Mission San Luis Rey is home to California's oldest peppertree, which still grows in the center of the mission quadrangle.[32] Father Péyri is known for introducing peppertrees, planted from seeds brought from Peru by sailors, to the missions. (The peppertree, *Schinus molle,* native to South and Central America, is not the same as *Capsicum,* another New World plant, or black pepper, *Piper nigrum,* which is native to the East Indies.) Pablo Tac described San Luis Rey's garden as "full of fruit trees, pears, apples or *perones,* as the Mexicans say, peaches, quinces, pears, sweet pomegranates, watermelons, melons, vegetables, cabbages, lettuces, radishes, mint, parsley . . . all for the neophytes, and any remaining fruit and vegetables for the missionary. . . . None of the neophytes can go to the garden or enter to gather the fruit. . . . [I]f he wants some he asks the missionary . . . for the missionary is their father."[33]

Rezanov was disappointed by the produce at Mission San Francisco: "[W]e were shown to the kitchen garden, but it did not equal our expectations. There was very little fruit, and that, of inferior quality. Most of the beds were overgrown with weeds. Of fine vegetables and herbs there were few. Northwest winds, which prevail on this coast, and a soil dry and sandy by nature, are insurmountable obstacles to horticulture. The only vegetables that grow well in the gardens are asparagus, cabbage, several kinds of lettuce, onions, and potatoes."

Guadalupe Vallejo described the mission gardens of the later Mexican period:

> I remember that at the Mission San José we had many varieties of seedling fruits which have now been lost to cultivation. Of pears we had four sorts, one ripening in early summer, one in late summer, and two in autumn and winter. . . . The flower gardens were gay with roses, chiefly a pink and very fragrant sort from Mexico, called by us the Castilian rose, and still seen in a few old gardens. Besides roses, we had pinks, sweet-peas, hollyhocks, nasturtiums which had been brought from Mexico, and white lilies. The vegetable gardens contained peas, beans, beets, lentils, onions, carrots, red peppers, corn, potatoes, squashes, cucumbers, and melons. A fine quality of tobacco was cultivated and cured by the Indians. Hemp and flax were grown to some extent.[34]

## Food

Mission meal staples were variations on porridge made from grain, occasionally with meat. *Atole,* made from acorn, cornmeal, or barley flour, was a gruel often

Castilian roses, San Juan Capistrano. Courtesy of Jim Graves, Mission San Juan Capistrano.

served for breakfast. When barley was used, it was roasted before grinding, then cooked unseasoned in large kettles. *Pozole* was a thick soup of cornmeal (maize), beans, marrow, bones, and scraps of meat, all cooked with hot water. "Each day a mighty cauldron of *pozole* is filled and emptied three times over," noted Serra.[35] *Piñole* was made of ground corn or wheat mixed with mesquite beans. Frijoles were cooked, then fried in lard and consumed regularly as a separate dish. Commented Rezanov: "The principal food of the Indians is a thick soup composed of meat, vegetables, and pulse [lentils]. Because of the scarcity of fish here, or the want of proper means of catching them, the missionaries obtained a special dispensation from the pope allowing the eating of meat on fast days. Besides this meal, bread, Indian corn, peas, beans, and other kinds of pulse are distributed in abundance, without any regular or stated allowance."[36]

Dairy methods and products at the missions were limited. Eggs and milk were used in their natural form and rarely made into cheese. Beef was more popular than dairy products, but not always available: in the earliest days of each mission, "the cows so far we have guarded like the apples of our eyes, contenting ourselves with their milk, so that they should breed."[37]

## Cooking Methods and Tools

Mortars and small stone mills were used as tools for mashing and grinding grain. Rezanov noted that "the most laborious work, the grinding of the corn[,] is left almost entirely to the women. It is rubbed between two quadrangular oblong stones until ground into meal. Although the flour made is very white, the bread is very heavy and hard." After flour mills were built, bread and tortillas made from wheat became popular.

Forty to fifty oxen may have been killed every week to support the community.[38] Most of the meat was turned into beef jerky, an ideal protein source because it kept for months without spoiling.[39] Bones and scraps went into the soup and meal pots, and beef fat was rendered and stored in skin bags to use as cooking oil and tallow for candles.

Stews, beans, and tortillas were cooked over outdoor fires or indoors in beehive ovens and over the hearth. The indoor oven and hearth grills at San Miguel featured small vent holes in the wall rather than chimneys.[40] Indian and Hispanic women also cooked food on adobe ranges with partitions. Clay dishes were used at meals along with squash gourds for drinking cups. Some mission courtyards display artifacts or replicas of early mission olive presses for making olive oil, along with grain mills.

## Change in Nutrition and Eating Habits

As the land around the missions began to be turned over to farming, the priests restricted Indian hunting, gathering, and fishing and discouraged the consumption of native foods except during times of drought and famine.[41] Acorns soon disappeared as a dietary mainstay. Although some Indians may have been allowed to continue to hunt and gather food as before,[42] and although the priests

Beehive oven, La Purísima.

at some missions, such as San Buenaventura, encouraged the Indians to plant their own gardens of pumpkins, watermelons, corn, and other grains,[43] for the most part the Indians subsisted on daily rations of atole with a little meat. This change in diet undermined the health of many of the mission residents and has been noted as a major reason for the spread of disease among them.[44]

The priests' establishment of a regular regime of three meals a day was part of a restructuring of the Indian concept of time. The Western model of daily schedules of worship, work, rest, and meals was a way of maintaining control.[45] "Three times a day they eat from what we provide them; they pray, sing, and work; and from the labor of their hands we can boast of fields of wheat, corn, beans, peas, and a garden chock-full of cabbage, lettuce, and all kinds of vegetables."[46]

Imported foodstuffs allowed some mission residents to escape having to eat the same meals every day. Depending on the prosperity of each mission, missionaries and soldiers could enjoy chocolate, rice, pasta, cinnamon, cloves, saffron, snuff, and whiskey. Typically, beef, red beans, and tortillas were eaten by the Spanish lower class; wealthier settlers enjoyed chocolate, milk, coffee, and wine.

## The Change in Landscape

Prevalent in historical and literary writings are stereotypes of how early settlers viewed the land of California before European settlement. To them the land was untouched, a pristine wilderness of which the Indians were just a small, inactive part.[47] Missionaries such as Palóu, Crespí, and Font were complimentary about the land and its offerings in its "natural" state. Later research tended to pigeonhole Indian cultures as either agricultural or hunter-gatherer. Recent studies, however, suggest that the Indians deeply understood how to use the land, interact with it, and domesticate their habitats. Many tribal legends cautioned against greed or waste in the use of the land.[48]

Indian use and modification of land included such deliberate influences on the ecosystem as transplanting, weeding, and pruning of plants and burning of vegetation. Indians practiced selective harvesting, cultivating favored plants in different areas. They were skilled at gathering plants in different habitats for extended periods without depleting plant populations. Small fires were used to clear out the underbrush, keeping woodlands open and less prone to large fires and promoting the growth of useful plants, some of which required fire to maintain their life cycle and remain healthy.

Today only isolated areas of pre-European vegetation exist in California. Urban areas and agriculture have covered over and replaced many historical varieties of plants.[49] In Alta California, settlers from Spain encountered a land similar to their Mediterranean home with its winter rainfall and summer drought. Mediterranean annuals were suited to California's climate and thrived there. Mediterranean grasses have been discovered in the adobe bricks of some of the earliest missions and from excavations of sites that predate 1769.[50]

The colonists and explorers accidentally or purposely brought plants from their own countries, which spread along with native grasses as a result of fewer fires. Chaparral, a low-growing, treeless vegetation that encompasses many species of shrubs, now blankets the foothills of California. In the days of the missions, there was much more desert scrub and perennial grassland.[51]

In addition to introducing new animals and crops, the arrival of Europeans in California brought the practices of fire suppression and heavy, year-round grazing by livestock. They also inadvertently brought in new bacteria, grasses, pests, and weeds.[52] In the absence of fire, these weeds and other plants prospered.

In just a few decades, European settlement of California forever changed the natural ecosystem as shaped by Indian civilizations for centuries.

# 12

## Mission Trades and Economy

> It must be remembered that the friars came to California as messengers of Christ. They were not farmers, mechanics, or stock breeders. As an absolutely necessary means to win the souls of these savages, these unworldly men accepted the disagreeable task of conducting huge farms, teaching and supervising various mechanical trades, having an eye on the livestock and herders, and making ends meet generally.
>
> —*Father Engelhardt*

Spain's colonial objective of becoming rich by land acquisition required workers in great numbers. The larger and more productive the settlement, the greater Spain's power in California. Not only did Indians brought into the missions contribute extra labor, but they also became subjects of Spain's colonial empire.

As in the rest of New Spain, use of the minerals and land depended almost wholly on Indian labor. Almost everything used was grown or manufactured locally. In settlements, like California, located far from the colonial center in Mexico City, importing items was slow and expensive and local manufacture was even more important.

Each mission relied on soldiers, laborers, cowboys, and mule drivers. Missions farther inland needed even more personnel to help transport provisions from the ports. In general, the larger the population, the greater the need for workers in all trades. Every Indian living at the mission was required to serve in a productive trade.

Techniques for raising crops with plows and draft animals, growing fruits and vegetables, and stock raising were new to California.[1] The cattle trade developed from the missions into the most vital industry in nineteenth-century California. Missions became important centers of artisan production, and when they were secularized, this production moved to the pueblos. In all, these activities helped build a small-scale Spanish colonial civilization.

Labor filled another role for the fathers. In the missionary view, trades were crucial to maintain discipline and a work ethic. The Franciscans promoted work as a means to a spiritual end, not just a way of fulfilling the material needs of the missions. Father Serra wrote happily, "Our adult new Christians in the mission, inspired by the example of the few workmen I have thus far succeeded in getting, are beginning to apply themselves diligently to work: some with hoes in hand, leveling the ground to increase our crops, others digging in the garden, others making adobe brick."[2]

The Franciscan father in charge of each mission determined his mission's work environment. One Franciscan, Father Lasuén, spread the philosophy of managing the missions as miniature factory towns. He envisioned each mission as a combination school, church, and factory, producing clothing, pottery, candles, soap, furniture, and other materials useful for survival and trade.

## Crafting Their Way to Heaven

Artisans came in from Mexico City or Guadalajara to train Indians and help increase the production of goods.[3] Crafts included tile making, brick making, carpentry, furniture making, house construction, building of dams and irrigation works, and agricultural techniques. Mission workshops, both indoor and outdoor, housed many crafts: tallow melting, soap making, smithing, and carpentry. Storehouses contained manufactured items and farm produce, as well as stores of tallow, soap, butter, salt, wool, hides, wheat, peas, and beans. Pablo Tac documented some of the products of Mission San Luis Rey: "[B]utter, tallow, hides, chamois leather, bear skins, wine, white wine, brandy, oil, maize, wheat, beans, and also bull horns which the English take by the thousand to Boston."[4]

Most work took place out in the open when weather allowed. Occupations varied from mission to mission as needs and resources dictated: coopers, cobblers, hatmakers, candle makers, winemakers, coppersmiths, muleteers, bell ringers, masons, acolytes, stonecutters, embroiderers, herders, barbers, and basket makers. Leather crafters made saddles and pack gear for horses, burros, and mules. Indian workers switched between tasks depending on the season and present needs of the mission. Seasonal work included branding livestock, shearing sheep, gathering lime and salt, preparing the tannery, and making tiles to strengthen the roofing against the winter rains.[5]

For the more complex trades, a master craftsman led a crew of artisans under the supervision of the majordomo (mission foreman). Master craftsmen held higher social and economic status and sometimes were given their own quarters. Wrote Tac:

> With the laborers goes a Spanish *majordomo* [master foreman of mission production] and others, neophyte *alcaldes* [elected Indian leaders], to see how the work is done, to hurry them if they are lazy, so that they will soon finish what was ordered, and to punish the guilty or lazy one who leaves his plow and quits the field. . . . They work all day. . . . The shoemakers work making chairs, leather knapsacks, reins and shoes for the cowboys, neophytes, *majordomos* and Spanish soldiers. . . . The blacksmiths make bridle kits, keys, bosses for bridles, nails for the church, and all work for all.[6]

In keeping with mission codes of morality, most jobs were segregated by sex, except for groups who worked together in textile workshops. Women ground corn and other grains into meal with stones and hand mills; cooked and washed in the kitchen; and made baskets, continuing in the native styles.[7] Pregnant women washed wool or pulled weeds, and children helped with lighter tasks like sweeping and picking in the garden.[8]

Another important activity for women was making clothing. While the California climate is temperate compared to that of much of North America, and some Indian groups were accustomed to wearing little, clothing for both warmth and modesty was an ongoing need. To that end, wool production was a bustling occupation at the missions. Master weavers taught women how to card wool, clean it, spin it, dye it, and weave cloth with it on crude looms. Women also crafted a variety of textiles, including rugs and blankets. Said Rezanov: "The wool of the sheep here is very fine and of superior quality, but the tools and looms are of a crude make. As the *misioneros* are the sole instructors of these people, who themselves know very little about such matters . . . [,] the cloth is

Indoor fireplace, La Purísima.

far from the perfection that might be achieved."[9] Priests and women from Baja California and Mexico trained the Indian women in other practical tasks such as sewing, knitting, lacework, and embroidery (church garments were embroidered with gold and silver thread in the style of vestments brought from Baja California). The handicrafts of Santa Inés were known throughout the province.

From the missionaries and occasional artisans brought in from New Spain, Indians learned to emboss leather, engrave horn, and inlay wood and iron with silver. For the making of *cueras* (thick deerskin coats for the soldiers) and other military clothing there was usually at least one proficient leatherworker at each presidio.

Building construction was one of the most important ongoing mission trades. Masons, bricklayers, and carpenters helped maintain and renovate presidios. Masons sculpted the building blocks for mission walls; they also made millstones. Most of the mission men helped mold and lay adobe bricks. Carpenters performed a range of tasks in support of building construction, furniture, and other needs. They made spinning wheels, frames, combs, and looms.

Cowhides, blankets, and other mission products were traded with outsiders for iron bars, which iron workers crafted into fixtures and attachments for grinders, presses, furniture, doors, and windows. They also made shovels, hoes,

Olive press, La Purísima.

nails, and door hinges and overhauled and soldered arms, cooking tools, and other metal items.

Keeping mission residents fed was another daily concern. Several grains and an abundance of fruits and vegetables grew at each mission. Barley, wheat, and corn were consumed daily, and also served as feed for livestock. Wheat was thrashed by hand on a tiled floor to separate the kernel from the stalk and chaff (dry outer layer) before milling.[10] In the courtyards, women culled wheat and, using mills, ground wheat and corn into meal. Some missions used water-powered flour mills, while others used horses or burros to turn the grindstone. Wine presses and olive presses (powered by burros) operated regularly.

Some Indians worked as servants to the missionaries and soldiers, while others worked outside at the presidios or nearby pueblos. Indians also managed the mission stores. Rezanov told how a mission ran like an industrious little town:

> [W]e inspected several . . . serviceable institutions for the promotion of pro-
> duction and economy in the establishment. There was a building for melting
> tallow and another for making soap; there were workshops for locksmiths
> and blacksmiths, and for cabinetmakers and carpenters; there were houses
> for the storage of tallow, soap, butter, salt, wool, and ox hides (these being ar-
> ticles of exportation), with storerooms for corn, peas, beans, and other kinds
> of pulse. . . .
>
> The neophytes are principally employed in such work as husbandry, tending
> cattle, and shearing sheep, or in handiwork, such as building, preparing tallow,
> and making soap and household articles. They are also employed in the trans-
> portation of provisions, as well as other goods, from one mission or presidio to
> another. The most laborious work, the grinding of the corn, is left almost en-
> tirely to the women. It is rubbed between two quadrangular oblong stones
> until ground into meal. Although the flour made is very white, the bread is
> very heavy and hard.

In keeping with the idea, expressed above, that labor was a way for the missionaries to maintain discipline, Rezanov offered a theory on why Indian work
took the place of windmills:

> When we consider that in the whole world there is no other country in which
> windmills are more numerous than in Spain, it appears incredible that these
> useful machines have never been put to use here. I learned, however, that in
> preferring the poorly ground flour produced by the methods just described,
> the good missionaries are really actuated by economic motives. As they have
> more Indians of both sexes under their care than they can keep constantly
> employed the whole year, they fear that the introduction of mills would only
> be productive of idleness, whereas under the present system the neophytes
> can be kept busy making flour during the periods of unemployment.[11]

Cattle raising grew into the largest occupation at the California missions. Almost every piece of the cow was used, especially its meat, horns, hide, and fat.
Hides were dried and tanned into leather and rawhide, and fat was rendered for
soap, leather dressing, candles, and lantern oil, a helpful product in the mines of
Mexico and South America. Guadalupe Vallejo described the process of slaugh-
tering cows for the cattle trade: "Every mission and ranch in old times had its
Calaveras, its 'place of skulls,' where cattle and sheep were killed by the Indian

butchers. Every Saturday morning the fattest animals were chosen and driven there, and by night the hides were all stretched on the hillside to dry."[12]

Hides and tallow were staple commercial goods, sold by contract to stores in Monterey or traded with ships,[13] and through 1834 the missions dominated their production in California. Well into the nineteenth century, each mission continued to be a hide and tallow production center for the surrounding hundred miles.

Cattle, cow- and deerhides, and leatherwork were essential to the mission lifestyle. At each presidio at least one proficient leatherworker made cueras, along with saddles and pack gear for riding animals. Rawhide was a valuable commodity; it was made into rope, supply containers for the backs of animals, shoes, and saddle coverings.

Many examples of mission trade craftsmanship remain today in museums and the rooms of surviving mission buildings. Ornate brocaded vestments, antique food-processing equipment, and primitive looms demonstrate key aspects of mission life to visitors.

## Fueling the Mission and Colonial Economies

As colonial organs, the mission, pueblo, and rancho were all designed to be economically self-sufficient. While this expectation was not always fulfilled, before the Mexican period the missions held most of California's wealth and livestock. Any production not used by the missions was sent back to fill the coffers of New Spain's bureaucracy.

In a colonial economy governed by mercantilist principles, factors such as price controls, royal taxes, regulations, and duties weighed heavily on traders. Spain set prices for both imported goods and items produced and traded in California. This royal monopoly made outside trade possible only on the black market, which was one method for missionaries to supplement their settlement's income. Restrictions were lifted later in the Spanish period, and customs centers were established in San Diego, Monterey, and, under Mexico, San Francisco.[14]

Missions sent their goods and raw materials to New Spain in exchange for manufactured goods or credit. Credit allowed them to import other important items such as iron and church supplies. Cowhides, wine, blankets, and other mission products were also traded for supplies such as iron, linen, clothing, and food.

Throughout the colonial period in South America, Mexico, and California, Spain funded its economic initiatives, including mission, pueblo, and presidio development. Other sponsored activities included hemp cultivation, the importing of skilled artisans, and hunting for sea otters. Franciscans and soldiers competed to acquire the pelts from the Indians who hunted them. The pelts were then traded to China, where they were prized, for mercury, a metal needed in New Spain.[15]

During the first four years of the missions, each settlement was almost completely dependent on supplies from Mexico. Two annual transports brought maize, wheat, beans, lentils, ham, sugar, chocolate, olive oil, wine, and brandy.[16] During a visit to Mexico City in 1773, Serra addressed the problems of unreliable shipments, periodic shortages, and low stipends for missionaries and soldiers. In 1772 ships from Mexico missed Monterey and arrived late in San Diego, causing near-famine conditions. The missions faced starvation again in 1786 and 1787. Floods, earthquakes, and fires contributed to food and supply shortages throughout the mission period. Missions with agricultural production would be asked to share their surplus harvest with the more badly off missions.[17]

In 1774 good harvests at Missions San Luis Obispo, San Carlos, San Gabriel, and San Antonio began to reduce the missions' dependency on supply ships. By 1778 the mission chain produced enough for its own consumption, though manufactured goods continued to be brought in from Mexico.[18] In terms of growth and production, 1790 to 1800 was the golden age of the California missions.

During the early years, trade was used by the missions to stay afloat. Later, when each mission made enough to support its own population, products such as clothes and food were traded or sold to nearby presidios and settlements. Occasional horse sales to trappers and traders were additional sources of revenue. After 1822 independent Mexico opened California to international trade, allowing more livestock in to support trade expansion in hides and tallow.[19]

Missions were like general stores to the presidios, especially when the Indians mastered crafts and trades such as soap making, leather working, candle making, and furniture building. Older crafts such as blanket weaving were also profitable. In return for presidio sales, missions received credits redeemed through a purchasing agent in Mexico City. These funds were used to purchase additional goods, including prayer books, trade beads, wool blankets, fine cloth, paper products, spices, wine, chocolate, and rice.[20]

Missionaries could not rely on regular and adequate stipends from the colonial government, and extra monies from crops and products went to the mission fund, rather than the missionaries. Funds were always limited, and annual salaries for both soldiers and missionaries were unreliable. Bureaucracy and communication problems slowed the market for hemp and grain exports.

Serra and his peers were constantly asking for funds, supplies, and soldiers to start new missions and presidios. To help subsidize the settlements, missionaries would meet with traveling merchants for news and profit. Anglo (American), Russian, and British guests and travelers made frequent appearances and were appreciated for the information they brought with them.

To make ends meet, California missionaries took part in the black market trade and smuggling.[21] Missionaries smuggled hides to trade ships off the coast and put the profits back into the mission fund.[22] Remembered Guadalupe Vallejo: "When a ship sailed into San Francisco Bay . . . the captain sent a large boat up this creek and arranged to buy hides. . . . Long files of Indians, each carrying a hide . . . could be seen trotting over the unfenced level land . . . and in a few weeks the whole cargo would thus be delivered."[23]

Trade ships also arrived from the East Coast and foreign countries, bringing tools, furniture, glass, nails, hardware, cloth, chests, pots, cooking utensils, musical instruments, and lighting fixtures for trade. These trade items in turn were used to pay missionary soldiers when stipends failed to arrive. By 1810, after the Napoleonic Wars in Europe had drained Spain's finances, supply ships stopped coming to California.[24] In the last decade of Spanish rule, only one supply ship arrived from San Blas. Fortunately, several dozen Spanish merchant ships landed in California during this time and helped with the deficit in supplies and money.[25]

The missions created a culture of dependence. Missionaries and other settlers depended on the Indians for their labors, and Indians, taken from their way of life, now depended on the missions for food and shelter. Pueblos and ranchos used seasonal labor from mission and non-mission Indians.[26] Throughout the stages of settlement, from mission to pueblo to rancho, Indians remained the primary source of labor.

Widespread conflict has been documented between Hispanic settlers and the missionaries throughout the mission period. The settlers, who saw the missionaries as squatters on potentially profitable land, got what they wanted after secularization in 1834, when all land, livestock, and workers were transferred to settlers and civil servants from Mexico. While the missions lost their economic mainstay, private enterprise continued to expand, as it had been doing since the opening of trade at the beginning of the Mexican period. Mission acreage was splintered into approximately seven hundred plots of land, and these plots turned into the next social and economic institution of California, the rancho.

Most ranchos were located along the coast, with a few in the Central Valley. Like the missions, the ranchos raised cattle, sheep, and horses and grew grain and grapes. Families with connections could obtain grants for each family member, creating an elite class of *rancheros* who controlled hundreds of thousands of acres of land.[27]

# 13

## Indians of the Missions

In the cemetery of El Campo Santo in today's Old Town San Diego, the stone of a mission Indian named Melchior, who was born in 1770 and died in 1867, reads as follows:

> My name is Melchior. I am a Roman Catholic Christian and an Indian of this locale. I was born one year after the arrival of the missionaries and soldiers. I may have been baptized by Father Serra at the Presidio, but I never knew. As a child and a young man, I heard about the murder of the Priest Father Luis Jayme at the mission. I remember the execution of four local Indian Chieftains who took part in an uprising in 1778 here in San Diego. I witnessed the coming of the Mexicans and then the Americans. I heard about the Battle of San Pasqual in 1846, and of Warner Springs Indian uprising of the early 1850s. I was in the crowd of Indians present for the execution of Indian Chieftain Antonio Garra in 1852. His grave is not far from here. In 97 years, I saw Old Town grow from a pueblo to a city. I've seen the happy and sad times in San Diego. I remember many things, but I am very old now, and I am very sleepy. Let me rest. Pray for me. My name is Melchior.

Cemetery campanario, Mission San Miguel.

Few mission Indians left such records of their existence. One exception was Luiseño Pablo Tac, who was born at San Luis Rey in 1822 and died in 1841, leaving handwritten accounts in Spanish of his experiences living at the San Diego mission. Father Antonio Péyri, administrator of the mission, took an interest in Tac's education. When Péyri left California in 1832, he took Tac with him to the Franciscan Mission College of San Fernando in Mexico City. The two stayed at the college for two years, then traveled to Spain and on to Italy. Tac registered at the Urban College of Rome and began study of Latin grammar and rhetoric,

moving on to humanities and philosophy in preparation for the mission field.[1]
He would never return to California, however; he died of smallpox in 1841, just
before his twentieth birthday.

Tac worked with linguist and cardinal Giuseppe Mezzofanti at the college on
a dictionary of Luiseño words, as well as a grammatical overview of the complex language. Tac's manuscripts were preserved by Mezzofanti and transferred
to a library in Bologna after the cardinal's death. Tac's diary, probably written
when he was twelve or thirteen years old, is a history and description of the
missions, with background on the missionaries in Baja and Alta California.

Tac called his home region and people of Alta California "Quechla," or "those
of the South." This word was used by his grandparents. Wrote Tac, "In Quechla
not long ago there were five thousand souls, with all their neighboring lands.
Through a sickness that came to California two thousand souls died, and three
thousand were left."[2]

## Mission Indian Groups

Some of the most prominent Indian groups in the missions were the Kumeyaay,
Shoshonean, Chumash, Yokut, Ohlone, Costanoan, and Miwok. Central Valley
Indians came to the missions early in the nineteenth century. Some valley tribes
bordered on the mission strip and were incorporated into the populations of the
missions. For example, the Yokut and Miwok were incorporated by missions directly west of the valley, such as Santa Clara, San José, and San Juan Bautista.

Most of the Indians baptized at these missions after 1805 came from the San
Joaquin Valley.[3] Starting in 1806 and into the 1820s, some Indians from the lower
San Joaquin Valley came to missions such as San José, Santa Clara, Soledad, San
Juan Bautista, and San Antonio.[4] The Chumash, who were reputed to be one of
the tribes most accepting of the Spaniards[5] and who made up nearly one-fourth
of the total mission population,[6] lived at five missions: San Buenaventura, Santa
Barbara, Santa Inés, La Purísima, and San Luis Obispo. Serra referred to the
Santa Barbara Channel Indians (the Chumash) as "those interesting and gifted
gentiles."[7] Almost all of the Chumash people were brought into the mission system by the early 1800s, except for those who fled into the mountains and inland
valleys.[8]

Living arrangements for Indian residents at the missions varied. The central
and northern mission area Indians were concentrated in and around mission
buildings, while those in the south clustered in rancherías farther from the

missions, though still in the vicinity. Indians at the southern missions tended to remain on their ancestral lands and live with some freedom in their own villages. An Indian village adjacent to the San Diego mission thrived from 1774 into the American period.[9]

### A Conscripted Labor Force

As far back as 1537, the papal bull of Paul III stated that "the said Indians and all other people who may be discovered by Christians, are by no means to be deprived of their liberty or the possession of their property, even though they may be outside of the faith of Jesus Christ."[10] Nevertheless, Indians in the northern and central missions lived and worked under a system of civil, religious, and military authority, leaving little room for individual choice or independent behavior. The missions were built upon conscripted Indian labor, and even after the dissolution of the missions, the ranches and pueblos continued on this basis until the end of the Mexican period. Mission Indians, ex-mission Indians, and villagers living outside the missions were all part of the labor pool. When trained labor was needed at new settlements, Indians would be relocated, sometimes by force.

Living conditions for the Indians were difficult. Cramped living quarters, poor ventilation in some of the work and living buildings, malnutrition, and a general lack of freedom of movement outside the mission all contributed to long-term depopulation from disease. French explorer and navigator Jean François de la Pérouse, who visited Mission Carmel in 1786, called the human environment "lifeless and depressing."[11] After 1800, life expectancy and reproductive rates continued to decrease.

The missions frequently hired out local workers to the presidios and ranchos. It was the missions, not the workers, who received wages, food, clothing, or hides for the work performed.[12] When traveling on work assignments, Indians lived on the outskirts of ranches in huts or in servants' quarters.[13] By a 1787 order of the governor of California, Indians were not allowed in settlers' homes, and Indians from distant villages could not settle permanently in the pueblos. Instead, they were permitted short-term work and lived near the guardhouse.[14] Even on work assignments, large groups of Indians were not allowed to travel into town unaccompanied by a soldier or missionary.

At the presidios and missions, Indian servants delivered food and supplies to the troops and tended to their horses. At the pueblos, Indians mainly worked as

Lockable doors, sole exits from La Purísima.

*vaqueros* (cowhands) or muleteers. Some were also employed as cooks and domestic servants. For the Indians, life at the pueblos was less oppressive and religion less prominent. Instead of living in-house, workers usually returned to
their own homes at the end of the day.

When settlers from Mexico began to move into larger towns and ranches,
some Indians remained as permanent workers outside of mission control.
The settlers of San José and Los Angeles depended on Indians for many tasks

that varied with the seasons. Indians occupied the lowest rung of this new colonial society. From the 1780s to 1870s, Los Angeles residents relied almost exclusively on Indian labor for agriculture, trades, and domestic service. A mission, a pueblo, and three privately owned ranchos used Indian labor, some of it voluntary.[15]

## Keeping and Recording the Populations

From 1769 to 1834, Franciscan missionaries kept detailed records of the mission Indian population, including annual censuses. The *libro de mision* (mission book) recorded baptisms, marriages, and deaths for each mission; all children in the mission were immediately baptized and recorded in the register. After 1792, ten years old was the age at which children became officially classified as adults. Indians often married very early, in their pre-teens.

The total Indian and Spanish population at the nine California missions rose from 1770 at a consistent four thousand people per decade. This rate increased steadily after 1798, and increased dramatically to twenty thousand by 1805. Mission populations began to drop at an increasing rate in 1824 with rising death rates. Record keeping ceased in 1834 with secularization.

During the most prosperous years of the mission system in California, the average mission housed approximately 2,300 Indian converts, including Christian Indians living in isolated ranchos or settlements. Runaways who escaped to adjacent areas were often captured by recovery expeditions, but temporary desertions were not noted in the population counts. Some research has suggested a twofold mission population, with a consistent flow of people toward and away from the missions at all times.[16]

## Indian Life

Unfortunately, many historical European and American accounts of Indian lifestyles at the missions were based on bias, prejudice, stereotypes, or a misunderstanding of Indian culture. Rezanov, observing Indian recreational activities during his visit, reinforces the perception that mission Indians were better off under missionary supervision than in their previous lives: "In their dances, amusements, sports, ornaments, etc., they are liberally indulged. They have a little property of their own in fowls and pigeons. Upon obtaining permission, they may go hunting and fishing. Altogether, they can live much more free from care than in their previous wild, natural state."[17]

Thousands of Indians, whether because of encouragement or force, moved to mission property to follow Christian customs, work in the fields, raise livestock, and learn a host of trades to serve the mission and the Spanish colony, all under the authority of a top-heavy religious and colonial bureaucracy. Despite the short distance between the missions and their original homes, the Indians, in a sense, were like immigrants. To suit the new environment and the needs of the Spanish empire, not only dress, language, diet, and work habits had to change, but their cultural and spiritual identity.[18] Each generation became more acculturated. After the dissolution of the missions in 1834, the Indians who stayed at the missions rather than return to ancestral lands had likely been born there and known only that way of life. These more assimilated descendants of earlier converts were also known as "old families."[19]

What disappeared and what remained of those Indian cultures that survived the disease epidemics? Customs and forms of identity that remained may have been distorted versions of their predecessors. This bears further study. For example, shamans traditionally commanded respect in their communities, but the shaman's authority was weakened with the onset of mission life.[20] Some traditional religions survived through dance, ceremony, and tales passed through the generations.

Amalgams of old and new religious traditions also exist today. "Syncretism" is the fusion of two very different systems of belief, a status that persisted in symbols and ways of life. Examples would be simultaneous practice of Catholic rites and tribal rituals.

As discussed previously, Catholic belief systems impacted women in profound ways. In a society where reproduction within marriage was demanded, a woman who failed to conceive or who miscarried could be flogged or forced to dress in sackcloth and cover herself with ashes.[21]

Abortion and infanticide represented, in some cases, a continuation of traditional Indian practices, as when, in the Chumash culture, women routinely killed their firstborn in the belief that failure to do so would prevent them from having further children. They could also, like escape and physical resistance, be calculated responses to mission life.

In looking at all such treatments of Indians, critics can make the argument for the mission as an instrument of conquest, control, and subjugation.

### Indian Leadership

Within their tightly controlled environment, some Indians were offered the opportunity to lead and supervise others. Governor Neve instituted the first measure for Indian self-governance during the mission period, appointing Indian *alcaldes,* political officers who served as judicial and administrative representatives of mission residents. The position (open only to men) grew in importance as the mission chain expanded. Alcaldes were subsequently chosen by priests, rather than by the Indians themselves,[22] until 1822, when Indians were allowed to vote for alcaldes to serve in the Mexican Congress. Pablo Tac wrote of alcaldes

> with rods as a symbol that they could [use to] judge the others. . . . The captain dressed like the Spanish, always remaining captain, but not ordering his people about as of old, when they were still gentiles. . . . In the afternoon, the alcaldes gather at the house of the missionary. They bring the news of that day, and if the missionary tells them something that all the people of the country ought to know, they return to the villages shouting, "Tomorrow morning" . . . [and crying] out what the missionary has told them, in his language, and all the country hears it: "Tomorrow the sowing begins and so the laborers go to the chicken yard and assemble there."[23]

As discussed earlier, the majordomo, the mission or ranch foreman, was another important Indian leader. Usually a retired Spanish soldier or respected Indian, the majordomo managed crops and herds. Majordomos also led remotely in distant districts.

Some Christian Indians were assigned small roles in leading other Indians at each mission and assisting with evangelization. Christian Indian women helped the priests bring in new female converts and socialize them in mission life.[24]

### Rebellion and Violence

Records and extensive evidence of Indian resistance to colonization and mission life dispel the stereotype of mission Indians as passive victims. Violence and tension among the Indians were constants as soldiers, missionaries, and other settlers moved into their land and lives.

Though some groups seemed to accept mission life, others rejected conversion outright. They remained on their own lands, refusing to be relocated to mission property. Some mission Indians fled, singly or in small groups, back to their homes or into the Central Valley. Invasion, enslavement, salvation, or civilization—how we judge the treatment of the California Indians depends on one's point of view and how we see the context of a society that relied on violent punishment and royal and church law to keep order. In any context, there were reasons to be discontented with mission life.

Missionaries and soldiers constantly scrutinized and modified Indian behavior. Missionaries and alcaldes took roll to determine if anyone was missing or shirking his or her duty. Disobedient Indians were flogged, put into stocks, and locked up at night. Indians who gambled and drank were also put into the stocks. Whipping with a barbed lash, branding, and solitary confinement were other punishments used to enforce military and Catholic discipline.[25]

Missionized Indians demonstrated resistance in multiple ways. Despite the inevitable physical punishment or imprisonment, some resisted through noncooperation in mission activities and absenteeism from church and work. Indian groups organized insurrections in the southern missions, with devastating effects on mission buildings and land. Most, but not all, resistance efforts were on a small scale.

The few larger revolts demonstrated the early vulnerability of mission settlements. The most violent included the 1781 Yuma tribe attack along the Colorado River and the 1819 attack in Buenaventura, when Mojave Indians attacked a priest and group of soldiers along the Santa Barbara Channel and in the delta area of the San Joaquin River. The soldiers killed ten of the Indians.[26]

In 1775 abuse of Indian women in San Diego may have been the impetus for a major revolt. Eight hundred Indians from more than seventy villages set the mission on fire. Other revolts involved destroying crops and scattering herds.[27] Some armed rebellions resulted from mistreatment by priests and the prohibition of certain traditional ceremonies, practices, and sexual behaviors.[28] Indians in Santa Cruz killed a friar in 1812, and leaders of the Chumash uprisings of 1824 also organized a flight to the interior. The Chumash at La Purísima, Santa Barbara, and Santa Inés revolted rather than attend Easter mass.[29]

At Mission San Diego, six years of tension and animosity culminated in violence in November 1775. Kumeyaay (Diegueño), who resented European intrusion and resisted conversion,[30] congregated from forty rancherías, looted the church, set it afire, and attacked the missionaries and their associates. Mission furnishings were destroyed, along with sacred vessels, paintings, and written records.[31] Father Luís Jayme, one of the fatally wounded victims, was subsequently declared a Catholic martyr. Efforts by the presidio garrison to subdue the angry group were futile, and survivors withdrew to the still-vulnerable presidio six miles west.[32]

Throughout 1776, Spanish officials, investigating the destruction of the mission, interrogated the principal rancherías within a twenty-five-mile radius.[33] Father Serra, reacting to the murder of Father Jayme, said, "Thanks be to God; now that the terrain has been watered by blood, the conversion of the San Diego Indians will take place."[34] Serra also called the San Diego disaster "a decided setback for future foundations."[35]

## Resistance and Economic Benefit: Livestock Raiding

Theft of tools, crops, and livestock was an ongoing problem at the missions well into the period of American settlement. Stealing livestock and farming tools was likely another form of resistance and means of survival. Within a decade of Serra's arrival in San Diego, missionaries began to complain of Indians stealing cattle. Groups of Indians who had escaped or been freed after secularization raided mission and ranch lands for cattle and horses for their own use in the Central Valley. Even Indians from as far away as the Rocky Mountains and Great Plains came to California specifically to raid southern missions and ranches. An American in the late nineteenth century stated that Indian raids of Mexican ranchos "were the scourge of the eastern and middle portion of California in the period following the decadence of the missions and before the settlement of the Territory by Americans and foreigners."[36] Guadalupe Vallejo remembered, "Perhaps the most exasperating feature of the coming-in of the Americans was owing to the mines, which drew away most of the servants, so that our cattle were stolen by thousands."[37]

## Escape

Escape from mission life was difficult. Mission residents were not allowed to return permanently to their homes, and trips outside were permitted only under work orders. Flight represented not only an individual act of rebellion, but a collective resistance to being compelled to live at the missions. Force was legally permitted to keep baptized Indians at the missions.[38] Captured runaways were brought back to mission quarters, where, if it was a first offense, they usually received one warning. A second offense earned the lash or time in the stocks; after that, they would be shackled for three days while working. Governor Fages prescribed ten lashes for Indians who ran away to the pueblos without permission from the missionaries.[39]

Indians under the watch of Junípero Serra were probably not as harshly treated: "[T]hese wayward sheep are my burden," he wrote, "and I am responsible for them not at the *tribunal de cuentas* [treasury] in Mexico but at a much higher tribunal than that."

At times the governor intervened and ordered troops to capture escapees and return them to the missions for punishment. Given the low numbers of soldiers from New Spain, even small numbers of fleeing Indians were of concern to mission officials. Both Spanish and Mexican troops searched the Central Valley for runaways. Frederick Beechey described how Indians along the coast were captured with a boat "furnished with a cannon and musketry, and in every respect equipped for war. . . . [T]he neophytes and the *gente de razon,* who superintended the direction of the boat, avail themselves of their superiority, with the desire of ingratiating themselves with their masters and of receiving a reward. . . . Women and children are generally the first objects of capture, as their husbands and parents sometimes voluntarily follow them into captivity."[40]

Rezanov recorded the process of searching for missing residents:

Notwithstanding all that has been said in favor of the treatment of the Indians at the missions, an irresistible desire for freedom sometimes breaks out in individuals. This may probably be referred to the natural genius of the race. Their attachment to a wandering life, their love of alternate diversion from hunting and fishing to entire idleness, seem in their eyes, to overbalance all the benefits they enjoy at the missions, and these to us appear very great. The result is every now and then attempts to escape are made. On such occasions, no sooner is a neophyte missed than search for him is at once begun, and as it is always known to what tribe he belongs, and on account of the enmity that subsists among the different tribes, he can never take refuge with any other. . . . He is almost always brought back to the mission, where he is bastinadoed [beaten with a stick], and an iron rod a foot or a foot-and-a-half long and an inch in diameter is fastened to one of his feet. This has a two-fold use, in that it prevents the Indian from making another attempt to escape, and has the effect of terrifying the others and deterring them from indulging in escapades of a similar nature.[41]

The methods of rebellion described above were some of the ways that missionized Indians could react to the culture that, imposed on them, changed their civilization forever.

# 14

## Changing Rule of the Missions

During its last years of rule, Spain struggled to hold on to its colonies while revolutionaries in Mexico demanded independence. Royal support for the missions steadily declined, with dire financial consequences for the California missions. Meanwhile, the social and economic seeds of change planted during the Spanish period began to flourish under Mexican rule: immigration, American and foreign commerce, the cattle trade, a decline in the authority of the Catholic Church, and the rise of liberal thought in Mexico.

Spain's last California mission was San Rafael Arcángel, founded in 1817. San Rafael started as an *asistencia* and did not receive mission status until six years later under Mexican rule. Mission San Francisco Solano in Sonoma, founded in 1823, was the final mission of the chain of twenty-one. It was the only one established independently of the Franciscans, or of any order.

The new Mexican constitution of 1824 established the Federal Republic of Mexico and granted Indians the rights to vote and own property, although these rights were not extended in practice. The new Mexican Congress controlled the territories of California, Texas, and New Mexico. Traders, businessmen, and trappers continued to flock to California, along with more soldiers, farmers, and

Mission Sonoma. © iStockphoto.com/Mayr Budny.

officials from Mexico. Mexico passed a law of colonization in 1824 that allowed more liberal land grants than under Spanish law. Anglo-Americans and other foreigners were allowed to buy tracts of land and encouraged to accept Mexican citizenship in the process. This diverse influx of people was guaranteed to change the face of California's population and institutions.

After 1822 Mexico ended several restrictions on foreign trade, increasing commerce between Californians and English, American, and Russian traders. Mexico kept the duties high, however, and made Monterey the only point of legal entry,[1] turning the city into an administrative center of the province and the seat of customs. All trade items were highly taxed, straining the already low finances of colonial institutions. Only the tallow and hide industry thrived, increasing product sales to foreigners. California remained relatively poor under Mexican rule, still remote from its home base (news of Mexican independence had not even reached Alta California for several months).

The Mexican constitution of 1824 set up Alta and Baja California as two territories under the federal government and legislature. From 1825 to 1836 each had its own governor, and from 1824 to 1827 the Commission for the Development of the Californias met regularly to discuss the area's unique issues. The commission disapproved not only of the motives behind the mission system, but also of the missionaries' method of conversion; it held that troops should not have been used to aid spiritual conquest. The group also charged that missionaries were overly concerned with commercial matters and unable to spend sufficient time nurturing religious needs.

One commission recommendation was to turn the nonreligious functions of the missions over to government control. Commission members contended that the missions should be able to support themselves for thirteen years at the expense of the Indians. The commission also believed that mission lands should belong to both mission Indians and resident Mexicans, not to the Indians alone.

### Land of Confusion

During the mission period there was confusion over who was in charge of rancho lands associated with the missions. Friars complained when settlers received grants of pueblo and ranch lands. They wanted to keep the available land for mission use and did not want to expose mission Indians to urban development.[2] Father-President José Señán commented to the viceroy:

> I . . . believe that under no circumstances should retired soldiers . . . who wish to settle in the Province be permitted to establish themselves separately in remote areas or in villages outside the towns. . . . Such persons should be required to reside in towns. . . . The consequences to be expected from scattered and isolated colonization are distressing to contemplate. Colonists this openly exposed are likely to suffer mischief at the hands of gentiles. . . . In short, they will live in those remote regions without King to rule or Pope to excommunicate them.[3]

Under Mexico an already messy administration became more complex. The mission settlements suffered the most. Missions were expensive to maintain, especially without support from the crown and the benefit of the Pious Fund used by missions in Mexico and South America. Supplies and funds for colonists appeared either irregularly or not at all. As Frederick Beechey noted, "the padres . . . dreading the worst, were very discontented, and many would willingly have quitted the country for Manila."[4]

Mexico's neglect of California affected its civil officials as well. Beechey described the sad state of the governor's mansion in San Francisco and surrounding buildings in 1826:

> The governor's abode was in a corner of the [San Francisco] presidio and formed one end of a row, of which the other was occupied by a chapel. The opposite

side was broken down and little better than a heap of rubbish and bones, on which jackals [coyotes], dogs, and vultures were constantly preying. The other two sides of the quadrangle contained storehouses, artificers' shops, and the jail, all built in the humblest style with badly-burned bricks and roofed with tiles. The chapel and the governor's house were distinguished by being whitewashed.

Whether viewed at a distance or near, the establishment impresses a spectator with any other sentiment than that of its being a place of authority; and but for a tottering flagstaff, upon which was occasionally displaced the tri-colored flag of Mexico, three rusty field-pieces, and a half accoutered sentinel parading the gateway in charge of a few poor wretches heavily-shackled, a visitor would be ignorant of the importance of the place. The neglect of the government to its establishments could not be more thoroughly evinced than in the dilapidated condition of the building in question, and such was the dissatisfaction of the people that there was no inclination to improve their situation or even to remedy many of the evils which they appeared to us to have the power to remove.[5]

Both missionaries and civil administrators, representing church and state, respectively, were expected to accomplish the conversion of Indians and their development into citizens. Civil administrators were often at odds with the missions, whether for altruistic reasons or because they were jealous of the missions' lands and resources. They were not always able to challenge the power of the missions, but they did make their concerns known. One point of opposition was the separation of mission Indians, who were not allowed to live outside the mission in farming settlements alongside the settlers from Mexico.[6] This conflict ended in 1834 when the provincial government transferred most of the mission properties to Hispanic settlers.

Historian Herbert Bolton commented on the philosophy behind Spain's colonial occupation via missionaries: "Such an ideal called not only for the subjugation and control of the natives, but their civilization, as well. To bring this end about, the rulers of Spain made use of the religious and humanitarian zeal of the missionaries, choosing them to be to the Indians not only preachers, but also teachers and disciplinarians."[7]

## The Drive for Secularization

Opponents of the mission system were rare in the early mission period, but Governor Felipe de Neve was an ardent believer in secularization of missionary holdings. His *Reglamento* of 1779 limited each mission to a single minister. The law was not followed and was eventually annulled after appeal by the missionaries.

It was not until later in the Spanish period and into the Mexican years of rule that serious opposition began to arise. Activists during the Mexican period hoped to turn the California missions over to parish priests and the mission land over to private, Indian ownership. Proponents of mission secularization could be found in the government, too, including the Mexican Secretary of Relations, Lucas Alamán, who made this statement to Congress in November 1823:

> It is necessary to consider other interests than those of the missionaries in the vast and fertile peninsula of Californias. . . . If the Mission system is that best suited to draw savages from barbarism, it can do no more than establish the first principle of society; it cannot lead men to their highest perfection. Nothing is better to accomplish this than to bind individuals to society by the powerful bond of property. The government believes that the distribution of lands to the converted Indians, lending them from the mission fund the means for cultivation, and the establishment of foreign colonies . . . would give great impulse to that important province.[8]

By this line of thinking, the missionaries could only start the Indians on the path to living a civilized life. The culmination of the mission system would be Indian management and land ownership. However, opinion was always split on what the Indians' status under the new colonial government should be. Both Spain and Mexico had commissions to address the issue.

In 1825, supporters of secularizing the missions formed the *Junta de Fomento de Californias* (Committee for Promoting the Progress of the Californias).[9] The junta was charged with researching the mission system and approaching the Mexican government with a solution that would be in keeping with the liberal ideals of the Mexican Revolution. The junta approached the first president of the Mexican Republic, Guadalupe Victoria, asserting sympathy for the missionized Indians and calling for a different system:

> The *junta* is not ignorant that from the Spanish system of discoveries and spiritual conquests has resulted all the progress made in the Jesuit missions of Old California and in those founded later in New California by the Fernandiños. . . . Still the *junta* has not been able to reconcile the principles of such a system with those of our independence and political constitution, nor with the true spirit of the Gospel. Religion under that system could not advance beyond domination. It could be promoted only under the protection of guards and presidios. The gentiles must renounce all the rights of their natural independence to be cate-

chumens from the moment of baptism; they must be subject to laws almost monastic, while their teachers deemed themselves freed from the laws which forbade their engaging in temporal business; and the neophytes must continue this without hope of ever possessing fully the civil rights of society. . . . The present condition of the missions does not correspond to the great progress which they made in the beginning.[10]

In 1826 Mexico attempted to start the process of secularization. California missions received orders to liberate any Indians of good character who possessed the ability to subsist by trade or agriculture.[11] In 1830 the newly appointed governor of California, Manuel Victoria, traveled to California to investigate the state of the missions for the Mexican government. He looked into the population, the public lands, and the status and civilization of the mission Indians.[12]

Another precursor to secularization was the dissolution of the Franciscan College of San Fernando in 1828. The following year, Franciscan priests were ordered by law to leave California and return to Spain. The law was not enforced, perhaps because of the administration's dependence on the clergy and military for support and enforcement.

The government was also interested to learn if the missions could support themselves without dependence on the Pious Fund or the government. The government's expectation was that by the end of October 1834 every Alta California mission would be a civil community.[13]

## The Plan of Transfer

The government of Mexico passed a secularization act in 1833, officially opening up mission and rancho land to settlers. The Híjar-Pádres colony brought more colonists and artisans to California, but otherwise settlement from Mexico was slow. The Mexican Congress's law stated that the government should release all the missions of Alta and Baja California from missionaries. The Pious Fund and its estates would help Indian families make the transition.[14] Mission properties were distributed among colonists, and remaining funds were allocated to help pay for stipends, school salaries, and farming equipment.[15]

The two Californias became a single department with an appointed governor and an assembly, both in name only, and one congressional representative without voting power. The department was divided into districts and the missions were incorporated under a single independent diocese. In February 1839 two prefectures were designated for Alta California, with capitals at Los Angeles and Santa Barbara, and one for Baja California, with a capital at San Juan de Castro. Governor Pio Pico declared: "Let the mission system end. Land should be owned by private individuals."[16]

One by one, the missions of California were to be converted to pueblos and large ranchos, privatized with the help of Mexican civil administrators. The first pueblos were to be attached to the closest presidio and overseen by appointed officers. Mexico planned to distribute land plots among the Indians and any Mexican immigrants living at the missions. Each transferee was to receive a *solar* (house lot), a *suerte* (plot of land for cultivation), and an allotment of livestock.

Land divisions were to include communal land for pasture and crops; town land with an open square in the center, Spanish-style; and a subsistence plot for each Indian family. Mission buildings would become schoolhouses, hospitals, administrative quarters, prisons, barracks, and other civil buildings. Government records regarding the mission handover specified how Indians would receive pueblo access. As long as an Indian was of age and a resident of one of the missions, he could receive acreage for farming and living. Half of the livestock, equipment, and seeds would be divided among Indians, with the remaining half managed by a local civil authority.[17] Indians knowing farming or a trade would receive preference. The August 1834 *Reglamento Provisional* stated that pasture land and livestock would be provided to heads of families and to all males over twenty years of age.

## The Outcome of Secularization

Documentation and definition of the government policy of secularization was about as far as it progressed for the Indian population. The implementation was muddy and ill enforced. As far as the Indians knew, they had no rights under the new system. Policy regarding the Franciscans, however, was clear and carried out to the letter. The Franciscans' status under Mexican rule had been shaky for years. The government had stopped paying them, and once secularization passed they were instructed to perform religious services only until their replacements arrived. Some priests refused to obey the new government or to leave California.

Governor Figueroa ordered ten Mexican Franciscans to replace the Spanish Franciscans in August 1834, and the government seized the missions.[18] During this period of transition, Franciscans were only allowed to occupy their private quarters and use the priests' garden and church. Mexican authorities divided the mission buildings into religious and public sections, sometimes with a wall built through some of the rooms to designate which spaces the priests could still inhabit.

All mission funds were transferred to the government in Mexico. New parish priests who did not belong to particular missionary orders were sent to oversee each parish division within the district. Everything else was soon moved into government and private hands. Mission buildings were intended to house public services for the new pueblo, and crops and herds were to be administered by a civil commissioner.[19]

Secularization caused a sharp decline in mission populations. One by one, the missions were sold and the Indians living there were "free" to walk away. Some Indians received land and buildings within mission complexes during the 1830s, but most of the land was taken by settlers from Mexico.[20] Nevertheless, through the 1830s and 1840s some of the missions continued to operate, although reduced in size, under different leadership, and without the bulk of their laborers.

San Juan Capistrano was converted into a pueblo in 1833, and steps were taken to do the same at San Diego and San Luis Rey. By the end of 1834, nine missions had been secularized: San Luis Rey, San Juan Capistrano, San Gabriel, San Fernando, Santa Barbara, Purísima, Santa Cruz, San Francisco, and San Rafael. Six more were secularized by the end of 1835, leaving five. However, only a few pueblos were founded and the rest of the land was fair game for *californios* and Mexican settlers now eager to come to California. The goals of secularization were just as short-lived in the mission pueblos. In 1840 just a few hundred Indians remained at the pueblo of San Juan Capistrano, and five hundred on mission lands.

In 1839 government inspectors who arrived in California to evaluate the progress of mission changeover discovered neglected and abandoned land. Most of the Indians had disappeared, crops and livestock were ignored, and the Indians who remained lived in poverty. The pueblos were in a shambles. By July 1846 sixteen of the missions had been sold, some by public auction and some to be rented to the highest bidder.[21]

Before Mexican rule began in 1821, the mission acreage boasted great herds of livestock and many acres of arable land. Guadalupe Vallejo remembered, "The old Mission field is now occupied by some of the best farms of the valley, showing how excellent was the fathers' judgment of good land."[22] One settler complained during the Mexican period that "twenty-one mission establishments possess all the fertile lands of the peninsula and . . . more than a thousand families of *gente de razon* possess only that which has been benevolently given them by the missionaries." Another said that "in this way they have appropriated

San Juan Capistrano, early nineteenth century. Courtesy of Jim Graves,
Mission San Juan Capistrano.

nearly all this territory, their object being to keep private parties from coming
between the mission grants. This is a system which the *gente de razon* should
reform."[23]

In the mid-1820s Mexico loosened the rules for settlers wishing to get title to
their own land. Poor management of secular policy, along with the influx of
Mexican colonists and the eagerness of californios to buy their own land, spelled
failure for Indian ownership of mission land. Mexican colonists received free passage to California to settle there as farmers, teachers, tradesmen, and craftsmen.

The transfer of one colonial Hispanic institution for another was overtaken
by capitalism. The Mexican turnover of missions to civil leaders and then parish
priests spelled the end of the California missions. By 1840 the private rancho,
still a bastion of Hispanic culture, replaced the mission as the most important
social and economic institution in California.

# 15

## The Decline of a Civilization

Between 1770 and 1900 the Indian population of California declined from approximately 310,000 in mission areas to less than 20,000.[1] Disease was the primary factor in this decline, hitting children and the elderly particularly hard. European diseases, to which Europeans had had centuries to develop resistance, wreaked havoc on the immune systems of America's native peoples.

Despite the late, slow settlement in California, the region's physical isolation can be said to have ended with the arrival of the first explorers in 1519. Studies in epidemiology suggest that the introduction of new diseases actually preceded permanent settlement.[2] Each exploratory voyage and crew potentially brought new bacteria and viruses. There is little doubt that the Indians learned to associate the Europeans with disease and death. To replace Indian populations depleted by disease, soldiers and missionaries went inland to the Coast Ranges and beyond to the interior to find new recruits. After settlement, mission convert runaways also inadvertently carried disease to the unconverted tribes.

After 1848, when American and New Mexican trappers and traders moved into the Central Valley and Coast Ranges and replaced the missions and pueblos with commercially based settlements, they brought more new diseases with them.[3]

## The Epidemic: A Fact of Life and Death

By 1730 several epidemic diseases were established on the Baja Peninsula, from smallpox, dysentery, and malaria to typhus, syphilis, and measles. These diseases were a major contributor to the linear decline in the mission Indian population on the peninsula during this period, from 41,500 to approximately 4,000 by 1773.[4]

The first serious epidemic in Alta California was a respiratory illness at Mission Santa Clara in 1777. Another probably respiratory epidemic took place there in 1781, and larger-scaled epidemics in 1828, in the San Joaquin Valley in 1838 and 1839, and in 1844 in Monterey. In 1802 diphtheria and pneumonia afflicted those living in and between Missions San Carlos and San Luis Obispo. Measles, probably carried from Mexico on incoming ships, was another serious threat. In 1806 it killed approximately sixteen hundred people between San Francisco and Santa Barbara.[5]

Venereal disease, perhaps the most common affliction of mission populations, caused many stillbirths and birth defects in the mission populations.[6] It started in the presidios before moving on to mission inhabitants. Spanish settlers and colonists brought syphilis to the Baja California Indians, and both groups brought the disease north to Alta California. Soldiers were primarily responsible for spreading the affliction to both settlers and Indian women.[7]

Alta California's isolation and the screening of travelers from Mexico provided a degree of protection from smallpox epidemics. Nevertheless, Governor Fages received a decree in 1786 with instructions to protect the population from smallpox by quarantining sufferers and "situat[ing them] so that the prevailing winds in the region cannot communicate the contagion to the villages and farms of the vicinity." Vaccination was introduced into the colonies, by royal order, in about 1804, only a few years after its discovery in 1796. Indians and Spaniards received vaccinations at Missions San Diego, San Francisco, and San Juan Bautista.[8]

Devastating epidemics in the densely populated Central Valley and adjacent foothills continued through the Mexican period, including malaria, syphilis, and other venereal diseases.

## Inside the Mission

Settlement design helped spread contagious diseases. At some settlements several hundred people would be crowded together in unsanitary conditions, with limited ventilation and damp walls and floors. Food and water contamination were also common. Shortages of food along with the stress of an unfamiliar and likely unwelcome lifestyle also contributed. Along the coast, the moist air was a probable cause of respiratory problems,[9] especially in the rainy season of late winter and spring. Indian groups that had relocated from the warmer interior of California to the wetter and cooler coast were unprepared for the change in climate and the illnesses they encountered. Population movement among the missions also spread disease, thanks to escapees and groups forcibly moved by the missionaries. The communication infrastructure maintained by missions such as Santa Cruz helped create a free flow of disease.

Some missions fared better than others. Locations such as San Luis Obispo, which was less populated and more isolated through the 1790s, were less susceptible to disease.[10] At Mission Soledad, Indians treated their illnesses at springs in the foothills of Paraiso. They baked in the sun and drank soda and sulfur water. Despite a lack of water during times of illness and intense heat, San Miguel had the second-lowest death rate, next to San Luis Rey. The mission sat close to thermal springs of Paso Robles and a plant called soap root grew nearby, which was believed to have helped against various diseases.[11]

San Rafael, called the "Mission of Bodily Healing," was set up in 1817 as a hospital center. Its location was healthier than that of Mission San Francisco (Dolores), which had suffered from disease for forty years. After increasing its numbers of converts and agricultural output, San Rafael was the only *asistencia* to become a full-fledged mission in its own right.

### Social Effects

Despite the new converts, high infant and child mortality rates slowed the population's growth, and there was a rapid tendency to remarriage. Serra wrote in 1774 that "eleven little babies of this mission, one after the other, took their flight to heaven. . . . [A] number of adults went also. Some we baptized just before dying; others had been baptized before." All had died from dysentery.[12]

During times of disease, mission labor and production had to rely on a barebones workforce.[13] Food and supplies were hard to come by. The missionaries gave their residents basic nursing care, spiritual solace, and what food they could, and each mission established its own infirmary where Indian women practiced herbal and other remedies. Some Indians reacted to sickness by seeking out their sweathouses and bathing in nearby water sources.[14]

Frederick Beechey commented on the decrepit state of some of the missions:

In some of the missions much misery prevails. . . . [San Francisco mission] in 1817 contained a thousand converts, who were housed in small huts around the mission; but at present only two hundred and sixty remain—some have been sent, it is true, to the new mission of San Francisco Solano, but sickness and death have dealt with an unsparing hand among the others. The huts of the absentees, at the time of our visit, had all fallen to decay and presented heaps of filth and rubbish; while the remaining inmates of the mission were in as miserable a condition as it was possible to conceive and were entirely regardless of their own comfort. Their hovels scarcely afforded any protection against the weather and were black with smoke. Some of the Indians were sleeping on the greasy floor; others were grinding baked acorns into cakes, which constitute a large portion of their food. So little attention indeed had been paid even to health that in one hut there was a quarter of beef suspended opposite a window in a very offensive and unwholesome state, but its owners were too indolent to throw it out.[15]

## A Group Abandoned

Starting in 1826, fifteen thousand Indians were released from the missions.[16] The changes brought by a confused and inefficient Mexican government spelled disaster for the mission Indians. After living and working under the Franciscan missionaries all their lives, far removed from the tribal kinship and survival practices of their ancestors, they were no longer prepared for life outside that structured environment.

The Indians of the missions had no claim to land, facilities, or water. They were supposed to receive land grants from the missions where they had lived and worked, but this rarely happened. Only a few pieces of land were given to Indians or retired soldiers as rewards for service.[17]

Missionized Indians were left with few options. It was futile to remain at the missions and get the lands promised them by law. Some went to work for new landowners at Mexican pueblos and ranchos or crowded into the towns looking for work; others fled into the valley or to their ancestral lands. Areas like these had already been destroyed by disease and warfare. In some cases independent pre-mission communities remained and were available for settlement. Once the Spanish Franciscans were exiled from California, the Salinan people left Mission San Miguel for their ancestral homelands throughout the central coast.

Some missionized Indians retreated to smaller settlements in isolated rural areas and reverted to hunting and gathering. Others engaged in trade with other tribes, trappers, and traders. Indians with usable skills engaged in small-scale farming and animal husbandry. Ranch labor was still needed for vineyards and orchards, irrigation, sheep herding, shearing, and livestock raising. Indians herded and slaughtered cattle, preserved hides, rendered tallow, and took care of the ranches' domestic chores. They lived at ranches or migrated to them seasonally.

California's Indians continued to suffer discrimination. They were an under-class, treated as slaves by civil administrators and ranch owners. Sometimes they were captured and put to work as farm labor on the growing number of private ranches.[18] Late in the mission period and after, some Indians were employed as ranch hands and cowboys. Although compensated in land or wages, they were also forced to work against their will, making them completely dependent on their employers for wages, clothing, shelter, and food.

Many California Indians were unemployed, and social problems such as alcoholism, violence, and vagrancy increased. Disease and alcoholism were common in settlements such as Los Angeles and San Diego. By the mid-1830s stock raiding was commonplace as Indians and other residents resorted to stealing livestock and supplies for basic survival.[19] Cattle and horse raids were carried out in central California by runaway Indians, valley tribes, American trappers, Anglo-Americans, and assorted criminals,[20] exemplifying the free-for-all society that existed during the transition from Mexican to American rule in California, even before the influx of gold seekers.

Alexander Forbes, an English writer and traveler, noted in 1839 the long-term effects of the missions on Indian cultures:

> [They] transformed the aborigines of a beautiful country from free savages; into pusillanimous, superstitious slaves, they have taken from them the enjoyment of the natural productions of a delicious country, and ministered to them the bare necessaries of life, and that on the condition of being bondsmen forever. Is there anyone who can suppose, that those men who formerly wandered in their native wilds, "free as the wind on their mountains," were not happier than the wretched herds of human animals which are now penned in the missionary folds? . . . They are made to assist in the toil which those improvements bring along with them, but for this toil they have no reward: for them there are no hopes! Can anyone of a well constituted mind approve of this transformation, or reflect on it without sorrow?[21]

## Legislation That Meant Well

At the beginning of the nineteenth century the treatment of Indians became a popular topic on both sides of the Atlantic. The liberal movement in Spain and New Spain (soon to be Mexico), which promoted the ideal of equal rights for all men, gained force. Legislation favoring Indians began to trickle out of Spain. In 1810 California Indians were freed from paying tribute and were included in a decree giving equal rights to all natives in Spain and the Americas.[22] In 1811 they were allowed (by law only) to raise any crop or conduct any profession on equal terms with other men.

Spain's constitution of 1812, extended to New Spain and other colonies, declared Indians to be both Spaniards and citizens. By decree that same year, Indians were granted land of their own, and in 1813 punishment of Indians by whipping was made illegal.[23] This legislation reflected a greater Spanish interest in the particulars of Indian life in the Americas. Some anticlerical voices in New Spain's government had begun to protest against what they saw as excess and the selfish motives of mission leadership. The money taken back to Mexico by missionaries, the failure of missions to convert into parishes, and the exploitation of the Indians by the missionaries and soldiers were all questioned. In response, the colonial government of New Spain sent a questionnaire to the missionaries of California, asking about their views of the Indians and the Indians' moral and political state. The stage was set for Mexico's eventual secularization of the California missions.

However, good intentions did not guarantee enforcement of the new laws; eventually the mission Indian population was left to fend for itself. Indians found themselves being moved out of their ancestral lands by missionaries and colonists, and continued to be afflicted by the thousands with foreign illnesses brought in by settlers from Europe and America's East Coast. After becoming accustomed to an institutional existence in the mission system, they were thrown out without recourse or opportunity to support themselves, overlooked by both the Mexican and American governments. It was not until the early 1890s that the American federal government took much interest in their welfare.

American author and activist Helen Hunt Jackson dedicated her life to exposing the poverty and discrimination of California's Indians, wanting to help secure Indian land rights and legal protection. To this end, she wrote numerous letters, editorials, and field reports, as well as several novels. In 1881 she published a nonfiction work, *Century of Dishonor,* on the history of American federal

Indian policy, and in 1883, as a member of a federal commission, she coauthored a report to the Commissioner of Indian Affairs on the poor status of Indians from the mission system. Ultimately, her most effective work was her immensely popular novel *Ramona* (1884), a story of a californio family and a San Diego County Indian tribe devastated by the changes brought by secularization and American rule of California. Ramona, a half-Indian and half-European girl, is caught in the middle of these social forces. *Ramona,* while written in the romantic, elaborate style of the period, rang true in some ways and garnered widespread, although belated, interest in the deteriorating missions, the California Indians, and mission history. Because of its style, today's critics view the novel as more of a tribute to the pastoral stereotype of California's Hispanic and Indian past.

At the time of Jackson's report, the term "mission Indians" referred to tribes in the three southernmost counties of California, mainly from the vicinities of Missions San Luis Rey and San Diego. Jackson wrote that mission Indians at that time lived in small and isolated villages, on reservations, and on the outskirts of white settlements, "where they live like gypsies . . . eking out a miserable existence by days' work." She also made note of the mission culture that remained: "On the occasional visits of the priest, they gather and hold services in the half-ruined adobe chapel built by them in the days of their prosperity." Jackson compared the current poverty of mission Indians with what she assumed to have been their lifestyle under the missions: "These same Indians had built all the houses in the country, planted all the fields and vineyards . . . they filled all the laborious occupations known to civilized society. . . . In 1830 there were in the twenty-one missions in California some 20,000 or 30,000 Indians living comfortable and industrious lives under the control of the Franciscan fathers."[24]

The report went on to describe the failed policies of secularization:

These provisions were in no case faithfully carried out. The administration of the Missions' vast estates and property was too great a temptation for human nature, especially in a time of revolution and misrule. The history of the thirteen years between the passing of the secularization act and the conquest of California is a record of shameful fraud and pillage, of which the Indians were the most hapless victims. Instead of being permitted each one to work, maintain, and govern himself without dependence on anyone, as they had been promised, their rights to their plots of land were in the majority of cases ignored; they were forced to labor on mission lands like slaves; in many instances they were hired out in gangs to cruel masters. From these cruelties and oppressions they fled by hundreds, returning to their old wilderness homes.[25]

Several organizations championed Jackson's activist message, and in 1891 the American government passed the Act for the Relief of the Mission Indians in the State of California. This legislation, along with providing legal protection to mission Indians, eventually resulted in an allotment of thirteen permanent mission Indian reservations, including one named Ramona in honor of Jackson's novel.

Like Jackson, novelist and anthropologist Constance Goddard DuBois took an ardent interest in the mission Indians. From 1897 to 1907 she investigated the myths, legends, and religion of the Luiseño and Diegueño Indians, and she wrote extensively on their culture. Calling them "nominally Christian,"[26] she noted the persistence of cosmogony, origin myths, and adolescent ceremonies. She also described what remained of Catholic culture:

> I am no Catholic, but I have seldom seen anything more sincere than the devout religious worship among these poor neglected people. They cherish this as their most precious possession, the only good gift left to them of those their early fathers gave them. . . .
>
> . . . In places where no priest has visited for many, many years they still have their little church, an adobe hut, or one of boughs; the altar is decked with a few poor ornaments, and candles set in tin cans for candlesticks. The men enter with uncovered heads, and the people kneel on the earth floor. One better educated than the rest with a better memory for the Spanish liturgy will say the prayers, and the people make the responses as reverently as at a cathedral service.[27]

DuBois made contact with the Bureau of Indian Affairs and anthropologists interested in Indian history. She wrote that "few [Indians] have been so neglected by the government" as the mission Indians of southern California, and concluded, "When Mrs. Jackson made her report, seventeen years ago, it would have been still comparatively easy to have righted most of the evil."[28]

Alfred Kroeber was another anthropologist who brought attention to the Indian situation in California. But for many Indian generations the help that he, Jackson, and DuBois offered came too late to make a difference.

# 16

## The Cycle of Decline and Restoration

A late-nineteenth-century historian made a prediction about the future of the California missions: "Some missions have crumbled to dust, others have been transformed in attempts to preserve them, and all will soon be forgotten in the new civilization of steam, and electricity; of free institutions and universal intelligence."[1] Were it not for the Californians who began to take interest in the restoration and rebuilding of the state's missions, this prediction might have come true.

The attention brought by historical preservationists to restoring and rebuilding the original missions led to the popular discovery of the utility and romantic appearance of mission architecture for new construction. The architectural movement known as mission revival flourished in California during the last quarter of the nineteenth century. Architects applied Spanish colonial features, borrowed from still-standing missions and presidios, to hotels and residences. By 1900 the style appeared in civic buildings, train stations, churches, and other urban buildings in California. Today the mission style is pervasive in California and other regions of the United States settled by the Spanish.

Unlike the stately colonial buildings of the eastern seaboard, constructed from wood and, later, durable brick in an area relatively free of devastating earthquakes and floods, adobe mission buildings have been disadvantaged from the start. These historic sites today are only suggestions of what they once were, combining some original structures and artifacts with restored and reconstructed buildings.

Earthquakes, fire, and floods are still constant reminders that mission and other historic buildings are fragile and vulnerable to the elements. Regular maintenance and funds are required to maintain these symbols of the past. Some missions receive more funding and interest than others, and thus the level and quality of restoration vary from mission to mission. The location, size, and wealth of a parish and its historical importance are all factors in a mission's popularity. Those missions in more serious financial straits are likely to be understaffed and to suffer from theft and vandalism, crumbling walls, cracked floors, and rusting of artifacts.

Across the board, efforts have been made to include earthquake-safe designs. In some buildings the structural maintenance is suitable, but the visual effect is suggestive of a theme park rather than an authentic reproduction. Examples include unnaturally shiny exterior walls with bumps underneath the whitewash that are too regular to look like human handiwork. Other buildings and sites are restored only in part, with other sections still works in progress.

Without popular awareness of mission history and its significance to California history, colonial history, and the forces that shaped the culture of California before it became part of the United States, no mission or presidio is immune to deterioration.


### The American Period and the Silent Years


War between Mexico and the United States started in 1846 and ended in 1848. Settlers seized Sonoma in 1846, and naval forces occupied Monterey and San Diego. The California Battalion and the U.S. Marines moved into Los Angeles in August of that same year. Mexican forces surrendered in 1847, and the coast between Sonoma and San Diego came under American military jurisdiction.

Once the coastal zone was occupied, the American military had the power to oversee and defend ranches, pueblos, and mission lands. Settlers and californios were recruited to help in the effort.[2] California became the thirty-first state under President Fillmore in September 1850.

During the first decades of the American period, mission buildings served the convenience of soldiers, travelers, and businessmen. Between 1852 and 1862, American troops occupied many of the buildings and used what remained of the land resources, felling the orchards for fuel. The military added a second story to Mission San Diego, and horses were quartered on the ground level. After the troops left, the building continued for years to be used as a stable.[3]

During the period of collapse following secularization and the change in government, the missions in more remote areas were used less frequently. Many valuable objects were looted, especially anything that could be used in the construction of new buildings: doors, hinges, timbers, floor tiles, and roofing tiles. Anything that remained became crumbled and overgrown with vines and weeds.

In the 1850s and 1860s the Federal Land Commission reviewed mission property rights, and some lands and buildings were returned to the Catholic Church by acts of Congress. The church was usually able to regain the mission quadrangle or the land where the original structures stood.[4]

Outbuildings not used for religious functions were often leased to stores, bars, or inns. A pig farm operated at Mission San Fernando, and Father Serra's chapel at San Juan Capistrano became a hay barn. Some owners removed the roofs to pay debts or to cover new haciendas, townhouses, and railroad stations. The Catholic Church obtained title to the Mission San Antonio property in 1858. Its last priest, a Mexican Indian named Father Dorotéo Ambrís, gathered several dozen Indian families to work on the mission, plant a garden, and keep religious ceremonies going.[5]

During his tour of the missions in 1857, Henry Miller noticed that the original churches and connected buildings were often all that remained of once-busy multi-ethnic communities. He described the old adobe church of Mission San José as "a large building, poorly decorated, and surrounded by ruins of a once massive edifice."[6] At Mission San Francisco de Asís, the dwellings of missionaries had been converted into "public houses." In the 1840s Indians had deserted the mission of San Francisco de Asís and its cemetery, which served the growing nearby town of Yerba Buena. In the 1850s the land was used privately for wine grape cultivation and cattle raising. During the gold rush period a large mining camp sprang up nearby, and gold seekers squatted on the land. A plank toll road connected the city of San Francisco with the former mission. Fandangos were held at the mission, along with saloons, bullfights, and animal racing.[7]

Mission San Luis Obispo, Miller wrote, had "metamorphosed into a little town . . . of about one hundred and fifty houses, inhabited principally by natives and Mexicans; however quite a number of Americans have also settled here. . . . I took a ramble about the mission buildings, some of which are in ruins, though once remarkably strong, constructed of rock joined with a very hard cement. . . . Of the once magnificent orchards are only a great number of olive trees remaining."[8]

After 1834, every square foot of land belonging to Mission San Carlos was sold, stopping at the church walls. The church bought a small strip of land next to the church so that the priests and congregation could enter without trespassing.[9] A small parish remained there for as long as the building remained usable.

Not all missions fared as well. Carmel's church roof gave way first, exposing the adobe walls to the rain. After the roof beams rotted and collapsed under the weight of the tiles, services were held in the sacristy through the nineteenth century. Miller saw mostly ruins:

> With [the] exception of a few adobe houses, the whole is a heap of ruins. The old church, which must have been a handsome one, is partly fallen in; however, the front with two strong belfreys [sic] over it is in good condition. There are still remaining two cracked bells, which are said to contain a considerable quantity of silver composition, as most of the ancient Spanish bells have. The inside of the church has some fresco painting and inscriptions from the Bible. Some saints, as large as life, cut in wood and painted, are still to be seen; they are riddled with bullets, having served as a target.[10]

Mission Soledad (Mission Nuestra Señora Dolorosísima de la Soledad [Our Lady of Solitude]), as its name suggests, knew mostly bad luck during its years of operation, and it became a symbol of the mission system's downslide. Founded south of Mission San Carlos in 1791, Soledad was a small mission with just seven hundred Cholon Costanoan people. Though it had a fifteen-mile aqueduct and twenty thousand irrigated acres of land, severe weather combined with heavy drought, a barren landscape, and epidemics beset the residents. As a result, some thirty missionaries came and went, none staying very long.[11] Miller encountered only "a great heap of ruins," except for one building and a small church built more recently. He noted that the mission land was owned mainly by the "numerous native family of the Soberanes."[12] Today Soledad remains a pile of ruins.

At Mission San Juan Bautista, smallpox and drought created a ghost town after secularization. During the gold rush it sat on a main highway as a point where stages changed horses. Still, some of its residents remained to live out their lives. One of the last Indians of San Juan Bautista, Doña Ascension Solorzano de Cervantes, was born in 1855. The Smithsonian Institution interviewed her and recorded some of the language and stories of the Indians who had lived there.

Miller wrote that Mission Santa Inés was "built on the edge of a table land. The church, which has a belfry with two bells in it, is in a good condition together with the adjoining house; the rest is a great heap of ruins. The walls of some of the buildings are of an enormous thickness, built of adobe."

Mission Buenaventura was settled by about seventy or eighty houses occupied by "natives and Mexicans."[13] At Mission San Gabriel,

> A little village, the haunt of some notorious cattle thieves; murders are committed here frequently, often as the result of the *fandangos* which are given almost every night, breaking up in a row and a stabbing or shooting affair. . . . The Mission Church is well preserved, being built in a peculiar style different from the other churches. The other buildings, however, are dilapidated or totally in ruins. Near the buildings are very long hedges of prickly pears, now full of ripe fruit, which have been planted by the missionaries round their vineyards and orchards.[14]

Some of the missions Miller saw appeared in relatively good condition. Of Mission Santa Barbara he wrote, "Judging from the remaining buildings and ruins, this Mission must have been a very flourishing one. A church with two belfreys [*sic*] and the adjoining house, in which the officiating priests live, are in a good state of preservation and built of well cemented rock. A bathing house, large basin and aqueduct rest of arches of the same material."[15]

During the American period Mission La Purísima was occupied by highwaymen before becoming home to a succession of families. Miller described it as "built between some sand hills on one side of a large green valley partly covered with timber. The mission buildings are completely hid to the traveler till coming very near it and by turning round a hill." He declared the remaining building, which housed the church, "remarkably strong and one of the best preserved ones which I met throughout California. There is still an orchard, a small vineyard remaining. . . . [O]n the thirteen hundred square miles which was claimed by this Mission was at one time such an abundance of cattle that it was allowed to any to kill the same for their hide and tallow; the meat was left to the wolves and buzzards."[16] By 1890 only roofless walls remained, used as a stable and sheepfold.[17] Everything else was a pile of rubble and trash. La Purísima was later completely restored, and today it stands as one of the most authentic reproductions of a California mission.

Near the village of San Jacinto, in the valley of the same name, Miller continued to the mission of San Luis Rey, another mission that had weathered the elements better than most. San Luis Rey had been the largest of all the missions, its buildings spanning six acres. Miller saw "two very old Indian women, one of which was blind, being both dressed in the most primitive California Indian style, being a short petticoat or rather apron, composed of rabbit skins sewed together and bark of a tree." They spoke Spanish. The buildings had "a very imposing appearance," and in the middle was "a mound of earth, with a low wall round it, out of which grows a beautiful black pepper tree, full of fruit." The mission interior was in fine condition and "near the buildings are a few huts in which live some Indian families."[18]

Carrying only some pears he picked at San Luis Rey, Miller pushed on to San Juan Capistrano, the last mission on his journey, whose buildings were "a few miles from the beach in a beautiful green valley which is well watered by a small stream. . . . The principal feature of this Mission is the ruins of a once magnificent church, built very solid of rock and cement, with arched roofs."[19] Amid gardens and stately ruins, surrounding a patio, stood an arcade, which had outlasted the buildings it bordered. Its pillars and arches were made from cut stone and baked brick and were able to resist the rain that dissolved adobe brick.[20]

The least prosperous of all the missions, Santa Cruz suffered greatly from the effects of earthquakes and a tidal wave that swept six hundred feet inland, carrying away a large quantity of mission tile.[21] The church, weakened by several earthquakes, collapsed in 1857. Today a modern replica stands, one-third the size of the original structure.

Between February and October 1857 Miller completed his sketches and journal, having accomplished his "intention of visiting the ancient Catholic missions which form a cordon from San Francisco to San Diego, comprising all the fertile valleys of the southern counties not distant from the seashore."[22]

### Restoration and an Uncertain Future

After several decades of decay and changing of hands, isolated efforts at renovation began. In 1870 the rector of Monterey parish, Father Casanova, raised funds to renovate the Carmel church. During the work, the remains of Serra and three other Franciscans, Fathers Crespí, Lopez, and Lasuén, were discovered. The graves were resealed and marked, and today Father Serra's crypt sits below the church.[23]

Father Anthony Ubach, who started an Indian school at Mission San Diego in the 1880s, worked there for twenty years to help restore mission objects and increase interest in restoration.[24] Citizens of San Diego organized the San Diego

Architectural remains of San Juan Capistrano. Courtesy of Jim Graves, Mission San Juan Capistrano.

Historical Society in 1880 out of concern for the preservation of historic landmarks such as Presidio Hill, the spot where Junípero Serra and Captain Gaspar de Portolá set up the first mission and presidio in Alta California. Many considered this site as important to American history as Plymouth Rock. A member of the board of directors of the Historical Society wrote in 1929: "San Diego has a double claim to fame. It was alike the first point of discovery on the Pacific Coast of what is now the United States [Cabrillo in 1542], and the first place of settlement as well [Serra and Portolá in 1769]."[25] Today Serra Museum in Presidio Park stands as a monument to the history of California and San Diego.

After the publication of Helen Hunt Jackson's novel *Ramona* in 1884, the missions started to pique the public's interest. Artists took notice of the missions and the picturesque aspects of their decay. Paintings and photos of the remains helped revive public interest. Edwin Deakin's oil paintings of the mission are displayed at the Los Angeles County Museum and Santa Barbara Historical Association. Mission Sonoma houses watercolors by Chris Jorgensen.

As tourists trickled into the ruins, various individuals worked to drum up interest in rebuilding some of the missions. Los Angeles journalist and benefactor Charles Fletcher Lummis wrote and lectured on the subject of California's Hispanic heritage. Launching a program to save the missions as representative institutions of California's past, he raised enough funds to prevent the total collapse of several missions. In 1895 Lummis created the California Landmarks Club, a

Mission San Juan Capistrano in 1876. Courtesy of Jim Graves, Mission San Juan Capistrano.

preservation association. He commented, "Unless our intelligence shall awaken at once, there will remain of these noble piles nothing but few indeterminable heaps of adobe. We shall deserve and shall have the contempt of all thoughtful people if we suffer our noble missions to fail."

Mission San Juan Capistrano captured the fancy of an ill American priest passing through in the late nineteenth century. Vandals had carried away stone and tile, and the church had been used as a lumber warehouse and place for garbage. Nonetheless, the ailing priest moved in to join the peacocks that had been living there since colonial times. When he had regained his strength, he began to look through the old records of the mission's aqueduct, reservoirs, cisterns, and irrigating systems. The Landmarks Club of Los Angeles had preserved some of the walls in 1895 and reroofed several hundred feet of the cloisters,[26] but there was still much to be done. He and volunteers worked to clean up the mission, and the bishop granted him charge of the location. He collected money to restore the mission and reinforce some of the buildings, and spent nearly twenty-five years there working at the church. Through his efforts, the garden with its pool was recreated and Castilian roses and gray olive trees were planted.

In 1900 the San Diego branch of the Landmarks Club was able to match a $500 offer from Lummis to start restoration work on Mission San Diego. Of the original complex, little beyond a fragment of the monastery still stood. By 1892 half of the church was caved in, and roof tiles had been taken to cover houses in Old Town.[27] A historian who visited in 1874 noticed, "It is not only badly ruined

Remodeling of Mission San Juan Capistrano. © iStockphoto.com/Sara Skiba.

but has been repaired at different times for different purposes so that the original plan is somewhat hard to make out."[28] No description was found of the original church interior of Mission San Diego, so craftsmen tried to blend the style with the remaining façade. Church records did show the altar was built from wooden planks brought by sea captains from their ships. Today's adobe church is a replica of the one dedicated in 1813. An Army engineer's 1853 sketch, a valuable resource for preservationists in the next century, is the only record of the mission's bell tower.

About twenty years after the restoration of Mission San Diego began, George Marston, an early member of the Landmarks Club, began restoration of San Diego's Presidio Park. The Junípero Serra Museum was built on Presidio Hill in 1929. The doorway's floor tiles come from the original flume that ran from the mission dam to Mission San Diego.[29] Below the mission, in the park, is a large cross made from floor tiles excavated from the ruins of the original San Diego presidio, near where Serra first raised a cross to celebrate mass.

By 1900 tourism to the missions had increased, as evidenced by railroad schedules and guidebooks from that time.[30] In 1903 the California Historic Landmarks League began guiding trips to Mission San Antonio, and a Franciscan father and mission historian, Zephyrin Engelhardt, returned to say mass there. Preservation and restoration of San Antonio began with Franciscan funding that helped fill in walls and rebuild some of the main structures. Newspaper magnate William

Bell ringer's steps, La Purísima.

Randolph Hearst bought mission property at Mission San Antonio and earmarked money for restoration. The oldest surviving woman of San Antonio, a descendant of missionized Indians whose family had worked there, helped in the restoration. In 1917 the Catholic Church renovated the rough-hewn beams, which were giving way. Steel beams were placed in grooves outside the adobe walls. Spaces were filled and covered with cement, and steel trestles were added to support the heavy roof. Cement was used to repair broken or missing floor tiles, interior walls were redecorated, wood rail was replaced by wrought iron, and new glass was placed in windows.[31]

The first missionaries at Mission San Carlos left no written plan of the original mission structures, placed around an irregularly shaped quadrangle. Exten-

Main church interior, La Purísima.

sive archeological and documentary work helped gather a picture of the whole for restoration, using drawings such as one from George Vancouver's British expedition in 1792. Interestingly, excavators in 1921 discovered old foundation lines in the surrounding bean fields.[32] Today Mission San Carlos stands as one of the most authentic restorations, famous for both its beauty and history. A popular tourist destination and active parish, the mission is an example of what all these historic sites could be with the right interest and funds. In 1961 the Vatican honored the church as a basilica due to its historic significance as the headquarters of the mission chain and its connection with Serra's work.

Mission La Purísima has been called "the most extensive historic reconstruction in the West." The ambitious project began in 1934 with cooperation between state, county, and federal agencies, with the Civilian Conservation Corps working under the National Park Service. All its buildings have been rebuilt and furnished to match their appearance in 1820, during the mission's active years. The colors of the main buildings were matched to plaster remnants among the ruins. Men created adobe bricks in the traditional manner, by stomping to compress the materials. Hundreds of thousands of bricks, along with roof and floor tiles, had to be moved and stacked. The foundations of the majordomo quarters, tallow workshop, barracks, weaving rooms, nunnery, reservoirs, fountains, and first church were uncovered.

Campanario, Mission San Miguel.

Plantings and livestock are still of authentic breeds and varieties. Burros, churro sheep, longhorn cattle, horses, and goats graze the mission property. The area around the mission buildings is filled with olive trees, date palms, and authentic roses, herbs, and fruits. The original aqueduct and pond are maintained, and the *lavanderías* (pools for washing clothes) have also been completely restored. The complex remains today as a thriving example of restoration and public participation.

Abandoned for decades after their transfer to secular hands, most of the missions spent more years decaying and crumbling to the ground than they had spent as living institutions. Thanks to the revival of interest in the late nineteenth century, various efforts have helped to restore and maintain them as historic sites for the public's enjoyment and education. Continuing archaeological excavation also helps contribute to a public understanding of mission history. Seven of the twenty-one missions are national historic landmarks, and two are run by the state park system. Since 1998 the California Missions Foundation has been "dedicated to the preservation, protection, and maintenance of California's twenty-one historic missions."[33]

Such achievements in restoration are examples for countless more projects that are needed to maintain these sites for future generations. Many buildings in the chain are still beset by deep structural problems that require costly repair. For adequate fire protection, water from the nearby town or city needs to be accessible. Seismic retrofitting is now required by the state of California. Termites and wood beetles creep into the wood behind the altars, threatening structural integrity. Walls need to be stabilized and the adobe needs to be sealed and waterproofed. Stucco walls are cracked, and some of the fresco paintings, like those of Mission San Miguel, are peeling and fading. Leaky palisade roofs soften the brick walkways into mud. But with more funding and interest, these symbols of an integral part of California history can endure.

# 17

## Conclusion

The Colonial Rosary

The chain of California missions started by Spain and completed by Mexico spans 650 miles of California's coastline, from San Diego to Sonoma. By the end of Hispanic rule of California in 1846, there were four presidios, seven pueblos, and twenty-one missions. Serra's plan for a mission chain to bolster Spain's presence in the region was finally realized not during the Spanish period, but with the building of the last mission during the Mexican period. Father Serra's overriding goal was "the great increase in Christianity, and an almost uninterrupted chain of missions covering an immense stretch of country. . . . [T]he religious who have to come would be saved the hardship of the ocean trip; the journey would be by land, and they would sleep at least every third day in a mission."[1]

The settlements overlapped geographic zones and incorporated peoples from both the interior and the coast. The mission zone, which included the coastal ranges of central and southern California, San Francisco Bay, and the western edge of the San Joaquin and Sacramento valleys, was the region from which the missions drew most of their converts. Phases of recruitment began in the vicinities of the first port towns, then, by the end of the first decade of the nine-

Great stone church, San Juan Capistrano. Courtesy of Jim Graves, Mission San Juan Capistrano.

teenth century, farther into coastal lands and to the interior inhabited by Yokuts Indians.[2]

As mission settlements grew into pueblos and towns, *el Camino Reál* evolved from a narrow dirt trail to a populated and often-traveled road. The road originated at Mexico City and stretched two hundred miles east to Veracruz, two hundred miles southwest to Acapulco, and around a thousand miles north to south from Santa Fe to Central America. The route's extension into California was relatively new and uncharted. In the first days the missionaries traveled amid threats from hostile Indians, wild animals, and rockslides. To help travelers find their way between the missions, missionaries marked the path by carving a cross on especially large trees along the way. On the trail between Mission San Antonio and Mission San Luis Obispo, workers in recent times chopped a tree and discovered a cross in one of the tree layers.[3]

After California was annexed to the United States, the road was used primarily as a north-south stagecoach route until the railroads replaced the coach. El Camino Reál became Highway 101 and Interstate 5, which link northern and southern California today. A small, dusty path remains at La Purísima as a remnant of the original road.

El Camino Reál eventually connected all the missions like beads on a rosary. The missions were built in two clusters, each growing outward from Missions San Diego and Monterey (San Carlos), one from the north and one from the south. These first two missions, both at ports, established the basis for further expansion in California and frontier settlement of the coast. These sites were chosen for very specific reasons. Predicted Henry Miller: "At some future time San Diego cannot fail to become a place of great importance. Its position near the Mexican frontier and its splendid harbor and other advantages justify this prediction."[4] As a crossroads between California and Mexico today, San Diego was surely the ideal location for the first mission of Alta California.

These two flagship missions created a prototype for the next three. The next settlements linked the two ports and became Missions San Gabriel, San Luis Obispo, and San Antonio. When the missions could depend on their own output of food and shelter supplies, shipments from Mexico became less essential. At this point later missions were built slightly farther inland in the coastal valleys. San Francisco Bay, discovered north of Monterey, was recognized for its importance as a strategic port, and plans were made for two more mission settlements nearby: San Francisco in 1776 and Santa Clara in 1777. Serra also hoped to set up three Channel missions, protected by a presidio, to bridge the gap between San Luis Obispo and San Gabriel. He lived to oversee only the founding of Mission Buenaventura.

After several years during which the existing missions became self-supporting, the Santa Barbara Channel missions were set up in 1782–87, closing the gap between the northern and southern missions. Two more beads were added to the rosary in 1791: Missions Santa Cruz and Soledad. San José, San Juan Bautista, San Fernando Rey, and San Miguel followed in the summer of 1797 under Father Lasuén with the help of supplies from existing missions.[5] San Miguel filled in a long gap between San Antonio and San Luis Obispo. The last two southern missions completed the network between San Francisco and San Diego. The seventeen missions already founded were at their height of productivity.

San Luis Rey and Santa Inés were founded between 1798 and 1804. San Luis Rey closed the geographic gap between San Diego and San Juan Capistrano in 1798. San Luis Rey grew into California's and perhaps New Spain's most prosperous mission.[6] The two northernmost missions, San Francisco Solano and San Rafael, completed the rosary between 1817 and 1823. Within a few years all mission lands and holdings were secularized and passed into private ownership.

Benches in the courtyard, San Juan Capistrano. Courtesy of Jim Graves, Mission San Juan Capistrano.

The California missions were founded during the dying years of the Spanish empire, soon before many of Spain's colonies gained independence. The mission system of California was a kind of last-gasp effort to stretch Spain's colonial grasp over the globe. It was also an anachronism on the continent of the American colonies. Monterey became capital of Alta California in 1790, the same year Philadelphia became capital of the United States. The missions reached their historical peak during the second decade of the nineteenth century. Even after Mexico took possession of the missions from Spain, the missions as institutions continued to influence frontier culture and society, as did relations between missionized Indians, Indians outside the missions, settlers, and civil administrators.

The transfer of land ownership from public to private replaced the fundamental social and economic institutions of California—the mission and the rancho. Secularization and the influx of settlers from Mexico, and later America, ensured that the missions and presidios would be replaced by large cattle ranches and a variety of commercial ventures.

Today, the missions vary in their degree of restoration, size of parishes, affiliation with religious orders, and extent of tourism. Four of the original twenty-one missions are in Franciscan hands: Missions San Antonio de Padua, San Miguel, Santa Barbara, and San Luis Rey. All missions except La Purísima and San Francisco de Asís are administered by local Catholic dioceses. They represent three different religious orders.

The mission chain grew rapidly and declined just as quickly. The period of mission prosperity—sixty-five years—was short relative to the march of history, but left lasting cultural and historical elements in California for future generations. California's missions continue today as sites for educational study, tours, archaeological digs, worship, and tourism. The dramatic mission tale reflects social and cultural trends within every chapter. Missionaries founded their settlements under arduous and sometimes tragic conditions, creating a massive impact on native cultures. During times of prosperity, the missions bustled with activity and production. Sweeping epidemics of diseases brought by European and Mexican settlers almost destroyed Indian populations. The Mexican and American periods were also times of betrayal, as the missions sat ignored and forgotten. The gradual return of interest in restoration efforts has slowly brought the missions to their present state. The future of the missions is still waiting to be told.

# Appendix A

Research and Resources

The history of California and Mexico is an amalgam of the activities of Indian, Spanish, and Anglo people. Differences in communication, language, and methods of passing down history have made for a variety of sources and viewpoints. Years before rancherías became connected with the missions and pueblos multiplied in population, the time of early contact between native peoples and the missionaries and soldiers was primarily documented through the eyes of the Europeans. Explorers and missionaries left abundant records about the Indian cultures they encountered and the experience of converting and educating them. Anyone traveling with colonial funding was expected to document his travels and report back to his superiors in the home country, and many of them left their impressions in journals. The mission libraries were full of documents and letters, essential pieces of communication between the frontier and the complex bureaucracy at home. As president of the missions, Serra was required to maintain correspondence with colleagues in the Franciscan Order at the College of San Fernando as well as government officials of New Spain.

These records, however, tend to show only one perspective, one that assumes cultural superiority over a population often viewed as ignorant, childish, and barbaric. As a result, bias toward and misrepresentation of Indian cultures in California are common in histories of Spain's presence in the Americas.

Immediately after Gálvez assumed leadership of the province, he ordered the Franciscans to gather a census of both the white and native populations, along with specific information on the customs and habits of the Indians. Shipments of goods to Alta California by sea and by land were documented in detail, with listings of items, amounts, and other specifications.

Because the number of conversions was an accepted measure of success, the missionaries tried to keep careful records of mission populations. Prior to 1783, mainly baptisms and deaths were recorded; population counts were estimates only. Further, not all Indians were accounted for in mission documents, as a certain number were always absent through escape or desertion. The reports and documentation we have from that period are also fragmentary. At the California Archives, some original correspondence between Spanish and Mexican authorities in California, Mexico City, and Spain was destroyed in San Francisco's 1906 earthquake and fire.

Infant mortality was not evident in the mission records as all infants were baptized; child deaths were recorded in the same way regardless of the child's age. Age distribution information is not wholly available either, due to incomplete, lost, or destroyed baptismal and burial registers.

Father Francisco Palóu was a close colleague of Father Serra. His written history of California, *Las noticias de nueva California* (Historical Memoirs of New California), was the first general history of the founding of Alta California. Palóu's eyewitness observations and journals were extensive, offering perspectives on the Franciscan regime in Baja California, the Portola-Serra expedition, pioneer years in Alta California, and his lifelong association with Serra. From this relationship Palóu also produced a detailed biography of Serra's life and accomplishments, *La vida del padre Serra*. His writings were respected by his religious peers and provide ample primary material for study of the missionary perspective and the first colonial days of California.

Narratives and journals survive from the mission period, such as letters and diaries written by visitors to the California coast from Russia, Great Britain, and the United States. In *Two Years before the Mast,* Richard Henry Dana tells of his own experience as a young sailor on an American merchant ship back in the time of the missions. He describes trading for cattle hides with the missions up and down the California coast. Other narratives are available that detail encounters between mission Indians and fur traders and explorers between 1820 and the gold rush. George Vancouver, a British naval captain who sailed on two of explorer James Cook's voyages, was commissioned in 1791 to survey and claim sections of the California coast and to visit California settlements. His ship, the *Discovery,* reached San Francisco Bay in 1792. Vancouver compiled his experiences and observations into *A Voyage of Discovery* (1798), in which he described California's landscape and the early life of the missions and presidios. Vancouver was unimpressed by the appearance of Spanish colonial settlement in California, a viewpoint probably colored both by comparison to English settlements along the Atlantic and by Britain's rivalry with Spain as a colonial power. Vancouver's visits to California produced nautical charts, maps, and surveys later used by ship captains, along with descriptions of the territory and a critique of the Spanish military defenses.

The Bancroft Library of the University of California, Berkeley, is the single best resource for primary documents. Toward the end of the nineteenth century Hubert Howe Bancroft gathered personal testimony from former mission

Indians, and his assistants copied and analyzed mission records. Many of these documents used were later destroyed in the 1906 earthquake. Those that are still available present important fragments of mission history.

Other attempts were also made in the late nineteenth century to collect oral reports from living missionized Indians and their descendants. Nevertheless, the Indian perspective on first contact is subject to conjecture. Many generalizations have been made about missionized Indian cultures and behaviors. Unfortunately, histories written until the 1960s substantially overlooked the depth and color of Indian history. The Indians were truly active agents in their environment and central players in the history of colonial California. Research in ethnology, archaeology, and anthropology will shed more light on the Indian perspective and present a more balanced picture of their role in California's history. Another subject of study is how contact between Europeans and Indians was represented in Indian art and symbolism.

# Appendix B

## Additional Resources Pertaining to California Indians

### *Indian Canyon*

Indian Canyon is a worldwide nerve center for California's Indian tribes and indigenous peoples. The property of an Ohlone family descended from Missions Soledad and San Juan Bautista, Indian Canyon is the only Costanoan territory in the greater San Francisco Bay area that survived European and American settlement as a native land. These ancestral lands of the Ohlone people were occupied by California Indians from ancient times to the present. Stone tools, mortars, human remains (including a pre-mission burial site), and oral tradition all confirm the presence of humans in the canyon since well before the first missionaries arrived in California. The canyon was protected by swamps and land treacherous to pass; surveyors' maps labeled it as inaccessible and useless for settlement. As a result, it was avoided by missionaries, settlers, and prospectors and served as a place of refuge during the mission period and after.

Ann Marie Sayers, the current owner, continues the traditions of her mother, Elena, a full-blooded Mutsun Ohlone Indian. Elena sang Mutsun songs and kept traditions alive in the canyon and surrounding communities. She once told her daughter, "As long as songs are sung and the ceremonies are continued, the earth will go on."

Says Russell Imrie, manager of the canyon Web site, "When California was absorbed into the Union in 1850, California natives became a class of homeless at a stroke." The canyon remained occupied by a small community of Mutsun Indians, one of them Ann Marie's grandfather, who received a federal allotment. Ann Marie worked patiently for eight years to obtain a second piece of land.

In the canyon, students from the University of California Santa Cruz have created an ethnobotanical display of Costanoan culture and life crafts like basketry, fire starters, cordage, and housing. Along the creek are sweat lodges and tule houses. The canyon community is in the process of constructing an Indian community center that will host numerous ceremonies and communal events.

The Ohlone/Costanoan-Esselen Nation currently has 450 registered members who trace their ancestry back to thirteen original families at the Carmel and Soledad missions as well as villages under Spanish and Mexican control during the mission period. These groups were differentiated by two common distinct languages, Esselen and Rumsen. The Ohlone lived throughout California, and the Mutsun are a particular language subset of the Ohlone group that lived in the canyon region.

http://www.indiancanyon.org
http://www.indiancanyonvillage.org

### The Alliance of California Tribes (ACT)

The Alliance of California Tribes is a statewide organization of sovereign tribes who work together to strengthen tribal governments in the areas of education, protection of tribal cultural and religious interests, and economic development.

http://www.allianceofcatribes.org/

### The Bureau of Indian Affairs

The Bureau of Indian Affairs administers and manages 55.7 million acres of land held in trust by the United States for American Indians and Indian tribes.

http://www.doi.gov/bureau-indian-affairs.html

### The California Indian Museum and Cultural Center in Santa Rosa, California

http://www.cimcc.indian.com/

### The Center for California Native Nations

http://www.americanindian.ucr.edu/strategic_vision/nations.html

## *Web Sites of California Tribes with Mission Descendants*

### Costanoan and Ohlone Links

http://www.ontalink.com/native_americans/costanoan.html
http://www.costanoanrumsen.org/
http://www.islaiscreek.com/ohlonehistorybackground.html
http://www.muwekma.org/
http://www.esselennation.com/

### "Chumash Indian Life" at the Santa Barbara Museum of History and Culture

http://www.sbnature.org/research/anthro/chumash/

### Esselen Tribe of Monterey County

http://www.esselen.com/

### The Gabrieleño-Tongva Tribal Council of San Gabriel

http://www.tongva.com/

### Juaneño Indian Sites

http://www.indiancenter.org/juaneno.html
http://www.juaneno.com/

### Kumeyaay Indian Site

http://www.kumeyaay.com/

### Luiseño Indian Sites

http://www.lajollaindians.com/
http://www.soboba-nsn.gov/

### Salinan Cultural Preservation Association

http://www.pelicannetwork.net/salinan.htm

## Resources for Study of California Missions

### The California Missions Foundation

The California Missions Foundation is dedicated to the preservation, protection, and maintenance of California's missions.

http://www.missionsofcalifornia.org/

### The California Mission Studies Organization

The California Mission Studies Organization exists for the study and preservation of California's missions, presidios, pueblos, and ranchos, along with the state's Native American, Hispanic, and early American past.

http://www.ca-missions.org/

### California Missions

Comprehensive annotated links to Web sites related to the California missions.

http://www.ca-missions.org/links.html

### The San Diego Historical Society

http://www.sandiegohistory.org/

### Monterey County Historical Society

http://users.dedot.com/mchs/

## Mission Web Sites and Home Pages

### Mission La Purísima

http://www.lapurisimamission.org/

### Mission San Buenaventura

http://www.sanbuenaventuramission.org/

## Mission San Carlos

http://www.carmelmission.org/

## Mission San Fernando

http://www.californiamissions.com/cahistory/sanfernando.html

## Mission San Francisco (Dolores)

http://www.californiamissions.com/cahistory/dolores.html

## Mission San Francisco de Solano

http://www.californiamissions.com/cahistory/solano.html

## Mission San Diego

http://www.missionsandiego.com/

## Mission San Gabriel

http://www.sangabrielmission.org/

## Mission San José

http://www.msjc.org/

## Mission San Juan Bautista

http://www.oldmission-sjb.org/

## Mission San Juan Capistrano

http://www.missionsjc.com/

## Mission San Luis Obispo

http://www.missionsanluisobispo.org/

## Mission San Luis Rey

http://www.sanluisrey.org/

## Mission San Miguel

http://www.missionsanmiguel.com/

## Mission San Rafael

http://www.californiamissions.com/cahistory/sanrafael.html

## Mission Santa Barbara

http://www.sbmission.org/

## Mission Santa Clara

http://www.scu.edu/visitors/mission/

## Mission Santa Cruz

http://www.geocities.com/missionbell/

## Mission Santa Inés

http://www.missionsantaines.org/

## Mission Soledad

http://users.dedot.com/mchs/missionsol.html

# Notes

## Introduction

1. Steven W. Hackel, "Land, Labor, and Production: The Colonial Economy of Spanish and Mexican California," in *Contested Eden: California before the Gold Rush,* ed. Ramón Gutiérrez and Richard J. Orsi (Berkeley: University of California Press, 1998), 122.

2. George Harwood Phillips, *Indians and Intruders in Central California, 1769–1849,* The Civilization of the American Indian (Norman: University of Oklahoma Press, 1993), 157.

3. Interview, Ruben G. Mendoza, Director, Institute for Archaeological Science, Technology and Visualization, Social and Behavioral Sciences, California State University Monterey Bay.

4. Interview, Philip Laverty, tribal anthropologist/ethnohistorian, Ohlone/Costanoan-Esselen Nation, California.

5. Harry W. Crosby, *Antigua California: Mission and Colony on the Peninsular Frontier, 1697–1768* (Albuquerque: University of New Mexico Press, 1994), xv.

## Chapter 1

1. Philip Fradkin, *The Seven States of California: A Natural and Human History* (New York: Henry Holt, 1995), 3.

2. Edward D. Castillo, "The Impact of Euro-American Exploration and Settlement," in *California,* ed. Robert F. Heizer, vol. 8 of *Handbook of North American Indians,* ed. William C. Sturtevant (Washington, DC: Smithsonian Institution, 1978), 99.

3. Alfred L. Kroeber, "The Food Problem in California," in *The California Indians: A Source Book,* 2nd ed., ed. Robert F. Heizer and Mary Anne Whipple (Berkeley: University of California Press, 1971), 266.

4. George Harwood Phillips, *Indians and Intruders in Central California, 1769–1849,* The Civilization of the American Indian (Norman: University of Oklahoma Press, 1993), 22.

5. James R. Mills, *San Diego: Where California Began,* 5th ed. (San Diego: San Diego Historical Society, 1985), part I. On-line at http://www.sandiegohistory.org/books/wcb/wcb1.htm.

6. Albert L. Hurtado, *Intimate Frontiers: Sex, Gender, and Culture in Old California* (Albuquerque: University of New Mexico Press, 1999), 3, 4.

7. Pablo Tac, "Indian Life and Customs at Mission San Luis Rey: A Record of California Mission Life," in *Ethnology of the Alta California Indians,* vol. 2, *Postcontact,* ed. Lowell John Bean and Sylvia Brakke, Spanish Borderlands Sourcebooks 4 (New York: Garland, 1991), 148.

8. Alfred L. Kroeber, *Handbook of the Indians of California* (Washington, DC: Smithsonian Institution, 1925; St. Clair Shores, MI: Scholarly Press, 1972), 2:810.

9. Joshua Paddison, ed., *A World Transformed: Firsthand Accounts of California before the Gold Rush* (Berkeley: Heyday Books, 1999), 194.

10. Robert F. Heizer, "Mythology: Regional Patterns and History of Research," in Heizer, *California,* 654.

11. Kroeber, *Handbook,* 2:624.

12. Mills, *San Diego,* part I.

13. Father Antonio Péyri, in *A Mission Record of the California Indians,* trans. Alfred L. Kroeber, University of California Publications in American Archaeology and Ethnology (Berkeley: University of California Press, 1908). On-line at http://www.notfrisco.com/almanac/kroeber01/ (accessed November 14, 2003).

14. James A. Sandos, "Christianization among the Chumash: An Ethnohistoric Perspective," *Indian Quarterly* 15, no. 1 (1991): 5.

15. Heizer, "Mythology," 656.

16. Elizabeth Roberts and Elias Amidon, *Earth Prayers from Around the World: 365 Prayers, Poems, and Invocations for Honoring the Earth* (San Francisco: HarperSanFrancisco, 1991), 146.

### Chapter 2

1. Iris H. W. Engstrand, "Seekers of the Northern Mystery: European Exploration of California and the Pacific," in *Contested Eden: California before the Gold Rush,* ed. Ramón Gutiérrez and Richard J. Orsi (Berkeley: University of California Press, 1998), 80.

2. Herbert E. Bolton, "The Mission as Frontier Institution in the Spanish-American Colonies," *American Historical Review* 23, no. 1 (1917): 43.

3. Norris Hundley, "Hispanic Water Rights," in *Green versus Gold: Sources in California's Environmental History,* ed. Carolyn Merchant (Washington, DC: Island Press, 1998), 9.

4. J. H. Elliott, ed., *The Spanish World: Civilization and Empire* (New York: Harry N. Abrams, 1991), 76.

5. Ibid., 42.

6. Woodrow Borah, *New Spain's Century of Depression,* Ibero-Americana 35 (Berkeley: University of California Press, 1951), 1.

7. Harry W. Crosby, *Antigua California: Mission and Colony on the Peninsular Frontier, 1697–1768* (Albuquerque: University of New Mexico Press, 1994), 6.

8. Woodrow Borah, "The California Mission," in *Ethnology of the Alta California Indians,* vol. 2, *Postcontact,* ed. Lowell John Bean and Sylvia Brakke, Spanish Borderlands Sourcebooks 4 (New York: Garland, 1991), 7.

9. Crosby, *Antigua California,* 20, 373.

10. Carlos Fuentes, *The Buried Mirror: Reflections on Spain and the New World* (Boston: Houghton Mifflin, 1992), 211.

11. C. Alan Hutchinson, *Frontier Settlement in Mexican California: The Híjar-Padrés Colony and Its Origins, 1769–1835* (New Haven: Yale University Press, 1969), 48.

12. Charles Edward Chapman, *The Founding of Spanish California: The Northwestward Expansion of New Spain, 1687–1783* (New York: Macmillan, 1916; New York: Octagon Books, 1973), 105.

13. Crosby, *Antigua California,* 4.

14. Dora Beale Polk, *The Island of California: A History of the Myth* (Spokane, WA: Arthur H. Clark, 1991), 326.

15. Crosby, *Antigua California,* 28, 31.

16. Ignacio del Río Chávez, "Utopia in Baja California: The Dreams of José de Gálvez," trans. Arturo Jiménez-Vera, *Journal of San Diego History* 18, no. 4 (1972). On-line at http://www.sandiegohistory.org/journal/72fall/utopia.htm.

17. Crosby, *Antigua California,* 374.

18. Hubert Howe Bancroft, *History of California,* vol. 1 (San Francisco: History Co., 1884), 111.

19. Crosby, *Antigua California,* 389.

20. Engstrand, "Seekers," 87.

21. Crosby, *Antigua California,* 5.

22. Bancroft, *History,* 112.

23. Crosby, *Antigua California,* 5.

24. Engstrand, "Seekers," 87.

25. Erick D. Langer and Robert H. Jackson, "Colonial and Republican Missions Compared: The Cases of Alta California and Southeastern Bolivia," *Comparative Studies in Society and History* 30, no. 2 (1988): 290.

26. Borah, "California Mission," 6.

27. Eric Beerman, "The Viceroy Marquis de Croix: A Biographical Sketch," *Journal of San Diego History* 25, no. 1 (1979). On-line at http://www.sandiegohistory.org/journal/79winter/viceroy.htm.

28. (Mrs.) Fremont Older, *California Missions and Their Romances* (New York: Coward-McCann, 1938), 113.

29. Richard F. Pourade, *The History of San Diego,* vol. 1, *The Explorers* (San Diego: Union-Tribune, 1960). On-line at http://sandiegohistory.org/books/pourade/.

*Chapter 3*

1. Harry W. Crosby, *Antigua California: Mission and Colony on the Peninsular Frontier, 1697–1768* (Albuquerque: University of New Mexico Press, 1994), 147.

2. Junípero Serra, *Writings,* ed. and trans. Antonine Tibesar, 4 vols. (Washington, DC: Academy of American Franciscan History, 1955–66), 2:39.

3. Crosby, *Antigua California,* 145.

4. Edwin A. Beilharz, *Felipe de Neve: First Governor of California* (San Francisco: California Historical Society, 1971), 125.

5. Frances Rand Smith, "The Spanish Missions of California," *Hispania* 7, no. 4 (1924): 243, 246.

6. Bill Mason, "The Garrisons of San Diego Presidio: 1770–1794," *Journal of San Diego History* 24, no. 3 (1978). On-line at http://www.sandiegohistory.org/journal/78fall/garrisons.htm.

7. Serra, *Writings,* 2:39.

8. Iris H. W. Engstrand, *Serra's San Diego* (San Diego: San Diego Historical Society, 1982). On-line at http://sandiegohistory.org/index.html.

9. Dorothy Krell, ed., *The California Missions: A Pictorial History* (Menlo Park, CA: Sunset Books, 1979), 42.

10. Charles Edward Chapman, *The Founding of Spanish California: The Northwestward Expansion of New Spain, 1687–1783* (New York: Macmillan, 1916; New York: Octagon Books, 1973), 97.

11. Smith, "Spanish Missions," 243.

12. Crosby, *Antigua California,* 390–91.

13. Erick D. Langer and Robert H. Jackson, "Colonial and Republican Missions Compared: The Cases of Alta California and Southeastern Bolivia," *Comparative Studies in Society and History* 30, no. 2 (1988): 288.

14. Crosby, *Antigua California,* 192.

15. Edward D. Castillo, "The Impact of Euro-American Exploration and Settlement," in *California,* ed. Robert F. Heizer, vol. 8 of *Handbook of North American Indians,* ed. William C. Sturtevant (Washington, DC: Smithsonian Institution, 1978), 101.

16. Serra, *Writings,* 1:217.

17. Ibid., 2:113.

18. Alfred L. Kroeber, *Handbook of the Indians of California* (Washington, DC: Smithsonian Institution, 1925; St. Clair Shores, MI: Scholarly Press, 1972), 2:631.

19. Serra, *Writings,* 1:63.

20. Vicente Santa María, "The First Spanish Entry into San Francisco Bay," in *A World Transformed: Firsthand Accounts of California before the Gold Rush,* ed. Joshua Paddison (Berkeley: Heyday Books, 1999), 28–29.

21. Ibid., 30–31.

22. Ibid., 31–32.

23. Francisco Palóu, "A Spaniard Explores the Southern California Landscape, 1774," in *Green versus Gold: Sources in California's Environmental History,* ed. Carolyn Merchant (Washington, DC: Island Press, 1998), 73.

24. Virginia M. Bouvier, *Women and the Conquest of California, 1542–1840: Codes of Silence* (Tucson: University of Arizona Press, 2001), 49.

25. Serra, *Writings,* 2:141.

26. Pablo Tac, "Indian Life and Customs at Mission San Luis Rey: A Record of California Mission Life," in *Ethnology of the Alta California Indians,* vol. 2, *Postcontact,* ed. Lowell John Bean and Sylvia Brakke, Spanish Borderlands Sourcebooks 4 (New York: Garland, 1991), 149.

27. Lorenzo Asisara, "Narrative of a Mission Indian," in *History of Santa Cruz County, California,* ed. Edward S. Harrison (San Francisco: Pacific Press, 1892), 47.

28. Serra, *Writings,* 1:63, 69.

29. Tac, "Indian Life," 149.

30. Francisco Palóu, "The Founding of the Presidio and Mission of Our Father Saint Francis," *California Historical Society Quarterly* 14, no. 2 (1935): 102–8.

## Chapter 4

1. Francisco Palóu, "The Founding of the Presidio and Mission of Our Father Saint Francis," *California Historical Society Quarterly* 14, no. 2 (1935): 107.

2. (Mrs.) Fremont Older, *California Missions and Their Romances* (New York: Coward-McCann, 1938), 184.

3. Junípero Serra, *Writings,* ed. and trans. Antonine Tibesar, 4 vols. (Washington, DC: Academy of American Franciscan History, 1955–66), 2:225.

4. Pablo Tac, "Indian Life and Customs at Mission San Luis Rey: A Record of California Mission Life," in *Ethnology of the Alta California Indians,* vol. 2, *Postcontact,* ed. Lowell John Bean and Sylvia Brakke, Spanish Borderlands Sourcebooks 4 (New York: Garland, 1991), 149.

5. Ibid.

6. Francisco Palóu, *Historical Memoirs of New California*, ed. Herbert Eugene Bolton, 4 vols. (Berkeley: University of California Press, 1926), 1:28.

7. Serra, *Writings,* 2:279–80.

8. Harry W. Crosby, *Antigua California: Mission and Colony on the Peninsular Frontier, 1697–1768* (Albuquerque: University of New Mexico Press, 1994), 144.

9. Francisco Palóu, "A Spaniard Explores the Southern California Landscape, 1774," in *Green versus Gold: Sources in California's Environmental History,* ed. Carolyn Merchant (Washington, DC: Island Press, 1998), 71.

10. Virginia M. Bouvier, *Women and the Conquest of California, 1542–1840: Codes of Silence* (Tucson: University of Arizona Press, 2001), 90.

11. Thom Davis, "California's Inland Chain of Missions," California Mission Studies Association, http://www.ca-missions.org/davis2.html.

12. Sherburne F. Cook, *Population Trends among the California Mission Indians,* Ibero-Americana 17 (Berkeley: University of California Press, 1940), 19.

13. Older, *California Missions,* 230.

14. Crosby, *Antigua California,* 7.

15. Ibid., 14.

16. Dorothy Krell, ed., *The California Missions: A Pictorial History* (Menlo Park, CA: Sunset Books, 1979), 47.

17. Ibid., 46.

18. Serra, *Writings,* 1:179.

19. Crosby, *Antigua California,* 65.

20. Jean Krase, "Ships and Sherds: Ceramics at the San Diego Presidio," *Journal of San Diego History* 27, no. 2 (1981). On-line at http://www.sandiegohistory .org/journal/81spring/sherds.htm.

21. Edwin A. Beilharz, *Felipe de Neve: First Governor of California* (San Francisco: California Historical Society, 1971), 64.

### *Chapter 5*

1. *Catholic Encyclopedia,* s.v. "Rule of Saint Francis." On-line at http://www
.newadvent.org/cathen/06208a.htm.

2. Eric O'Brien, "The Life of Padre Serra," in *Writings,* by Junípero Serra, ed. and trans. Antonine Tibesar, 4 vols. (Washington, DC: Academy of American Franciscan History, 1955–66), 1:xxxviii–xxxix.

3. Serra, *Writings,* 1:47.

4. Donald Francis Toomey, *The Spell of California's Spanish Colonial Missions* (Santa Fe: Sunstone Press, 2001), 45.

5. O'Brien, "Life," xxxiii.

6. (Mrs.) Fremont Older, *California Missions and Their Romances* (New York: Coward-McCann, 1938), xxii, 24.

7. Hubert Howe Bancroft, *History of California,* vol. 1 (San Francisco: History Co., 1884), 415.

8. O'Brien, "Life," xxvii.

9. Dorothy Krell, ed., *The California Missions: A Pictorial History* (Menlo Park, CA: Sunset Books, 1979), 48.

10. Joshua Paddison, ed., *A World Transformed: Firsthand Accounts of California before the Gold Rush* (Berkeley: Heyday Books, 1999), 61.

11. Toomey, *Spell,* 21.

12. Serra, *Writings,* 2:33, 1:57, 2:5.

13. Fermín Francisco de Lasuén, *Writings,* trans. and ed. Finbar K. Kenneally, 2 vols. (Washington, DC: Academy of American Franciscan History, 1965), 2:137, 202.

14. Serra, *Writings,* 2:41, 61, 73, 79.

15. Pedro Font, "Diary of the Anza Expedition, 1775–1776," in *Font's Complete Diary: A Chronicle of the Founding of San Francisco,* ed. Herbert Eugene Bolton (Berkeley: University of California Press, 1931), 110–12.

16. Serra, *Writings,* 2:167, 111, 117, 137, 139.

17. Nikolai Petrovich Rezanov, "The Rezanov Voyage to Nueva California in 1806," in *A World Transformed: Firsthand Accounts of California before the Gold Rush,* ed. Joshua Paddison (Berkeley: Heyday Books, 1999), 98.

18. Ibid., 109.

19. Alexander Forbes, *California: A History of Upper and Lower California* (London: Smith, Elder, 1839; New York: Arno Press, 1973), 235.

20. Krell, *California Missions,* 53.


## Chapter 6


1. Harry W. Crosby, *Antigua California: Mission and Colony on the Peninsular Frontier, 1697–1768* (Albuquerque: University of New Mexico Press, 1994), 202.

2. Robert F. Heizer and Alan J. Almquist, *The Other Californians: Prejudice and Discrimination under Spain, Mexico, and the United States to 1920* (Berkeley: University of California Press, 1971), 5–6.

3. Virginia M. Bouvier, *Women and the Conquest of California, 1542–1840: Codes of Silence* (Tucson: University of Arizona Press, 2001), 15.

4. Pablo Tac, "Indian Life and Customs at Mission San Luis Rey: A Record of California Mission Life," in *Ethnology of the Alta California Indians,* vol. 2, *Postcontact,* ed. Lowell John Bean and Sylvia Brakke, Spanish Borderlands Sourcebooks 4 (New York: Garland, 1991), 156.

5. Mission San Miguel Web site, http://www.missionsanmiguel.org/tour/page10.html.

6. Charles Edward Chapman, *The Founding of Spanish California: The Northwestward Expansion of New Spain, 1687–1783* (New York: Macmillan, 1916; New York: Octagon Books, 1973), 123.

7. Alfred L. Kroeber, *Handbook of the Indians of California* (Washington, DC: Smithsonian Institution, 1925; St. Clair Shores, MI: Scholarly Press, 1972), 2:712.

8. Sherburne F. Cook, *Population Trends among the California Mission Indians,* Ibero-Americana 17 (Berkeley: University of California Press, 1940), 21.

9. Heizer and Almquist, *Other Californians,* 21.

10. Francisco Palóu, "A Spaniard Explores the Southern California Landscape, 1774," in *Green versus Gold: Sources in California's Environmental History,* ed. Carolyn Merchant (Washington, DC: Island Press, 1998), 67.

11. J. A. Sandos, "Christianization among the Chumash: An Ethnohistoric Perspective," *Indian Quarterly* 15, no. 1 (1991): 209.

12. Fermín Francisco de Lasuén, *Writings,* trans. and ed. Finbar K. Kenneally (Washington, DC: Academy of American Franciscan History, 1965), 1:76.

13. Dorothy Krell, ed., *The California Missions: A Pictorial History* (Menlo Park, CA: Sunset Books, 1979), 58.

14. Crosby, *Antigua California,* 215.

15. Woodrow Borah, "The California Mission," in Bean and Brakke, *Ethnology,* 11.

16. Tac, "Indian Life," 157.

17. Bouvier, *Women,* 157.

18. Crosby, *Antigua California,* 184.

19. Buenaventura Sitjar, *Vocabulary of the Language of San Antonio Mission, California* (New York: Cramoisy Press, 1861; New York: AMS Press, 1970); Felipe Arroyo de la Cuesta, *Grammar of the Mutsun Language* (New York: Cramoisy Press, 1861; New York: AMS Press, 1970); id., *A Vocabulary or Phrase Book of the Mutsun Language of Alta California* (New York: Cramoisy Press, 1862; New York: AMS Press, 1970); Donald Francis Toomey, *The Spell of California's Spanish Colonial Missions* (Santa Fe: Sunstone Press, 2001), 58.

20. Junípero Serra, *Writings,* ed. and trans. Antonine Tibesar, 4 vols. (Washington, DC: Academy of American Franciscan History, 1955–66), 2:89.

21. (Mrs.) Fremont Older, *California Missions and Their Romances* (New York: Coward-McCann, 1938), 77.

22. Guadalupe Vallejo, "Ranch and Mission Days in Alta California," *Century Magazine* 41 (1890): 189–92. On-line at http://www.sfmuseum.org/hist2/rancho.html.

23. Crosby, *Antigua California,* 205.

24. Borah, "California Mission," 11.

25. Bouvier, *Women,* 108.

26. José Señan, "Contestación al Interrogatorio," in Archivo de la Misión de Santa Barbara, Pap. Misc., vol. 7, copied from the Santa Barbara Mission Archives for the Bancroft Library by E. G. Murray in 1877, 27–37.

27. Serra, *Writings,* 2:3.

28. Borah, "California Mission," 10.

29. Tac, "Indian Life," 157.

30. Serra, *Writings,* 2:307, 117.

31. Ibid., 2:131–33.

32. Palóu, "Spaniard," 68.

33. Tac, "Indian Life," 157.

34. Steven W. Hackel, "Land, Labor, and Production: The Colonial Economy of Spanish and Mexican California," in *Contested Eden: California before the Gold*

*Rush,* ed. Ramón Gutiérrez and Richard J. Orsi (Berkeley: University of California Press, 1998), 123.

35. Nikolai Petrovich Rezanov, "The Rezanov Voyage to Nueva California in 1806," in *A World Transformed: Firsthand Accounts of California before the Gold Rush,* ed. Joshua Paddison (Berkeley: Heyday Books, 1999), 117.

36. Hackel, "Land," 125–27.

### Chapter 7

1. Virginia M. Bouvier, *Women and the Conquest of California, 1542–1840: Codes of Silence* (Tucson: University of Arizona Press, 2001), 22, 44.

2. Juan Bautista Anza, "Diario de la Ruta, y Operaciones que Yo el Ynfraescripto Theniente Coronel, y Capitan del Rl. Residio de tubac, en la Provincia, y Governación de Sonora, practicó segunda vez," Horcasitas, October 23, 1775, to June 1, 1776, Mexico, AGN, Prov. Int., vol. 169, exp. 7, fols. 176–81v.

3. Pedro Font, "Diario que formó el P. Pdo. Apco. Fr. Pedro Font Missionero . . . en el viage que hizó á Monterey," Horcasitas, September 29, 1775, to Tubatama, May 11, 1777, John Carter Brown library, Brown University, Providence, RI.

4. Steven W. Hackel, "Land, Labor, and Production: The Colonial Economy of Spanish and Mexican California," in *Contested Eden: California before the Gold Rush,* ed. Ramón Gutiérrez and Richard J. Orsi (Berkeley: University of California Press, 1998), 128.

5. Pedro Fages, *A Historical, Political, and Natural Description of California,* trans. Herbert Ingram Priestley (Berkeley: University of California Press, 1937; Ramona, CA: Ballena Press, 1972), 48.

6. Antonia Castañeda, "Engendering the History of Alta California, 1769–1848: Gender, Sexuality, and the Family," in Gutiérrez and Orsi, *Contested Eden,* 235.

7. Albert L. Hurtado, *Intimate Frontiers: Sex, Gender, and Culture in Old California* (Albuquerque: University of New Mexico Press, 1999), 2, xxiii.

8. Ibid., xxiii.

9. Bouvier, *Women,* 83.

10. Junípero Serra, *Writings,* ed. and trans. Antonine Tibesar, 4 vols. (Washington, DC: Academy of American Franciscan History, 1955–66), 2:203.

11. Guadalupe Vallejo, "Ranch and Mission Days in Alta California," *Century Magazine* 41 (December 1890): 186–87. On-line at http://www.sfmuseum.org/hist2/rancho.html.

12. Robert H. Jackson and Edward Castillo, *Indians, Franciscans, and Spanish Colonization: The Impact of the Mission System on California Indians* (Albuquerque: University of New Mexico Press, 1995), 180.

13. Nikolai Petrovich Rezanov, "The Rezanov Voyage to Nueva California in 1806," in *A World Transformed: Firsthand Accounts of California before the Gold Rush,* ed. Joshua Paddison (Berkeley: Heyday Books, 1999), 108.

14. Irving Berdine Richman, *California under Spain and Mexico: 1535–1847* (Boston: Houghton Mifflin, 1911), 336.

15. Frederick William Beechey, "Narrative of a Voyage to the Pacific and Beering's Strait to Cooperate with the Polar Expeditions, 1825–1828," in Paddison, *World Transformed,* 185–86.

16. Rezanov, "Rezanov Voyage," 108.

17. Eulalia Pérez, "Una vieja y sus recuerdos dictados à la edad avanzada de 139 años," in *Three Memoirs of Mexican California* (Berkeley: Friends of the Bancroft Library, University of California, 1988), 100.

18. Regina Teresa Manocchio, "Tending Communities, Crossing Cultures: Midwives in Nineteenth Century California" (master's thesis, Yale University School of Nursing, 1998), 23–24.

19. Richard Konetzke, "La émigración de mujeres españolas à América durante la época colonial," *Revista Internacional de Sociología* 9 (1945): 129.

20. Castañeda, "Engendering," 239.

21. Serra, *Writings,* 2:149.

22. Bouvier, *Women,* 75.

23. Hubert Howe Bancroft, *History of California,* vol. 1 (San Francisco: History Co., 1884), 605.

24. Harry W. Crosby, *Antigua California: Mission and Colony on the Peninsular Frontier, 1697–1768* (Albuquerque: University of New Mexico Press, 1994), 214.

## Chapter 8

1. Junípero Serra, *Writings,* ed. and trans. Antonine Tibesar, 4 vols. (Washington, DC: Academy of American Franciscan History, 1955–66), 2:151.

2. Michael J. Gonzalez, "'The Child of the Wilderness Weeps for the Father of Our Country': The Indian and the Politics of Church and State in Provincial California," in *Contested Eden: California before the Gold Rush,* ed. Ramón Gutiérrez and Richard J. Orsi (Berkeley: University of California Press, 1998), 158.

3. Edwin A. Beilharz, *Felipe de Neve: First Governor of California* (San Francisco: California Historical Society, 1971), 98.

4. Serra, *Writings,* 2:xv.

5. C. Alan Hutchinson, *Frontier Settlement in Mexican California: The Híjar-Padrés Colony and Its Origins, 1769–1835* (New Haven: Yale University Press, 1969), 62.

6. Antonia Castañeda, "Engendering the History of Alta California, 1769–1848: Gender, Sexuality, and the Family," in Gutiérrez and Orsi, *Contested Eden,* 241.

7. Paul F. Starrs, "California's Grazed Ecosystems," in *Green versus Gold: Sources in California's Environmental History,* ed. Carolyn Merchant (Washington, DC: Island Press, 1998), 202.

8. Virginia M. Bouvier, *Women and the Conquest of California, 1542–1840: Codes of Silence* (Tucson: University of Arizona Press, 2001), 78.

9. Irving Berdine Richman, *California under Spain and Mexico: 1535–1847* (Boston: Houghton Mifflin, 1911), 265; David Hornbeck, *California Patterns: A Geographical and Historical Atlas* (Palo Alto: CA: Mayfield, 1983), 51.

10. Hubert Howe Bancroft, *History of California,* vol. 6 (San Francisco: History Co., 1888), 530.

11. Alexander Forbes, *California: A History of Upper and Lower California* (London: Smith, Elder, 1839; New York: Arno Press, 1973), 206.

12. Hutchinson, *Frontier Settlement,* 61.

13. Donald Francis Toomey, *The Spell of California's Spanish Colonial Missions* (Santa Fe: Sunstone Press, 2001), 67.

14. (Mrs.) Fremont Older, *California Missions and Their Romances* (New York: Coward-McCann, 1938), 59.

15. Steven W. Hackel, "Land, Labor, and Production: The Colonial Economy of Spanish and Mexican California," in Gutiérrez and Orsi, *Contested Eden,* 118.

16. David Hornbeck, "The Past in California's Landscape," California Mission Studies Association, http://www.ca-missions.org/hornbeck.html.

17. George Harwood Phillips, *Indians and Intruders in Central California, 1769–1849,* The Civilization of the American Indian (Norman: University of Oklahoma Press, 1993), 107.

18. Ibid.

19. Robert F. Heizer and Alan J. Almquist, *The Other Californians: Prejudice and Discrimination under Spain, Mexico, and the United States to 1920* (Berkeley: University of California Press, 1971), 18.

20. Harry W. Crosby, *Antigua California: Mission and Colony on the Peninsular Frontier, 1697–1768* (Albuquerque: University of New Mexico Press, 1994), 276.

21. Hubert Howe Bancroft, *History of California,* vol. 1 (San Francisco: History Co., 1884), 602–3.

22. Crosby, *Antigua California,* 393.

23. Charles Edward Chapman, *The Founding of Spanish California: The Northwestward Expansion of New Spain, 1687–1783* (New York: Macmillan, 1916; New York: Octagon Books, 1973), 348.

24. Charles Edward Chapman, *A History of California: The Spanish Period* (New York: Macmillan, 1921), 348.

25. Hubert Howe Bancroft, *History of California,* vol. 2 (San Francisco: History Co., 1885), 392.

26. Guadalupe Vallejo, "Guadalupe Vallejo Recalls the Rancheros, 1890," in Merchant, *Green versus Gold,* 182.

27. Norris Hundley, "Hispanic Water Rights," in Merchant, *Green versus Gold,* 88.

28. Older, *California Missions,* 192, 8.

29. Vallejo, "Guadalupe Vallejo," 182.

30. Guadalupe Vallejo, "Ranch and Mission Days in Alta California," *Century Magazine* 41 (1890): 189–92. On-line at http://www.sfmuseum.org/hist2/rancho.html.

31. Bouvier, *Women,* 75.

32. Woodrow Borah, "The California Mission," in *Ethnology of the Alta California Indians,* vol. 2, *Postcontact,* ed. Lowell John Bean and Sylvia Brakke, Spanish Borderlands Sourcebooks 4 (New York: Garland, 1991), 13.

33. Richman, *California,* 127.

34. Hackel, "Land," 125.

35. Albert L. Hurtado, *Intimate Frontiers: Sex, Gender, and Culture in Old California* (Albuquerque: University of New Mexico Press, 1999), xxvi.

## Chapter 9

1. Pablo Tac, "Indian Life and Customs at Mission San Luis Rey: A Record of California Mission Life," in *Ethnology of the Alta California Indians,* vol. 2, *Postcontact,* ed. Lowell John Bean and Sylvia Brakke, Spanish Borderlands Sourcebooks 4 (New York: Garland, 1991), 156.

2. Harry W. Crosby, *Antigua California: Mission and Colony on the Peninsular Frontier, 1697–1768* (Albuquerque: University of New Mexico Press, 1994), 187.

3. Edwin A. Beilharz, *Felipe de Neve: First Governor of California* (San Francisco: California Historical Society, 1971), 112.

4. Robert L. Schuyler, "Indian-Euro-American Interaction: Archeological Evidence from Non-Indian Sites," in *California,* ed. Robert F. Heizer, vol. 8 of *Handbook of North American Indians,* ed. William C. Sturtevant (Washington, DC: Smithsonian Institution, 1978), 74.

5. Bill Mason, "The Garrisons of San Diego Presidio: 1770–1794," *Journal of San Diego History* 24, no. 3 (1978). On-line at http://www.sandiegohistory.org/journal/78fall/garrisons.htm.

6. Charles Edward Chapman, *The Founding of Spanish California: The Northwestward Expansion of New Spain, 1687–1783* (New York: Macmillan, 1916; New York: Octagon Books, 1973), 319.

7. Alexander Forbes, *California: A History of Upper and Lower California* (London: Smith, Elder, 1839; New York: Arno Press, 1973), 203–4.

8. George Vancouver, "Vancouver in California: 1792–1794," in *A World Transformed: Firsthand Accounts of California before the Gold Rush,* ed. Joshua Paddison (Berkeley: Heyday Books, 1999), 71–76.

9. Hubert Howe Bancroft, *History of California,* vol. 1 (San Francisco: History Co., 1884), 110.

10. Crosby, *Antigua California,* 393.

11. Ibid., 80.

12. Junípero Serra, *Writings,* ed. and trans. Antonine Tibesar, 4 vols. (Washington, DC: Academy of American Franciscan History, 1955–66), 2:xvi.

13. Crosby, *Antigua California,* 393.

14. Leon Campbell, "The First Californios: Presidial Society in Spanish California, 1769–1822," *Journal of the West* 11 (1972): 586.

15. Nikolai Petrovich Rezanov, "The Rezanov Voyage to Nueva California in 1806," in *A World Transformed: Firsthand Accounts of California before the Gold Rush,* ed. Joshua Paddison (Berkeley: Heyday Books, 1999), 107.

16. Sherburne F. Cook, *The Conflict between the California Indian and White Civilization,* vol. 2, *The Physical and Demographic Reaction of the Non-mission Indians in Colonial and Provincial California,* Ibero-Americana 22 (Berkeley: University of California Press, 1943), 29.

17. Dorothy Krell, ed., *The California Missions: A Pictorial History* (Menlo Park, CA: Sunset Books, 1979), 59–60.

18. Serra, *Writings,* 2:149.

19. Crosby, *Antigua California,* 36–37.

20. Joseph Adamo, "Soldados de Cuera," *California Mission Studies Association Newsletter* (August 1986).

21. Beilharz, *Felipe de Neve,* 79.

22. Krell, *California Missions,* 46.

23. Adelbert von Chamisso, "A Voyage around the World with the Romanzov Exploring Expedition in the Years 1805–1808," in Paddison, *World Transformed,* 142.

24. Frederick William Beechey, "Narrative of a Voyage to the Pacific and Beering's Strait to Cooperate with the Polar Expeditions, 1825–1828," in Paddison, *World Transformed,* 177–78.

25. C. Alan Hutchinson, *Frontier Settlement in Mexican California: The Híjar-Padrés Colony and Its Origins, 1769–1835* (New Haven: Yale University Press, 1969), 88–89.

## Chapter 10

1. Dorothy Krell, ed., *The California Missions: A Pictorial History* (Menlo Park, CA: Sunset Books, 1979), 68.

2. Irving Berdine Richman, *California under Spain and Mexico: 1535–1847* (Boston: Houghton Mifflin, 1911), 332.

3. Ibid., 334.

4. Krell, *California Missions,* 33.

5. Hubert Howe Bancroft, *History of California,* vol. 1 (San Francisco: History Co., 1884), 203.

6. Francisco Palóu, "A Spaniard Explores the Southern California Landscape, 1774," in *Green versus Gold: Sources in California's Environmental History,* ed. Carolyn Merchant (Washington, DC: Island Press, 1998), 68.

7. Krell, *California Missions,* 11.

8. Junípero Serra, *Writings,* ed. and trans. Antonine Tibesar, 4 vols. (Washington, DC: Academy of American Franciscan History, 1955–66), 1:181.

9. Virginia M. Bouvier, *Women and the Conquest of California, 1542–1840: Codes of Silence* (Tucson: University of Arizona Press, 2001), 82.

10. Robert L. Schuyler, "Indian-Euro-American Interaction: Archeological Evidence from Non-Indian Sites," in *California,* ed. Robert F. Heizer, vol. 8 of *Handbook of North American Indians,* ed. William C. Sturtevant (Washington, DC: Smithsonian Institution, 1978), 71.

11. Bouvier, *Women,* 82–83.

12. Henry Miller, *Account of a Tour of the California Missions and Towns, 1856* (Santa Barbara, CA: Bellerophon Books, 2000), 12–13.

13. Steven W. Hackel, "Land, Labor, and Production: The Colonial Economy of Spanish and Mexican California," in *Contested Eden: California before the Gold Rush,* ed. Ramón Gutiérrez and Richard J. Orsi (Berkeley: University of California Press, 1998), 121.

14. Krell, *California Missions,* 58.

15. Harry W. Crosby, *Antigua California: Mission and Colony on the Peninsular Frontier, 1697–1768* (Albuquerque: University of New Mexico Press, 1994), 50.

16. Krell, *California Missions,* 68.

17. (Mrs.) Fremont Older, *California Missions and Their Romances* (New York: Coward-McCann, 1938), 114.

18. Ibid., 114–15.

19. Ibid., 130.

20. Mission San Miguel Web site, http://www.missionsanmiguel.org/tour/page16.html.

21. Older, *California Missions,* 82.

22. William Preston, "Serpent in the Garden: Environmental Change in Colonial California," in Gutiérrez and Orsi, *Contested Eden,* 286.

23. Older, *California Missions,* 83.

24. Crosby, *Antigua California,* 84.

25. Edward D. Castillo, "The Impact of Euro-American Exploration and Settlement," in Heizer, *California,* 101.

26. Older, *California Missions,* 187.

27. Crosby, *Antigua California,* 196.

28. Older, *California Missions,* 32, 36.

29. Krell, *California Missions,* 69.

30. James A. Sandos, "Between Crucifix and Lance: Indian and White Relations in California, 1769–1848," in Gutiérrez and Orsi, *Contested Eden,* 208–9.

31. Older, *California Missions,* 230.

32. Mission San Miguel Web site, http://www.missionsanmiguel.org/tour/page13.html.

33. Older, *California Missions,* 96.

34. Krell, *California Missions,* 68.

35. Donald Francis Toomey, *The Spell of California's Spanish Colonial Missions* (Santa Fe: Sunstone Press, 2001), 26.

36. Mission San Miguel Web site, http://www.missionsanmiguel.org/tour/page7.html.

37. Serra, *Writings,* 1:49.

38. Older, *California Missions,* 109.

39. Serra, *Writings,* 1:129, 131.

40. Richman, *California,* 333.

41. Older, *California Missions,* 71.

42. Pablo Tac, "Indian Life and Customs at Mission San Luis Rey: A Record of California Mission Life," in *Ethnology of the Alta California Indians,* vol. 2, *Postcontact,* ed. Lowell John Bean and Sylvia Brakke, Spanish Borderlands Sourcebooks 4 (New York: Garland, 1991), 151.

43. Bancroft, *History,* 203.

44. Bruce Walter Barton, *A Tree at the Center of the World: A Story of the California Missions* (Santa Barbara: Ross-Erikson, 1980), 2.

45. Older, *California Missions,* 265.

46. Guadalupe Vallejo, "Guadalupe Vallejo Recalls the Rancheros, 1890," in Merchant, *Green versus Gold,* 183.

47. Tac, "Indian Life," 152.

48. Norman Neuerburg, "A Visit to the Home of California's First Martyr," *Journal of San Diego History* 35, no. 1 (1989): 22–27. On-line at http://www.sandiegohistory.org/journal/89winter/visit.htm.

49. Older, *California Missions,* 82–83.

## Chapter 11

1. Alexander Forbes, *California: A History of Upper and Lower California* (London: Smith, Elder, 1839; New York: Arno Press, 1973), 210.

2. Frederick William Beechey, "Narrative of a Voyage to the Pacific and Beering's Strait to Cooperate with the Polar Expeditions, 1825–1828," in *A World Transformed: Firsthand Accounts of California before the Gold Rush,* ed. Joshua Paddison (Berkeley: Heyday Books, 1999), 177–78.

3. California Missions Foundation, *The Missions of Alta California: An Educational Guide* (San Francisco: California Missions Foundation, 2000).

4. Steven W. Hackel, "Land, Labor, and Production: The Colonial Economy of Spanish and Mexican California," in *Contested Eden: California before the Gold Rush,* ed. Ramón Gutiérrez and Richard J. Orsi (Berkeley: University of California Press, 1998), 116.

5. Dorothy Krell, ed., *The California Missions: A Pictorial History* (Menlo Park, CA: Sunset Books, 1979), 56.

6. Julia G. Costello, "Variability among the Alta California Missions: The Economics of Agricultural Production," in *Columbian Consequences,* ed. David Hurst Thomas, vol. 1, *Archaeological and Historical Perspectives on the Spanish Borderlands West* (Washington, DC: Smithsonian Institution Press, 1989), 435–49.

7. Forbes, *California,* 228.

8. Donald Francis Toomey, *The Spell of California's Spanish Colonial Missions* (Santa Fe: Sunstone Press, 2001), 64.

9. Krell, *California Missions,* 316.

10. (Mrs.) Fremont Older, *California Missions and Their Romances* (New York: Coward-McCann, 1938), 1.

11. Beechey, "Narrative," 197.

12. Nikolai Petrovich Rezanov, "The Rezanov Voyage to Nueva California in 1806," in Paddison, *World Transformed,* 117.

13. William Preston, "Serpent in the Garden: Environmental Change in Colonial California," in Gutiérrez and Orsi, *Contested Eden,* 277.

14. Forbes, *California,* 272.

15. Krell, *California Missions,* 316.

16. Irving Berdine Richman, *California under Spain and Mexico: 1535–1847* (Boston: Houghton Mifflin, 1911), 208.

17. Pablo Tac, "Indian Life and Customs at Mission San Luis Rey: A Record of California Mission Life," in *Ethnology of the Alta California Indians,* vol. 2, *Postcontact,* ed. Lowell John Bean and Sylvia Brakke, Spanish Borderlands Sourcebooks 4 (New York: Garland, 1991), 153.

18. Guadalupe Vallejo, "Ranch and Mission Days in Alta California," *Century Magazine* 41 (1890): 189–92. On-line at http://www.sfmuseum.org/hist2/rancho.html.

19. Robert L. Schuyler, "Indian-Euro-American Interaction: Archeological Evidence from Non-Indian Sites," in *California,* ed. Robert F. Heizer, vol. 8 of *Handbook of North American Indians,* ed. William C. Sturtevant (Washington, DC: Smithsonian Institution, 1978), 70.

20. Rezanov, "Rezanov Voyage," 110.

21. Junípero Serra, *Writings,* ed. and trans. Antonine Tibesar, 4 vols. (Washington, DC: Academy of American Franciscan History, 1955–66), 2:45, 109, 295.

22. Preston, "Serpent," 285.

23. Guadalupe Vallejo, "Guadalupe Vallejo Recalls the Rancheros, 1890," in *Green versus Gold: Sources in California's Environmental History,* ed. Carolyn Merchant (Washington, DC: Island Press, 1998), 183.

24. Older, *California Missions,* 14.

25. Serra, *Writings,* 2:305.

26. Henry Miller, *Account of a Tour of the California Missions and Towns, 1856* (Santa Barbara, CA: Bellerophon, 2000), 42, 45.

27. Older, *California Missions,* 96, 115, 146.

28. George Harwood Phillips, "Indians in Los Angeles, 1781–1875: Economic Integration, Social Disintegration," in *Ethnology of the Alta California Indians,* vol. 2, *Postcontact,* ed. Lowell John Bean and Sylvia Brakke, Spanish Borderlands Sourcebooks 4 (New York: Garland, 1991), 364.

29. Mission San Miguel Web site, http://www.missionsanmiguel.org/tour/page2.html.

30. Ibid., http://www.missionsanmiguel.org/tour/page15.html.

31. Older, *California Missions,* 57.

32. California Missions Foundation, *The Missions of Alta California: An Educational Guide* (San Francisco: California Missions Foundation, 2000).

33. Tac, "Indian Life," 152.

34. Vallejo, "Ranch and Mission."

35. Serra, *Writings,* 2:71.

36. Rezanov, "Rezanov Voyage," 109.

37. Serra, *Writings,* 2:47.

38. Rezanov, "Rezanov Voyage," 109.

39. Harry W. Crosby, *Antigua California: Mission and Colony on the Peninsular Frontier, 1697–1768* (Albuquerque: University of New Mexico Press, 1994), 218.

40. Mission San Miguel Web site, http://www.missionsanmiguel.org/tour/page9.html.

41. Ann Lucy Wiener Stodder, *Mechanisms and Trends in the Decline of the Costanoan Indian Population of Central California: Nutrition and Health in Pre-contact California and Mission Period Environments* (Salinas, CA: Coyote Press, 1986), 33.

42. Hackel, "Land," 124.

43. José Señán, "Contestación al Interrogatorio," in Archivo de la Misión de Santa Barbara, Pap. Misc., vol. 7, copied from the Santa Barbara Mission Archives for the Hubert Howe Bancroft Library by E. G. Murray in 1877, 12.

44. Edward D. Castillo, "The Impact of Euro-American Exploration and Settlement," in Heizer, *California,* 101.

45. Virginia M. Bouvier, *Women and the Conquest of California, 1542–1840: Codes of Silence* (Tucson: University of Arizona Press, 2001), 162.

46. Serra, *Writings,* 2:79.

47. Preston, "Serpent," 264.

48. M. Kat Anderson, Michael G. Barbour, and Valerie Whitworth, "A World of Balance and Plenty: Land, Plants, Animals, and Humans in a Pre-European California," in Gutiérrez and Orsi, *Contested Eden, 33.*

49. Ibid., 12.

50. Preston, "Serpent," 268–9, 273.

51. Paul F. Starrs, "California's Grazed Ecosystems," in Merchant, *Green versus Gold,* 12.

52. Anderson et al., "World of Balance," 23.

## Chapter 12

1. Woodrow Borah, "The California Mission," in *Ethnology of the Alta California Indians,* vol. 2, *Postcontact,* ed. Lowell John Bean and Sylvia Brakke, Spanish Borderlands Sourcebooks 4 (New York: Garland, 1991), 11.

2. Junípero Serra, *Writings,* ed. and trans. Antonine Tibesar, 4 vols. (Washington, DC: Academy of American Franciscan History, 1955–66), 2:145.

3. Steven W. Hackel, "Land, Labor, and Production: The Colonial Economy of Spanish and Mexican California," in *Contested Eden: California before the Gold Rush,* ed. Ramón Gutiérrez and Richard J. Orsi (Berkeley: University of California Press, 1998), 120.

4. Pablo Tac, "Indian Life and Customs at Mission San Luis Rey: A Record of California Mission Life," in Bean and Brakke, *Ethnology,* 157.

5. Hackel, "Land," 123.

6. Tac, "Indian Life," 156.

7. Constance Goddard DuBois, *The Condition of the Mission Indians of Southern California* (Philadelphia: Office of the Indian Rights Association, 1901), 438.

8. (Mrs.) Fremont Older, *California Missions and Their Romances* (New York: Coward-McCann, 1938), 12.

9. Nikolai Petrovich Rezanov, "The Rezanov Voyage to Nueva California in 1806," in *A World Transformed: Firsthand Accounts of California before the Gold Rush,* ed. Joshua Paddison (Berkeley: Heyday Books, 1999), 108.

10. Mission San Miguel Web site, http://www.missionsanmiguel.org/tour/page15.html.

11. Rezanov, "Rezanov Voyage," 109 and 116.

12. Guadalupe Vallejo, "Guadalupe Vallejo Recalls the Rancheros, 1890," in *Green versus Gold: Sources in California's Environmental History,* ed. Carolyn Merchant (Washington, DC: Island Press, 1998), 184–85.

13. Paddison, *World Transformed,* 199.

14. Dorothy Krell, ed., *The California Missions: A Pictorial History* (Menlo Park, CA: Sunset Books, 1979), 56.

15. Hackel, "Land," 115, 119.

16. Irving Berdine Richman, *California under Spain and Mexico: 1535–1847* (Boston: Houghton Mifflin, 1911), 185.

17. Crosby, *Antigua California,* 218.

18. Hackel, "Land," 116.

19. William Preston, "Serpent in the Garden: Environmental Change in Colonial California," in Gutiérrez and Orsi, *Contested Eden,* 275.

20. Hackel, "Land," 117.

21. Krell, *California Missions,* 56.

22. Michael J. Gonzalez, "'The Child of the Wilderness Weeps for the Father of Our Country': The Indian and the Politics of Church and State in Provincial California," in Gutiérrez and Orsi, *Contested Eden,* 157.

23. Vallejo, "Guadalupe Vallejo," 182–83.

24. Doyce B. Nunis, "Alta California's Trojan Horse: Foreign Immigration," in Gutiérrez and Orsi, *Contested Eden,* 299.

25. Hackel, "Land," 129.

26. George Harwood Phillips, "Indians in Los Angeles, 1781–1875: Economic Integration, Social Disintegration," in Bean and Brakke, *Ethnology,* 365.

27. Paddison, *World Transformed,* 200.

## Chapter 13

1. Pablo Tac, "Indian Life and Customs at Mission San Luis Rey: A Record of California Mission Life," in *Ethnology of the Alta California Indians,* vol. 2, *Postcontact,* ed. Lowell John Bean and Sylvia Brakke, Spanish Borderlands Sourcebooks 4 (New York: Garland, 1991), 142.

2. Ibid., 155.

3. George Harwood Phillips, *Indians and Intruders in Central California, 1769–1849,* The Civilization of the American Indian (Norman: University of Oklahoma Press, 1993), 98.

4. William J. Wallace, "Northern Valley Yokuts," in *California*, ed. Robert F. Heizer, vol. 8 of *Handbook of North American Indians*, ed. William C. Sturtevant (Washington, DC: Smithsonian Institution, 1978), 468.

5. Alfred L. Kroeber, *Handbook of the Indians of California* (Washington, DC: Smithsonian Institution, 1925; St. Clair Shores, MI: Scholarly Press, 1972), 551.

6. Campbell Grant, "Chumash: Introduction," in Heizer, *California*, 506.

7. Junípero Serra, *Writings*, ed. and trans. Antonine Tibesar, 4 vols. (Washington, DC: Academy of American Franciscan History, 1955–66), 2:349.

8. Grant, "Chumash: Introduction," 505.

9. Schuyler, "Indian-Euro-American Interaction," 69.

10. Bruce Walter Barton, *A Tree at the Center of the World: A Story of the California Missions* (Santa Barbara: Ross-Erikson, 1980), xi.

11. Donald Francis Toomey, *The Spell of California's Spanish Colonial Missions* (Santa Fe: Sunstone Press, 2001), 47.

12. Hubert Howe Bancroft, *History of California*, vol. 1 (San Francisco: History Co., 1886), 614.

13. Douglas Monroy, "The Creation and Re-creation of Californio Society," in *Contested Eden: California before the Gold Rush*, ed. Ramón Gutiérrez and Richard J. Orsi (Berkeley: University of California Press, 1998), 190; Michael J. Gonzalez, "'The Child of the Wilderness Weeps for the Father of Our Country': The Indian and the Politics of Church and State in Provincial California," in Gutiérrez and Orsi, *Contested Eden*, 152.

14. Phillips, "Indians in Los Angeles," 365.

15. Ibid., 361.

16. Sherburne F. Cook, *Population Trends among the California Mission Indians*, Ibero-Americana 17 (Berkeley: University of California Press, 1940), 1, 2, 10, 13, 5, 27.

17. Nikolai Petrovich Rezanov, "The Rezanov Voyage to Nueva California in 1806," in *A World Transformed: Firsthand Accounts of California before the Gold Rush*, ed. Joshua Paddison (Berkeley: Heyday Books, 1999), 117.

18. Bean and Brakke, *Ethnology*.

19. Sherburne F. Cook, *The Conflict between the California Indian and White Civilization*, vol. 2, *The Physical and Demographic Reaction of the Non-mission Indians in Colonial and Provincial California*, Ibero-Americana 22 (Berkeley: University of California Press, 1943), 21.

20. Harry W. Crosby, *Antigua California: Mission and Colony on the Peninsular Frontier, 1697–1768* (Albuquerque: University of New Mexico Press, 1994), 38.

21. James A. Sandos, "Christianization among the Chumash: An Ethno-historic Perspective," *Indian Quarterly* 15, no. 1 (1991): 7, 201.

22. James A. Sandos, "Between Crucifix and Lance: Indian and White Relations in California, 1769–1848," in Gutiérrez and Orsi, *Contested Eden*, 21.

23. Tac, "Indian Life, 155.

24. Virginia M. Bouvier, *Women and the Conquest of California, 1542–1840: Codes of Silence* (Tucson: University of Arizona Press, 2001), 84.

25. Edward D. Castillo, "The Impact of Euro-American Exploration and Settlement," in Heizer, *California*, 101.

26. (Mrs.) Fremont Older, *California Missions and Their Romances* (New York: Coward-McCann, 1938), 148.

27. Dorothy Krell, ed., *The California Missions: A Pictorial History* (Menlo Park, CA: Sunset Books, 1979), 59.

28. Antonia Castañeda, "Engendering the History of Alta California, 1769–1848: Gender, Sexuality, and the Family," in Gutiérrez and Orsi, *Contested Eden*, 237.

29. Sandos, "Christianization," 211.

30. Richard L. Carrico, "Sociopolitical Aspects of the 1775 Revolt at Mission San Diego de Alcala: an Ethnohistorical Approach," *Journal of San Diego History* 43, no. 3 (1997): 142–57. On-line at http://sandiegohistory.org/journal/97summer/missionrevolt.htm.

31. Serra, *Writings*, 2:405.

32. Bancroft, *History*, 254.

33. California Archives (Manuscripts, Bancroft Library): Ortega, 1–5; State Papers, Sacramento, ix, 72; Provincial State Papers, 1, 228–32.

34. Francis J. Weber, "The Death of Fray Luís Jayme: Two Hundredth Anniversary," *Journal of San Diego History* 22, no. 1 (1976). On-line at http://www.sandiegohistory.org/journal/76winter/jayme.htm.

35. Serra, *Writings*, 2:417.

36. Edward Kemble, "Yerba Buena, 1846," in *Indians and Intruders in Central California, 1769–1849*, by George Harwood Phillips, The Civilization of the American Indian (Norman: University of Oklahoma Press, 1993), 163.

37. Guadalupe Vallejo, "Ranch and Mission Days in Alta California," *Century Magazine* 41 (1890): 189–92. On-line at http://www.sfmuseum.org/hist2/rancho.html.

38. Bouvier, *Women*, 99.

39. Steven W. Hackel, "Land, Labor, and Production: The Colonial Economy of Spanish and Mexican California," in Gutiérrez and Orsi, *Contested Eden,* 128.

40. Frederick William Beechey, "Narrative of a Voyage to the Pacific and Beering's Strait to Cooperate with the Polar Expeditions, 1825–1828," in Paddison, *World Transformed,* 188.

41. Rezanov, "Rezanov Voyage," 117–18.

## Chapter 14

1. Steven W. Hackel, "Land, Labor, and Production: The Colonial Economy of Spanish and Mexican California," in *Contested Eden: California before the Gold Rush,* ed. Ramón Gutiérrez and Richard J. Orsi (Berkeley: University of California Press, 1998), 130.

2. Manuel Servin, "The Secularization of the California Missions: A Reappraisal," in *Ethnology of the Alta California Indians,* vol. 2, *Postcontact,* ed. Lowell John Bean and Sylvia Brakke, Spanish Borderlands Sourcebooks 4 (New York: Garland, 1991), 121.

3. Letter from Fray José Señán to Viceroy the Marqués de Branciforte, Mexico, May 14, 1796, in *The Letters of José Señán, O.F.M., Mission San Buenaventura, 1796–1823,* trans. Paul D. Nathan, ed. Lesley Byrd Simpson (San Francisco: Ventura County Historical Society, 1962), 5.

4. Frederick William Beechey, "Narrative of a Voyage to the Pacific and Beering's Strait to Cooperate with the Polar Expeditions, 1825–1828," in *A World Transformed: Firsthand Accounts of California before the Gold Rush,* ed. Joshua Paddison (Berkeley: Heyday Books, 1999), 181.

5. Ibid., 177–78.

6. Michael J. Gonzalez, "'The Child of the Wilderness Weeps for the Father of Our Country': The Indian and the Politics of Church and State in Provincial California," in Gutiérrez and Orsi, *Contested Eden,* 147–48.

7. Dorothy Krell, ed., *The California Missions: A Pictorial History* (Menlo Park, CA: Sunset Books, 1979), 54.

8. Bancroft Collection, Mem. Relaciones, trans. Hubert Howe Bancroft, Mexico, 1823, 31–33.

9. Servin, "Secularization," 126.

10. Bancroft Collection, Junta de Fomentos de Californias, Mexico: 1827.

11. Alexander Forbes, *California: A History of Upper and Lower California* (London: Smith, Elder, 1839; New York: Arno Press, 1973), 135.

12. C. Alan Hutchinson, *Frontier Settlement in Mexican California: The Híjar-Padrés Colony and Its Origins, 1769–1835* (New Haven: Yale University Press, 1969), 142.

13. Irving Berdine Richman, *California under Spain and Mexico: 1535–1847* (Boston: Houghton Mifflin, 1911), 255.

14. Basilio José Arrillaga, "Recopilación de Leyes, Decretos, Bandos, Reglamentos, Circulares y Providencias de los Supremos Poderes y Otras Autoridades de la República Mexicana," in *History of California*, vol. 3, by Hubert Howe Bancroft (San Francisco: History Co., 1885), 337.

15. Virginia M. Bouvier, *Women and the Conquest of California, 1542–1840: Codes of Silence* (Tucson: University of Arizona Press, 2001), 78.

16. (Mrs.) Fremont Older, *California Missions and Their Romances* (New York: Coward-McCann, 1938), 222.

17. George Harwood Phillips, *Indians and Intruders in Central California, 1769–1849*, The Civilization of the American Indian (Norman: University of Oklahoma Press, 1993), 95.

18. Older, *California Missions*, 16.

19. Krell, *California Missions*, 64–65.

20. Robert H. Jackson, "Patterns of Demographic Change in the Missions of Central California," in Bean and Brakke, *Ethnology*, 73.

21. Richman, *California*, 284.

22. Guadalupe Vallejo, "Ranch and Mission Days in Alta California," *Century Magazine* 41 (1890): 189–92. On-line at http://www.sfmuseum.org/hist2/rancho.html.

23. Douglas Monroy, "The Creation and Re-creation of Californio Society," in Gutiérrez and Orsi, *Contested Eden*, 179.

## Chapter 15

1. Sherburne F. Cook, "Historical Demography," in *California*, ed. Robert F. Heizer, vol. 8 of *Handbook of North American Indians*, ed. William C. Sturtevant (Washington, DC: Smithsonian Institution, 1978), 91–93.

2. William Preston, "Serpent in the Garden: Environmental Change in Colonial California," in *Contested Eden: California before the Gold Rush*, ed. Ramón Gutiérrez and Richard J. Orsi (Berkeley: University of California Press, 1998), 268.

3. Sherburne F. Cook, *The Conflict between the California Indian and White Civilization,* vol. 2, *The Physical and Demographic Reaction of the Non-mission Indians in Colonial and Provincial California,* Ibero-Americana 22 (Berkeley: University of California Press, 1943), 12.

4. Sherburne F. Cook, *The Extent and Significance of Disease among the Indians of Baja California, 1697–1773,* Ibero-Americana 12 (Berkeley: University of California Press, 1937), 1, 35, 38.

5. Sherburne F. Cook, "The Impact of Disease," in *Green versus Gold: Sources in California's Environmental History,* ed. Carolyn Merchant (Washington, DC: Island Press, 1998), 57.

6. James A. Sandos, "Between Crucifix and Lance: Indian and White Relations in California, 1769–1848," in Gutiérrez and Orsi, *Contested Eden,* 199–200.

7. Michael J. Gonzalez, "'The Child of the Wilderness Weeps for the Father of Our Country': The Indian and the Politics of Church and State in Provincial California," in Gutiérrez and Orsi, *Contested Eden,* 158.

8. Sherburne F. Cook, "Smallpox in Spanish and Mexican California, 1770–1845," in *Ethnology of the Alta California Indians,* vol. 2, *Postcontact,* ed. Lowell John Bean and Sylvia Brakke, Spanish Borderlands Sourcebooks 4 (New York: Garland, 1991), 26, 29, 46–47.

9. Cook, *Conflict,* 14.

10. Robert H. Jackson, "Patterns of Demographic Change in the Missions of Central California," in Bean and Brakke, *Ethnology,* 69.

11. (Mrs.) Fremont Older, *California Missions and Their Romances* (New York: Coward-McCann, 1938), 199, 228.

12. Junípero Serra, *Writings,* ed. and trans. Antonine Tibesar, 4 vols. (Washington, DC: Academy of American Franciscan History, 1955–66), 2:167.

13. Edward D. Castillo, "The Impact of Euro-American Exploration and Settlement," in *California,* ed. Robert F. Heizer, vol. 8 of *Handbook of North American Indians,* ed. William C. Sturtevant (Washington, DC: Smithsonian Institution, 1978), 101.

14. Cook, "Smallpox," 185.

15. Frederick William Beechey, "Narrative of a Voyage to the Pacific and Beering's Strait to Cooperate with the Polar Expeditions, 1825–1828," in *A World Transformed: Firsthand Accounts of California before the Gold Rush,* ed. Joshua Paddison (Berkeley: Heyday Books, 1999), 184.

16. J. N. Bowman, "The Resident Neophytes (Existentes) of the California Missions," *Historical Society of Southern California Quarterly* 40 (1958): 138–48.

17. Dorothy Krell, ed., *The California Missions: A Pictorial History* (Menlo Park, CA: Sunset Books, 1979), 64.

18. Cook, *Conflict,* 5.

19. George Harwood Phillips, *Indians and Intruders in Central California, 1769–1849,* The Civilization of the American Indian (Norman: University of Oklahoma Press, 1993), 97.

20. Cook, *Conflict,* 5.

21. Alexander Forbes, *California: A History of Upper and Lower California* (London: Smith, Elder, 1839; New York: Arno Press, 1973), 232.

22. C. Alan Hutchinson, *Frontier Settlement in Mexican California: The Híjar-Padrés Colony and Its Origins, 1769–1835* (New Haven: Yale University Press, 1969), 80.

23. Ibid.

24. Helen Hunt Jackson and Abbot H. Kinney, "Report on the Condition and Needs of the Mission Indians of California," in Bean and Brakke, *Ethnology,* 403–5.

25. Ibid., 405–6.

26. Raymond C. White, "Two Surviving Luiseno Ceremonies," in Bean and Brakke, *Ethnology,* 543.

27. Constance Goddard DuBois, "The Condition of the Mission Indians of Southern California" (Philadelphia: Office of the Indian Rights Association, 1901), 444–45.

28. Ibid., 437, 447–48.

## Chapter 16

1. Frank W. Blackmar, *Spanish Institutions of the Southwest* (Baltimore: Johns Hopkins University Press, 1891), 152.

2. George Harwood Phillips, *Indians and Intruders in Central California, 1769–1849,* The Civilization of the American Indian (Norman: University of Oklahoma Press, 1993), 136.

3. (Mrs.) Fremont Older, *California Missions and Their Romances* (New York: Coward-McCann, 1938), 18.

4. Dorothy Krell, ed., *The California Missions: A Pictorial History* (Menlo Park, CA: Sunset Books, 1979), 66.

5. Older, *California Missions,* 49.

6. Henry Miller, *Account of a Tour of the California Missions and Towns, 1856* (Santa Barbara, CA: Bellerophon, 2000), 3.

7. Older, *California Missions*, 105–6.

8. Miller, *Account*, 29.

9. Krell, *California Missions*, 86.

10. Miller, *Account*, 19.

11. Robert L. Schuyler, "Indian-Euro-American Interaction: Archeological Evidence from Non-Indian Sites," in *California*, ed. Robert F. Heizer, vol. 8 of *Handbook of North American Indians*, ed. William C. Sturtevant (Washington, DC: Smithsonian Institution, 1978), 73.

12. Miller, *Account*, 22.

13. Ibid., 35, 41–42.

14. Ibid., 48–49.

15. Ibid., 37.

16. Ibid., 33 and 35.

17. Older, *California Missions*, 178–79.

18. Miller, *Account*, 54–55.

19. Ibid., 61.

20. Krell, *California Missions*, 63.

21. Older, *California Missions*, 191.

22. Miller, *Account*, 3.

23. Older, *California Missions*, 38.

24. Donald Francis Toomey, *The Spell of California's Spanish Colonial Missions* (Santa Fe: Sunstone Press, 2001), 36.

25. James E. Moss, "For Discovery, Collection and Preservation: The San Diego Historical Society," *Journal of San Diego History* 25, no. 2 (1979). On-line at http://sandiegohistory.org/journal/79spring/discovery.htm.

26. Older, *California Missions*, 122–23.

27. Krell, *California Missions*, 77.

28. Toomey, *Spell*, 36.

29. Bill Virden, "The Junípero Serra Museum," *Journal of San Diego History* 8, no. 2 (1962). On-line at http://www.sandiegohistory.org/journal/62april/museum.htm.

30. Toomey, *Spell*, 24.

31. Older, *California Missions*, 51, 109.

32. Krell, *California Missions*, 85.

33. California Missions Foundation, http://www.missionsofcalifornia.org/.

## Conclusion

1. Junípero Serra, *Writings,* ed. and trans. Antonine Tibesar, 4 vols. (Washington, DC: Academy of American Franciscan History, 1955–66), 1:217.

2. Robert H. Jackson, "Patterns of Demographic Change in the Missions of Central California," in *Ethnology of the Alta California Indians,* vol. 2, *Postcontact,* ed. Lowell John Bean and Sylvia Brakke, Spanish Borderlands Sourcebooks 4 (New York: Garland, 1991), 69.

3. Mission San Miguel Web site, http://www.missionsanmiguel.org/tour/page5.html.

4. Henry Miller, *Account of a Tour of the California Missions and Towns, 1856* (Santa Barbara, CA: Bellerophon, 2000), 57.

5. Dorothy Krell, ed., *The California Missions: A Pictorial History* (Menlo Park, CA: Sunset Books, 1979), 25.

6. Robert L. Schuyler, "Indian-Euro-American Interaction: Archeological Evidence from Non-Indian Sites," in *California,* ed. Robert F. Heizer, vol. 8 of *Handbook of North American Indians,* ed. William C. Sturtevant (Washington, DC: Smithsonian Institution, 1978), 72.

# Bibliography

*Primary Sources*

Anza, Juan Bautista. "Diario de la Ruta, y Operaciones que Yo el Ynfraescripto Theniente Coronel, y Capitan del Rl. Residio de tubac, en la Provincia, y Governación de Sonora, practicó segunda vez." Horcasitas, October 23, 1775, to June 1, 1776, Mexico, AGN, Prov. Int., vol. 169, exp. 7, fols. 176–81v.

Arrillaga, Basilio José. "Recopilación de Leyes, Decretos, Bandos, Reglamentos, Circulares y Providencias de los Supremos Poderes y Otras Autoridades de la República Mexicana." In Bancroft, *History,* vol. 3.

Asisara, Lorenzo. "Narrative of a Mission Indian." In Harrison, *History.* Bancroft Collection, Junta de Fomentos de Californias, Mexico, 1827.

Bancroft Collection. Mem. Relaciones. Translated by Hubert Howe Bancroft, Mexico, 1823.

Bayle, Constantino. "Misión de la Baja California." In Crosby, *Antigua California.*

Beechey, Frederick William. "Narrative of a Voyage to the Pacific and Beering's Strait to Cooperate with the Polar Expeditions, 1825–1828." In Paddison, *World Transformed.*

California Archives (Manuscripts, Bancroft Library). a, Ortega, 1–5; b, State Papers, Sacramento, ix, 72; c, Provincial State Papers, 1, 228–32.

Chamisso, Adelbert von. "A Voyage around the World with the Romanzov Exploring Expedition in the Years 1805–1808." In Paddison, *World Transformed.*

Fages, Pedro. *A Historical, Political, and Natural Description of California.* Translated by Herbert Ingram Priestley. Berkeley: University of California Press; Ramona, CA: Ballena Press, 1972.

Font, Pedro. "Diario que formó el P. Pdo. Apco. Fr. Pedro Font Missionero . . . en el viage que hizó á Monterey." Horcasitas, September 29, 1775, to Tubatama, May 11, 1777. Original in John Carter Brown Library, Brown University, Providence, RI.

———. *Font's Complete Diary: A Chronicle of the Founding of San Francisco.* Edited by Herbert Eugene Bolton. Berkeley: University of California Press, 1931.

Forbes, Alexander. *California: A History of Upper and Lower California*. London: Smith, Elder, 1839; New York: Arno Press, 1973.

Fuster, Vicente. "Register de Defunciones." 1775. Ms. on file at University of California, Hubert Howe Bancroft Library, Berkeley.

Jackson, Helen Hunt, and Abbot H. Kinney. "Report on the Condition and Needs of the Mission Indians of California." In Bean and Brakke, *Ethnology*.

Kemble, Edward. "Yerba Buena, 1846." In Phillips, *Indians and Intruders*.

Kroeber, Alfred L. *A Mission Record of the California Indians*. University of California Publications in American Archaeology and Ethnology, Web ed. 1999 [cited 14 November 2003]; available at http://www.notfrisco.com/almanac/kroeber01/.

Lasuén, Fermín Francisco de. *Writings*. Translated and edited by Finbar K. Kenneally. 2 vols. Washington, DC: Academy of American Franciscan History, 1965.

Mexican Colonization Law, August 18, 1824, http://www.learncalifornia.org/doc.asp?id=53.

Miller, Henry. *Account of a Tour of the California Missions and Towns, 1856*. Santa Barbara, CA: Bellerophon Books, 2000.

Palóu, Francisco. "The Founding of the Presidio and Mission of Our Father Saint Francis." *California Historical Society Quarterly* 14, no. 2 (1935): 102–8.

———. *Historical Memoirs of New California*. Edited by Herbert Eugene Bolton. 4 vols. Berkeley: University of California Press, 1926.

———. "A Spaniard Explores the Southern California Landscape, 1774." In Merchant, *Green versus Gold*.

Pérez, Eulalia. "Una vieja y sus recuerdos dictados à la edad avanzada de 139 años." In *Three Memoirs of Mexican California*. Berkeley: Friends of the Hubert Howe Bancroft Library, University of California, 1988.

Rezanov, Nikolai Petrovich. "The Rezanov Voyage to Nueva California in 1806." In Paddison, *World Transformed*.

Santa María, Vicente. "The First Spanish Entry into San Francisco Bay." In Paddison, *World Transformed*.

Señán, José. "Contestación al Interrogatorio." In Archivo de la Misión de Santa Barbara, Pap. Misc., vol. 7. Copied from the Santa Barbara Mission Archives for the Hubert Howe Bancroft Library by E. G. Murray in 1877.

———. *The Letters of José Señán, O.F.M., Mission San Buenaventura, 1796–1823*. Translated by Paul D. Nathan. Edited by Lesley Byrd Simpson. San Francisco: Ventura County Historical Society, 1962.

Serra, Junípero. *Writings*. Edited and translated by Antonine Tibesar. 4 vols. Washington, DC: Academy of American Franciscan History, 1955–66.

Tac, Pablo. "Indian Life and Customs at Mission San Luis Rey: A Record of California Mission Life." In Bean and Brakke, *Ethnology*.

Thomas, David Hurst, ed. *Columbian Consequences*. Vol. 1, *Archaeological and Historical Perspectives on the Spanish Borderlands West*. Washington, DC: Smithsonian Institution Press, 1989.

Vallejo, Guadalupe. "Guadalupe Vallejo Recalls the Rancheros, 1890." In Merchant, *Green versus Gold*.

———. "Ranch and Mission Days in Alta California." *Century Magazine* 41 (1890): 183–92. On-line at http://www.sfmuseum.org/hist2/rancho.html.

Vancouver, George. "Vancouver in California: 1792–1794." In Paddison, *World Transformed*.

*Secondary Sources*

Adamo, Joseph. "Soldados de Cuera." *California Mission Studies Association Newsletter* (August 1986).

Anderson, M. Kat, Michael G. Barbour, and Valerie Whitworth. "A World of Balance and Plenty: Land, Plants, Animals, and Humans in a Pre-European California." In Gutiérrez and Orsi, *Contested Eden*.

Bancroft, Hubert Howe. *History of California*. 7 vols. San Francisco: History Co., 1884–1890.

Barton, Bruce Walter. *A Tree at the Center of the World: A Story of the California Missions*. Santa Barbara: Ross-Erikson, 1980.

Bean, Lowell John, and Sylvia Brakke, eds. *Ethnology of the Alta California Indians*. Volume 2, *Postcontact*. Spanish Borderlands Sourcebooks 4. New York: Garland, 1991.

Beerman, Eric. "The Viceroy Marquis de Croix: A Biographical Sketch." *Journal of San Diego History* 25, no. 1 (1979). On-line at http://www.sandiegohistory.org/journal/79winter/viceroy.htm.

Beilharz, Edwin A. *Felipe de Neve: First Governor of California*. San Francisco: California Historical Society, 1971.

Blackmar, Frank W. *Spanish Institutions of the Southwest*. Baltimore: Johns Hopkins University Press, 1891.

Bolton, Herbert E. "The Mission as Frontier Institution in the Spanish-American Colonies." *American Historical Review* 23, no. 1 (1917): 42–61.

Borah, Woodrow. "The California Mission." In Bean and Brakke, *Ethnology*.

———. *New Spain's Century of Depression*. Ibero-Americana 35. Berkeley: University of California Press, 1951.

Bouvier, Virginia M. *Women and the Conquest of California, 1542–1840: Codes of Silence*. Tucson: University of Arizona Press, 2001.

Bowman, J. N. "The Resident Neophytes (Existentes) of the California Missions." *Historical Society of Southern California Quarterly* 40 (1958): 138–48.

Breschini, Gary S. "The Founding of Monterey." Monterey County Historical Society, http://www.mchsmuseum.com/colonization.html.

California Missions Foundation. *The Missions of Alta California: An Educational Guide*. San Francisco: California Missions Foundation, 2000.

Campbell, Leon. "The First Californios: Presidial Society in Spanish California, 1769–1822." *Journal of the West* 11 (1972): 582–95.

Carrico, Richard L. "Sociopolitical Aspects of the 1775 Revolt at Mission San Diego de Alcala: an Ethnohistorical Approach." *Journal of San Diego History* 43, no. 3 (1997). On-line at http://sandiegohistory.org/journal/97summer/missionrevolt.htm.

Castañeda, Antonia. "Engendering the History of Alta California, 1769–1848: Gender, Sexuality, and the Family." In Gutiérrez and Orsi, *Contested Eden*.

Castillo, Edward D. "The Impact of Euro-American Exploration and Settlement." In Heizer, *California*, 99–127.

Chapman, Charles Edward. *The Founding of Spanish California: The Northwestward Expansion of New Spain, 1687–1783*. New York: Macmillan, 1916; New York: Octagon Books, 1973.

———. *A History of California: The Spanish Period*. New York: Macmillan, 1921.

Chávez, Ignacio del Río. "Utopia in Baja California: The Dreams of José de Gálvez." Translated by Arturo Jiménez-Vera. *Journal of San Diego History* 18, no. 4 (1972). On-line at http://www.sandiegohistory.org/journal/72fall/utopia.htm.

Cook, Sherburne F. "Colonial Expeditions to the Interior of California: Central Valley, 1800–1820." *Anthropological Records* 16 (1960).

———. *The Conflict between the California Indian and White Civilization*. Vol. 2, *The Physical and Demographic Reaction of the Non-mission Indians in Colonial and Provincial California*. Ibero-Americana 22. Berkeley: University of California Press, 1943.

———. *The Extent and Significance of Disease among the Indians of Baja California, 1697–1773*. Ibero-Americana 12. Berkeley: University of California Press, 1937.

————. "Historical Demography." In Heizer, *California*, 91–98.

————. "The Impact of Disease." In Merchant, *Green versus Gold*.

————. *Population Trends among the California Mission Indians*. Ibero-Americana 17. Berkeley: University of California Press, 1940.

————. "Smallpox in Spanish and Mexican California, 1770–1845." In Bean and Brakke, *Ethnology*.

Costello, Julia G. "Variability among the Alta California Missions: The Economics of Agricultural Production." In Thomas, *Columbian Consequences*, 435–49.

Crosby, Harry W. *Antigua California: Mission and Colony on the Peninsular Frontier, 1697–1768*. Albuquerque: University of New Mexico Press, 1994.

Cuesta, Felipe Arroyo de la. *Grammar of the Mutsun Language*. New York: Cramoisy Press, 1861; New York: AMS Press, 1970.

————. *A Vocabulary or Phrase Book of the Mutsun Language of Alta California*. New York: Cramoisy Press, 1862; New York: AMS Press, 1970.

Davis, Thom. "California's Inland Chain of Missions." California Mission Studies Association, http://www.camissions.org/davis2.html.

DuBois, Constance Goddard. *The Condition of the Mission Indians of Southern California*. Philadelphia: Office of the Indian Rights Association, 1901.

Elliott, J. H., ed. *The Spanish World: Civilization and Empire*. New York: Harry N. Abrams, 1991.

Engstrand, Iris H. W. "Seekers of the Northern Mystery: European Exploration of California and the Pacific." In Gutiérrez and Orsi, *Contested Eden*.

————. *Serra's San Diego*. San Diego: San Diego Historical Society, 1982. On-line at http://sandiegohistory.org/index.html.

Fradkin, Philip. *The Seven States of California: A Natural and Human History*. New York: Henry Holt, 1995.

Fuentes, Carlos. *The Buried Mirror: Reflections on Spain and the New World*. Boston: Houghton Mifflin, 1992.

Garr, Daniel. "Planning, Politics, and Plunder: The Missions and Indian Pueblos of Hispanic California." *Southern California Quarterly* 54, no. 4 (1972): 299–300.

Gentilcore, R. Louis. "Missions and Mission Lands of Alta California." *Annals of the Association of American Geographers* 51, no. 1 (1961): 46–72.

Gonzalez, Michael J. "'The Child of the Wilderness Weeps for the Father of Our Country': The Indian and the Politics of Church and State in Provincial California." In Gutiérrez and Orsi, *Contested Eden*.

Grant, Campbell. "Chumash: Introduction." In Heizer, *California*, 505–8.

Gutiérrez, Ramón, and Richard J. Orsi, eds. *Contested Eden: California before the Gold Rush*. Berkeley: University of California Press, 1998.

Hackel, Steven W. "Land, Labor, and Production: The Colonial Economy of Spanish and Mexican California." In Gutiérrez and Orsi, *Contested Eden*.

———. "The Staff of Leadership: Indian Authority in the Missions of Alta California." *William and Mary Quarterly*, third series, vol. 54, issue 2 (April 1997): 347–76.

Hanke, Lewis. *The Spanish Struggle for Justice in the Conquest of America*. Dallas: Southern Methodist University Press, 2002.

Harrison, Edward S., ed. *History of Santa Cruz County, California*. San Francisco: Pacific Press, 1892.

Heizer, Robert F., ed. *California*. Vol. 8 of *Handbook of North American Indians*, edited by William C. Sturtevant. Washington, DC: Smithsonian Institution, 1978.

———. "Mythology: Regional Patterns and History of Research." In Heizer, *California*, 654–57.

———. "Native World Views." In Merchant, *Green versus Gold*.

———. "Natural Forces and the Native World View." In Heizer, *California*, 649–53.

Heizer, Robert F., and Alan J. Almquist. *The Other Californians: Prejudice and Discrimination under Spain, Mexico, and the United States to 1920*. Berkeley: University of California Press, 1971.

Heizer, Robert F., and Mary Anne Whipple, eds. *The California Indians: A Source Book*. 2nd ed. Berkeley: University of California Press, 1971.

Hill, Joseph. "Dry Rivers, Dammed Rivers and Floods: An Early History of the Struggle between Droughts and Floods in San Diego." *Journal of San Diego History* 48, no. 1 (2002). On-line at http://www.sandiegohistory.org/journal/2002-1/hill.htm.

Honig, Sasha. "The Presidios of Alta California." California Mission Studies Association, http://www.ca-missions.org/honig.html.

Hornbeck, David. *California Patterns: A Geographical and Historical Atlas*. Palo Alto, CA: Mayfield, 1983.

———. "The Past in California's Landscape." California Mission Studies Association, http://www.ca-missions.org/hornbeck.html.

Hundley, Norris. "Hispanic Water Rights." In Merchant, *Green versus Gold*.

Hurtado, Albert. "Indians Encounter Spaniards." In Merchant, *Green versus Gold*.

———. *Intimate Frontiers: Sex, Gender, and Culture in Old California*. Albuquerque: University of New Mexico Press, 1999.

Hutchinson, C. Alan. *Frontier Settlement in Mexican California: The Híjar-Padrés Colony and Its Origins, 1769–1835*. New Haven: Yale University Press, 1969.

Jackson, Robert H. "Patterns of Demographic Change in the Missions of Central California." In Bean and Brakke, *Ethnology*.

Jackson, Robert H., and Edward Castillo. *Indians, Franciscans, and Spanish Colonization: The Impact of the Mission System on California Indians*. Albuquerque: University of New Mexico Press, 1995.

Konetzke, Richard. "La émigración de mujeres españolas à América durante la época colonial." *Revista Internacional de Sociología* 9 (1945): 123–50.

Krase, Jean. "Ships and Sherds: Ceramics at the San Diego Presidio." *Journal of San Diego History* 27, no. 2 (1981). On-line at http://www.sandiegohistory.org/journal/81spring/sherds.htm.

Krell, Dorothy, ed. *The California Missions: A Pictorial History*. Menlo Park, CA: Sunset Books, 1979.

Kroeber, Alfred L. "The Food Problem in California." In Heizer and Whipple, *California Indians*.

———. *Handbook of the Indians of California*. Washington, DC: Smithsonian Institution, 1925; St. Clair Shores, MI: Scholarly Press, 1972.

Kroeber, Theodora, and Robert F. Heizer. *Almost Ancestors: The First Californians*. Edited by F. David Hales. San Francisco: Sierra Club, 1968.

Langer, Erick D., and Robert H. Jackson. "Colonial and Republican Missions Compared: The Cases of Alta California and Southeastern Bolivia." *Comparative Studies in Society and History* 30, no. 2 (1988): 286–311.

Manocchio, Regina Teresa. "Tending Communities, Crossing Cultures: Midwives in Nineteenth Century California." Master's thesis, Yale University School of Nursing, 1998.

Mason, Bill. "The Garrisons of San Diego Presidio: 1770–1794." *Journal of San Diego History* 24, no. 3 (1978). On-line at http://www.sandiegohistory.org/journal/78fall/garrisons.htm.

Merchant, Carolyn, ed. *Green versus Gold: Sources in California's Environmental History*. Washington, DC: Island Press, 1998.

Mills, James R. *San Diego: Where California Began*. 5th ed. San Diego: San Diego Historical Society, 1985. On-line at http://sandiegohistory.org/index.html.

Monroy, Douglas. "The Creation and Re-creation of Californio Society." In Gutiérrez and Orsi, *Contested Eden*.

Moss, James E. "For Discovery, Collection and Preservation: The San Diego Historical Society." *Journal of San Diego History* 25, no. 2 (1979). On-line at http://sandiegohistory.org/journal/79spring/discovery.htm.

Neuerburg, Norman. "The Little Mission: History at an Inch to the Foot." *Journal of San Diego History* 33, no. 4 (1987). On-line at http://www.sandiegohistory .org/journal/87fall/mission.htm.

——. "A Visit to the Home of California's First Martyr." *Journal of San Diego History* 35, no. 1 (1989). On-line at http://www.sandiegohistory.org/ journal/89winter/visit.htm.

Nunis, Doyce B. "Alta California's Trojan Horse: Foreign Immigration." In Gutiérrez and Orsi, *Contested Eden*.

O'Brien, Eric. "The Life of Padre Serra." In Serra, *Writings*.

Older, (Mrs.) Fremont. *California Missions and Their Romances*. New York: Coward-McCann, 1938.

Paddison, Joshua, ed. *A World Transformed: Firsthand Accounts of California before the Gold Rush*. Berkeley: Heyday Books, 1999.

Phillips, George Harwood. *Indians and Intruders in Central California, 1769–1849*. Civilization of the American Indian. Norman: University of Oklahoma Press, 1993.

——. "Indians in Los Angeles, 1781–1875: Economic Integration, Social Disintegration." In Bean and Brakke, *Ethnology*.

Polk, Dora Beale. *The Island of California: A History of the Myth*. Spokane, WA: Arthur H. Clark, 1991.

Pourade, Richard F. *The History of San Diego*. Vol. 1, *The Explorers*. San Diego: Union-Tribune, 1960. On-line at http://sandiegohistory.org/index.html.

Preston, William. "Serpent in the Garden: Environmental Change in Colonial California." In Gutiérrez and Orsi, *Contested Eden*.

Richman, Irving Berdine. *California under Spain and Mexico: 1535–1847*. Boston: Houghton Mifflin, 1911.

Roberts, Elizabeth, and Elias Amidon, eds. *Earth Prayers from Around the World: 365 Prayers, Poems, and Invocations for Honoring the Earth*. San Francisco: Harper-San Francisco, 1991.

Sandos, James A. "Between Crucifix and Lance: Indian and White Relations in California, 1769–1848." In Gutiérrez and Orsi, *Contested Eden*.

——. "Christianization among the Chumash: An Ethnohistoric Perspective." *Indian Quarterly* 15, no. 1 (1991): 1–22.

Schuyler, Robert L. "Indian-Euro-American Interaction: Archeological Evidence from Non-Indian Sites." In Heizer, *California*, 69–79.

Servin, Manuel. "The Secularization of the California Missions: A Reappraisal." In Bean and Brakke, *Ethnology.*

Simmons, William S. "Indian Peoples of California." In Gutiérrez and Orsi, *Contested Eden.*

Sitjar, Buenaventura. *Vocabulary of the Language of San Antonio Mission, California.* New York: Cramoisy Press, 1861; New York: AMS Press, 1970.

Skowronek, Russell. "Sifting the Evidence: Perceptions of Life at the Ohlone (Costanoan) Missions of Alta California." *Ethnohistory* 45, no. 4 (1998): 675–708.

Smith, Frances Rand. "The Spanish Missions of California." *Hispania* 7, no. 4 (1924): 243–58.

Starrs, Paul F. "California's Grazed Ecosystems." In Merchant, *Green versus Gold.*

Stodder, Ann Lucy Wiener. *Mechanisms and Trends in the Decline of the Costanoan Indian Population of Central California: Nutrition and Health in Pre-contact California and Mission Period Environments.* Salinas, CA: Coyote Press, 1986.

Toomey, Donald Francis. *The Spell of California's Spanish Colonial Missions.* Santa Fe: Sunstone Press, 2001.

Vigil, Ralph H. "The Hispanic Heritage and the Borderlands." *Journal of San Diego History* 19, no. 3 (1973). On-line at http://www.sandiegohistory.org/journal/73summer/hispanic.htm.

Virden, Bill. "The Junípero Serra Museum." *Journal of San Diego History* 8, no. 2 (1962). On-line at http://www.sandiegohistory.org/journal/62april/museum.htm.

Wallace, William J. "Northern Valley Yokuts." In Heizer, *California*, 462–70.

Weber, Francis J. "The Death of Fray Luís Jayme: Two Hundredth Anniversary." *Journal of San Diego History* 22, no. 1 (1976). On-line at http://www.sandiegohistory.org/journal/76winter/jayme.htm.

# Index